Women of the Storm

Members of Women of the Storm in 2006: Madeline West,
Liz Sloss, Anne Milling (*standing, left to right*) and Lindy Boggs (*seated*).
Photograph courtesy of Maura McEvoy.

WOMEN OF THE STORM

Civic Activism after Hurricane Katrina

EMMANUEL DAVID

UNIVERSITY OF ILLINOIS PRESS
Urbana, Chicago, and Springfield

Library of Congress Control Number: 2017948476
978-0-252-04126-6 (hardcover)
978-0-252-08281-8 (paperback)
978-0-252-09986-1 (e-book)

For my parents

And for the women whose stories appear in these pages

Contents

Illustrations

Prologue

When I began my research on Hurricane Katrina, I didn't set out to study privileged Southern women. The world of elites was not really one of my interests. As a student at Loyola University New Orleans in 2003, I even turned down an opportunity to get a peek behind the curtain of the city's upper class. One of my professors knew a local photographer who sought assistance carrying equipment while she documented Mardi Gras balls, one location where elite culture in New Orleans exhibits and reproduces itself. I could have attended these invitation-only events, but I opted to spend Carnival on the St. Charles Avenue parade route with friends. I often wonder how my thinking—my sociological perspective—would have changed had I seized that opportunity. My interests changed just a few years later, when a group known as Women of the Storm, whose roster included many privileged subjects, began to capture my attention. This book is the result of a series of events that led me to "study up" on power and inequality.[1]

I was in graduate school at the University of Colorado Boulder when Hurricane Katrina came ashore on August 29, 2005. I hadn't been following the news out of New Orleans too closely. But Katrina changed everything. From then on I spent almost every free moment trying to understand what was going on in the wake of the storm, to contact my New Orleans friends, and to find a way back to the city.

While my pre-Katrina ties to New Orleans don't run deep, especially compared to those whose families have lived there for generations, I spent four years at Loyola in the early part of the decade. Unlike many of the women in this study, I did not come from a wealthy family, and I knew almost nothing about Southern culture. My father immigrated to the United States from the Philippines. My mother, the first in her family to receive a college degree, worked as a university librarian and at one point as president of the faculty union (following in the footsteps of my grandfather, who was very proud of his union membership). My life seemed worlds away from those whose stories fill these pages.

I didn't always care for New Orleans, an admission that departs from narratives routinely told about falling in love with the city for its food, music, and culture. It was a strange place. The pace of life was slow. Things didn't always work, inefficiency seemed to be the norm, and life was often disorganized and somewhat wild. Only with time, exploration, and eventually complete immersion did I warm up to the city. One day, some friends who were locals took me to a bar on Magazine Street, not far from Loyola. There I got a lesson about some of the city's quirks and contradictions from words printed on the side of a pint glass. It was a list to ponder while intoxicated, a crash course in New Orleans culture for the uninitiated. "Shopping is not good," the pint glass professed, "unless you are buying beer, hookers or antiques." The list also offered geography lessons: "Giving driving directions to non-local New Orleans [*sic*] is a waste of time. Every street intersects with each other. No two streets run parallel to each other," and "The West Bank is actually East of the city. It would take too long to explain." Another read, "If the levee breaks, everyone will die. No one seems worried about this problem either." The notion that levees could breach circulated in the popular imaginary like modern folklore, a collective awareness that there was a slim chance—but a chance nonetheless—that life could change quickly in big ways. A few years later, it did.

I became increasingly politicized at Loyola, thanks to my encounters with a few progressive professors and student groups. I found the field of sociology and became entranced with critical social theories that helped me make sense of inequality. I discovered social justice groups that would make annual pilgrimages to protest at the U.S. Army School of Americas (now the Western Hemisphere Institute for Security Cooperation) in Fort Benning, Georgia. And in my last semester at Loyola, in 2003, just two years before Katrina, I put to use material learned in a sociology class on 1960s-era protest movements during my participation in antiwar demonstrations, including marches down St. Charles Avenue and protests in front of New Orleans City Hall. I was among a handful of students who participated in civil disobedience training with Loyola law professor Bill Quigley, who would later become a key actor in the post-Katrina recovery.

My scholarly interest in Katrina was shaped by my past ties to the city and by my desire to participate in its recovery. In the weeks after the storm, I became a research assistant on a National Science Foundation–funded Quick Response research project, administered by the Natural Hazards Center at the University of Colorado. The research began in September 2005 and involved fieldwork at an emergency shelter run by the Red Cross at the River Center Convention Center in Baton Rouge. Before Katrina, the Baton Rouge metropolitan area had a population of about four hundred thousand, but in Katrina's aftermath the city had taken in almost two hundred thousand evacuees.[2] There were between eight thousand and ten thousand displaced residents living in shelters, many of whom came from New Orleans, eighty miles away. At one point there were nearly five thousand evacuees at the shelter.

This was my first fieldwork experience, and interviewing disaster survivors was incredibly difficult. I was disheartened by the facility's conditions and by the sheer number of displaced residents. Some had been rescued by boat from rooftops in New Orleans and subsequently dropped off at the Baton Rouge shelter, where heightened security made it feel more like a jail than a place of refuge. Many arrived with nothing more than the clothes on their backs and the money in their pockets. Most of the evacuees, however, kept their spirits up. One night during a heavy storm, a brass band convened outside under an overhang, playing music that countered the less-than-comforting speech of President George W. Bush, delivered in Jackson Square and shown on a small television outside the shelter.

Although I was moved by New Orleans residents' powerful stories of survival, that research project raised questions about the ethics and politics of knowledge production. Were we exploiting Katrina survivors? Were we capitalizing on the experiences of those who had nowhere else to go? Because emergency shelters provided what some might consider a captive population, it was a place of convergence for researchers and the media alike. As I left the shelter, I was handed a flyer that called for a mass mobilization of displaced residents on the day that would later coincide with the landfall of Hurricane Rita. When I saw displaced residents self-organizing, I began thinking about collective action in response to the catastrophe. The concerns about exploitation remained with me and, coupled with this flyer, informed my thinking about the study of emergence of disaster-related groups.

I started fieldwork in New Orleans in the first week of October 2005, when vast parts of the city were under "look-and-leave" visitation policies and residents were still prohibited from entering a number of neighborhoods. With only a few leads, my research was highly exploratory. I spent time at the home of a woman named Dyan French Cole, also known as Mama D, an African American sanitation worker who stayed through the storm and subsequently opened a community center in her flooded Seventh Ward residence. On the same trip, a few radical volunteers took me to the home of Malik Rahim, a Black Panther and Green Party activist who, like Mama D, had not evacuated. It was there that I learned about the newly formed Common Ground Collective, and I began interviewing members about their post-disaster activities organized around the slogan "Solidarity Not Charity." In November 2005 I continued fieldwork with Common Ground as a researcher-volunteer. This preliminary research allowed me to begin planning a longer phase of fieldwork in spring of 2006. I used December to regroup and make arrangements. Ed McCaughan, a former professor at Loyola, put me in touch with a friend, Harriet Swift, who lived in the Bywater neighborhood. Harriet's 1895 house had escaped floodwaters by mere inches, as I would later learn. When we talked by phone, she invited me to move into the upstairs of her shotgun "camelback" house, a style peculiar to New Orleans with a truncated second story of only one or two rooms. I made plans to stay with her indefinitely.

In early January 2006 in Colorado, I boarded the *California Zephyr*, an Amtrak train that runs from San Francisco to Chicago, with my bicycle, laptop, and a backpack full of clothes. I transferred in Chicago to the *City of New Orleans* train, which traveled nearly nine hundred miles through the Midwest en route to New Orleans. When I found my seat, I noticed a bearded young man in the seat next to mine. It turned out that my seatmate, an Oberlin College student with a biblical name, was on his way to volunteer at Common Ground. He and I talked for hours about politics, disasters, and train travel.

I arrived in New Orleans on January 10, coincidentally the same day that civic activist and philanthropist Anne Milling held the first meeting in her home that would jumpstart Women of the Storm, though I, like most outside the group's initial inner circle, was unaware of this gathering at the time. I was planning to complete my fieldwork at Common Ground, and as I sat on the train I realized that my research had already started with my chance encounter with this aspiring volunteer. Knowing that he was bound for Common Ground, I offered to bring him to the volunteer housing in the Upper Ninth Ward, a short walk from Harriet's home.

Two weeks after returning to New Orleans, my fieldwork took a sudden turn. Some might say I was in the right place at the right time. I first learned about Women of the Storm (WOS) on January 26, 2006, just four days before the group's inaugural trip to Washington, D.C. That morning, I opened the *Times-Picayune*, the newspaper of record in New Orleans, and read what might be the first words ever published about WOS. I was sitting in Harriet's Bywater home, just blocks away from the now infamous Industrial Canal, whose floodwalls breached during Katrina, inundating the Upper and Lower Ninth Wards with floodwater. Listening to the repetitive drone of construction work on the breached levees, I felt there was something about WOS that set it apart from the many other groups that had emerged after Katrina. Perhaps it was its all-female membership. Perhaps it was because they were organizing in a beautiful home that escaped the flooding, as evidenced by the color photograph that accompanied the story. Almost everything about WOS stood in stark contrast to the tent cities, communal kitchens, and radical ideals of the post-Katrina groups I had been documenting since October 2005. I had found my earlier fieldwork with decentralized, radical groups both inspiring and challenging, not least because of their fluid group structures and my conflicts with activists who distrusted "outsiders" asking questions about their activities. WOS promised something different; I was curious about how and why this group of women came together. Adding to my growing collection of Katrina ephemera, I saved the clipping, which has since yellowed with age.

In those late January days, I began to refocus my research on this group of women. I kept track of the news coverage as they embarked on their mission in Washington, and I eagerly awaited their return. Just a few days later, through a chain of events that brought me first in contact with a member on the group's edges, who then put me in touch with the inner circle, I found myself on the steps of Anne Milling's gracious Uptown New Orleans home after being invited to attend one of the first steering committee meetings following the group's whirlwind trip in Washington. I rode my bike to Milling's home, stopping first at Loyola to change into more appropriate clothing for the occasion. Wanting to make a good first impression, I took a moment to fix my hair, which had been flattened under my bicycle helmet during the seven-mile ride from Bywater. Standing on the steps of her beautiful home, I felt out of my element. With hesitation, I rang the doorbell. The door opened and a member of the newly formed executive committee invited me into the foyer. I was one of the first to arrive.

Once inside, I met Anne Milling for the first time. To my surprise, she was busy polishing silverware in the parlor, placing the gleaming utensils on a table next to a stack of just cleaned and hand-dried dishware. "We just had a luncheon with the garden club," she said before leading me through the kitchen into a dining room overlooking a serene pool worthy of a magazine spread. She offered me ice water from a clear glass pitcher, which she then placed on a wet bar in the corner of the room. Trying to be useful, I helped her clear the dining room table in preparation for the meeting, moving decorative pots from one table to another. "These are ancient Thai artifacts that are older than Christ," she said as I picked one up, my hands tightening to ensure I didn't lose my grip. She must have noticed my discomfort. "Don't worry," she said, "my children would play with them when they were younger." I relaxed my hands, but only a little.

Over the next few minutes, members of WOS's executive committee began to arrive, women who, over the subsequent years, would engage in what could fittingly be described as kitchen-table organizing. I didn't know it then, but this small group of women leaders would arguably become among the most powerful and influential in Louisiana's history, contributing in countless ways to the rebirth of New Orleans after one of the greatest catastrophes of our time.

For several months thereafter, I attended their meetings and observed their activities, gaining their trust and confidence. I also went to great lengths to interview group members at all participation levels in order to document the details of their lives, and I spent the rest of my time volunteering in recovery efforts and riding my bike through neighborhoods to better understand the scale of the damage. I stayed in post-Katrina New Orleans through the summer of 2006, and in the years that followed I continued to chronicle the women's activities, returning frequently to the city and recording their collective actions in an attempt to build a comprehensive record of the group.

In the wake of Katrina, people described intense feelings of burnout and sheer exhaustion from the hard work of recovery they were engaged in, but also from the anticipation of the many years of work that lay ahead. This was often referred to as "Katrina fatigue." During and after my fieldwork in New Orleans, I experienced something similar. I finished my dissertation in 2009 and completed an anthology on women and Hurricane Katrina, coedited with Elaine Enarson, a few years later, in 2012. Yet I shelved this book project for several years, choosing to work on new topics in different parts of the world. I even considered dropping this project on Women of the Storm completely. I told myself that it is sometimes better to bury the past and move on. As the ten-year anniversary of Katrina approached, however, I decided it was time to revisit the project. The passage of time had enabled another vantage point: I began to see new meaning in my interviews, which captured many of the unfolding processes of the group's initial formation, a yet untold story of the catastrophe. With these emergent dynamics in mind, I have done my best to tell the story of Women of the Storm through the eyes of its participants. This book reports what I learned after following the group for many years.

Women of the Storm: Civic Activism after Hurricane Katrina presents a detailed account of WOS's emergence after hurricanes Katrina and Rita. Focusing primarily on WOS's first year of existence, a period spanning from January 2006 to December 2006, and continuing through the BP oil spill in 2010, it tells how WOS came together to collectively transform the post-disaster landscape. Drawing on in-depth interviews with group members, documentary sources, archival materials, and ethnographic fieldwork in New Orleans in Katrina's aftermath, this study chronicles how WOS emerged and narrates the processes that unfolded as group members pursued their goals to help rebuild New Orleans and the Gulf Coast.

Abbreviations

AWF	America's WETLAND Foundation
BIA	Broadmoor Improvement Association
BNOB	Bring New Orleans Back Commission
CARA	Conservation and Reinvestment Act
CPD	Commission on Presidential Debates
FEMA	Federal Emergency Management Agency
FONO	Friends of New Orleans
GNOF	Greater New Orleans Foundation
LRA	Louisiana Recovery Authority
LRC	Louisiana Recovery Corporation
NCCRW	Newcomb College Center for Research on Women
OCS	Outer Continental Shelf
RESPOND	Restoring Ecosystem Sustainability and Protection on the Delta Act
WOS	Women of the Storm

Women of the Storm

Introduction

On December 11, 2005, the *New York Times* printed an editorial titled "The Death of an American City," which projected a dire outlook for post-Katrina New Orleans. The editors wrote, "We are about to lose New Orleans. Whether it is a conscious plan to let the city rot until no one is willing to move back or honest paralysis over difficult questions, the moment is upon us when a major American city will die, leaving nothing but a few shells for tourists to visit like a museum." Warning against the city's death by neglect, the editors continued, "Lawmakers need to understand that for New Orleans the words 'pending in Congress' are a death warrant requiring no signature."[1]

Focusing on the nation's post-Katrina social contract with the Crescent City, the editorial reminded readers of President George W. Bush's televised speech on September 15, 2005, delivered from a generator-lit Jackson Square, where troops from the Eighty-Second Airborne Division were on patrol after having locked down the French Quarter just a week and a half earlier. "There is no way to imagine America without New Orleans," President Bush said, while noting that the city was virtually empty and that many parts of it were still underwater.[2] Yet by December, three painful months later, with hundreds of thousands of residents displaced across the country and rebuilding efforts nearly at a standstill, the prospects for a swift recovery were giving way to a profound sense of abandonment. To many residents and observers, it seemed that New Orleans had been forgotten.

The editorial provided a scathing critique of government inaction, lamenting weak leadership and money spent on foreign wars. It described a great American city left in "complete shambles" and the post-Katrina reconstruction as a "rudderless ship." While the column recognized that citizens were rebuilding their devastated homes and uprooted lives, it focused attention on a single "make-or-break" issue: storm protection. "It all boils down to the levee system," the editors wrote, calling for comprehensive storm protection, including fortified levees, new drainage canals, and broader environmental restoration. "Homeowners, businesses, and insurance companies," they argued, "all need a commitment before they will stake their futures on the city." While residents and volunteers could rebuild homes from the ground up and from the inside out, they could not reconstruct or fund an intricate flood protection system needed to keep the city dry. If the city was going to survive, the citizens of New Orleans needed government help, which is why the editorial called upon Congress to fund the recovery.[3]

The cost would be enormous. Estimates for Category 5 storm protection were over $32 billion, an amount that many in Congress deemed just too expensive for a flood-prone city that sat well below sea level, a city that Tulane University geographer Richard Campanella describes as the "bowl-shaped metropolis."[4] Comparisons were made to the $95 billion in tax cuts just approved for the wealthy and the $300 billion allocated for the U.S. war on terror. With billions spent to fight wars in Iraq and Afghanistan, the editors scoffed, "All that money has been appropriated as the cost of protecting the nation from terrorist attacks. But what was the worst possible case we fought to prevent? Losing a major American city."

New Orleans was at a turning point. Wait any longer, and evacuees might become permanently displaced.[5] "The city must rise to the occasion," the editors wrote, "but it will not have that opportunity without the levees, and only the office of the president is strong enough to goad Congress to take swift action. Only his voice is loud enough to call people home and convince them that commitments will be met."[6]

While this pointed editorial drew national attention to the near death of New Orleans, it may have exaggerated the power of the president's office. In its focus on state actors, the editorial underestimated the power of ordinary citizens who were asserting that their communities in New Orleans and along the Gulf Coast were worth saving. In neighborhoods across the city, residents and community leaders self-organized, filling the deep chasm created by ineffective political leaders. That citizens across the political spectrum and of varying class positions organized simultaneously underscores the uniqueness of this political project. As Tom Wooten would later write, "This neighborhood mobilization under way in New Orleans was unlike anything else a modern American city had seen."[7]

In the shadow of Katrina was Hurricane Rita, a Category 3 storm that hit southwestern Louisiana on September 24, 2005, less than a month after Katrina's landfall. The editorial failed to mention the struggles of coastal communities that were still recovering from Rita, which had also prompted a second evacuation of a still bruised and battered New Orleans, reflooding neighborhoods and complicating the already difficult recovery. Four months after Rita, a dusk-till-dawn curfew was still in effect for some communities, sewage systems were not functioning, and people questioned moving back at all. Some federal relief provisions that had been passed by Congress for Katrina were not extended to areas hit by Rita.[8] While some residents in New Orleans and the diaspora were already experiencing "Katrina fatigue," residents in areas devastated by "Louisiana's 'other' storm" were said to be victims of "Rita amnesia."[9] For many outside these disaster zones, collective forgetting had begun. As Louisiana governor Kathleen Babineaux Blanco would say, "The harsh reality is that for many people in Washington, Katrina is yesterday's problem and Rita never happened."[10] How and whether Washington remembered hurricanes Katrina and Rita mattered greatly, and the citizens of New Orleans and the Gulf Coast did not want to let those in Washington so easily forget their plight.

On January 30, 2006, five months after Hurricane Katrina made landfall, Women of the Storm (WOS), as the emergent group came to be known, made its debut on the post-disaster scene. They organized to do what the *New York Times* editors imagined only the president could do: pressure Congress to support the rebuilding of New Orleans and the Gulf Coast. Led by a small cadre of elite New Orleans women, 130 Louisiana women from diverse backgrounds flew to Washington to lobby Congress for more disaster aid. The group held a press conference on Capitol Hill, where they unfurled bright blue umbrellas in a symbolic reference to the blue tarps supplied by the Federal Emergency Management Agency (FEMA) that were still covering damaged homes across the Gulf Coast. WOS's founder, Anne Milling, a New Orleans philanthropist, passionately delivered a call to action that January morning in Washington: "They must visit our decimated neighborhoods. They must see the devastation block-by-block, mile-by-mile."[11]

Right after the press conference, the women set out in twos and threes to invite elected officials to visit Katrina's destruction firsthand. Lawmakers, they argued, needed to make educated and well-informed decisions. And how could lawmakers understand the needs of the Gulf Coast, they reasoned, without seeing the Katrina devastation in person? By the end of their one-day trip, they had extended hundreds of formal invitations to visit New Orleans, complete with RSVP cards and return envelopes.

At the time of WOS's January 2006 trip to Washington, only 30 of 100 U.S. senators and 55 of 435 U.S. representatives had visited post-Katrina New Orleans.[12] Some senior Republican lawmakers, including Speaker of the House Dennis Hastert, had questioned rebuilding the city at all.[13] Unsatisfied with the number of congressional visits, comparing it unfavorably to trips made by lawmakers to wartime Iraq and post-tsunami Indonesia, WOS thought an invitation would make all the difference.

Many New Orleanians feared the nation had moved on despite the daunting challenges that remained. Several pieces of Katrina-related legislation were pending in Congress, including an ambitious housing plan that would have provided large-scale government buyouts of flood-damaged homes, but their passage was far from guaranteed. These women, like the *New York Times* editors, were well aware that the Gulf Coast recovery would depend heavily on the procurement of additional federal funds, and hence they positioned themselves as crucial intermediaries between society and the state.[14]

WOS kept a running count of visits by lawmakers, and in a series of public relations campaigns, they used media outlets to pressure reluctant lawmakers to visit. Some elected officials avoided the women, canceling prearranged appointments in Washington or refusing to return their calls. These implicit challenges did not go unmet by the self-described "Southern ladies," who were experts in the art of hospitality. They self-consciously deployed their Southern charm, hoping that elected officials would have a difficult time saying "no" to a proper, albeit insistent, invitation.

Following a second trip to Washington, in September 2006, visits by elected officials had nearly doubled, and many lawmakers credited WOS's influence. By December 2006, Congress had approved billions of additional federal funds for the Gulf Coast recovery. Working in conjunction with the business community, city officials, and Louisiana politicians, WOS helped bring about the passage of landmark, though controversial, legislation aimed at restoring coastal wetlands using royalties generated from oil and gas drilling off Louisiana's coast, thereby crafting market solutions to environmental problems while contributing to the regional and national dependence on oil.

New crises and political debates in the years that followed would recharge the women. In the wake of the 2010 *Deepwater Horizon* oil spill, blamed primarily on the London-based BP oil and gas company, which leased the rig, the group expanded its membership to include women from five Gulf Coast states whose coastal communities were affected by the spill. Together they called on Congress to direct a percentage of the penalties imposed on BP to finance coastal restoration projects.[15] As this book chronicles, WOS continued to adapt over the years, developing new structures, goals, and strategies to address issues it deemed important for the city, the region, and even the nation.[16]

WOS shaped the Gulf Coast recovery in profound ways. They worked to forge ties across the boundaries of race, class, age, and geography. Their efforts united a group of women from varied social backgrounds and life experiences—ranging from philanthropists to florists, from attorneys and small-business owners to former debutantes and Mardi Gras royalty, from housewives and mothers to professors and university presidents, bankers, writers, and nuns—in struggles to rebuild their communities.

Disasters often create conditions that give rise to new groups. In this book I treat WOS as a "disaster-related emergent group," which sociologists define as a group of "private citizens who work together in pursuit of collective goals relevant to actual or potential disasters but whose organization has not yet become institutionalized."[17] In contrast to established groups or disaster relief organizations—such as the American Red Cross, Catholic Relief Services, or Mercy Corps—whose tasks and structures are typically in place before disasters, the goals and structures of emergent groups are under construction during times of extreme duress. For emergent groups, organizational structures are not firmly established, membership is not always clearly defined, and the prioritization of tasks is up for negotiation. Emergent groups are typically fragile and short lived, and many dissolve after immediate needs are met. It is not surprising that emergent groups formed in the wake of Katrina; disaster sociologist Kathleen Tierney observes that the greater the scale of the disaster, the more likely emergent groups are to form.[18]

Studying group emergence is important precisely because of these instabilities and contingencies, which provide insight into the complex processes involved in groups, the reasons people work with some rather than others, and the choices subjects make about activities they deem important. Disasters are events in which implicit meanings about the social world become explicit.[19] These social upheavals can be likened to what Arlie Russell Hochschild describes as "magnified moments," which are "episodes of heightened importance, either epiphanies, moments of intense glee or unusual insight, or moments in which things go intensely wrong." For Hochschild, these episodes are instructive: "By interrogating the moment, so to speak, we ferret out the cultural premises that underlie it."[20] This includes premises about social and moral identities, which are often called into question and transformed in disasters.

And yet many studies of group emergence in disaster treat identity categories (such as race, class, and gender) as static and unchanging; they also tend to ignore how group emergence itself contributes to the constitution or reconstitution of identities that disasters often put into question.[21] A disaster's breach of everyday life provides an important empirical context for the examination of identity construction and reconstruction; the breach creates moments when people become more aware of these social processes—and themselves. As Vered Vinitzky-Seroussi writes, "People most frequently become conscious of their identities at moments of transition, which are often also moments of crisis."[22]

WOS members' work to rebuild their communities was also work to repair their sense of self, to engage in moral action enabled by their social location in the world. By focusing on process and interaction, I aim to show how group emergence in disasters contributes to the process of identity construction and reconstruction. My interviews with WOS members show how identities—especially moral identities—are actively reconstituted through group formation and its concomitant practices and interaction rituals.[23] This book situates identity repair and reconstruction in the context of small group life. In its early days, WOS was in flux. Social relations and their meanings were being negotiated. Identities and group boundaries were being figured out. Ten years after hurricanes Katrina and Rita, these processes and narratives have settled. But insights can be gained by returning to WOS's formative moments. Following research by sociologist Kathleen Blee, a scholar of social movements and incipient activism, I have decided to focus much of this book on

WOS's initial formation, guided by her claim that in the study of social movements groups, "what happens later obscures what happened earlier."[24] In Blee's words:

> The cultural blueprint set out in the early days of grassroots groups is difficult to reconstruct once the group becomes established. By then, many issues of the early days are gone. As initial questions are settled and dilemmas resolved, activists' recollection of how this happens fades. Ways of acting and thinking become assumed, obscuring the process by which these were established. What was once up for grabs comes to be seen as fixed, normal, even inevitable. The group *is* African American or mixed race, violent or peaceable, insular or inclusive. The reasons it is this way disappear from individual and collective memory. It is now unquestioned and largely unquestionable.[25]

Blee argues for a close focus on the process of emergence: "By looking at the early moments of collective activism we can see directly what later will become opaque."[26] Such an approach provides a way of understanding what she calls "cascading sequences of actions," or how small acts made early in a group's existence "can reverberate to provoke large effects."[27]

This book draws upon these assumptions to better understand WOS's story. Rather than painting the group's history with large brushstrokes, as if its outcomes were determined by putatively static characteristics of individual group members or the group's overall composition, I focus on micro-level processes that took place as the group came together. These processes had the power to shift the group's trajectory. Blee notes, "Given the complexity of cause and effect, the task is to understand unfolding processes, not to predict their realization or final 'accomplishment.' This task requires thick description of sequences over time."[28]

Ethnography and qualitative methods are useful for undertaking what Blee calls a "microhistorical analysis in a sociological study of a present-day social phenomenon."[29] I use microhistory as an analytic framework to address issues that can arise when observers and participants talk about social movement groups after they are established, relying on the group's current membership or its successes or failures to read backward in time. While I was not present to witness the group's genesis, I entered the ethnographic scene early and documented dynamics, issues, and dilemmas whose outcomes might easily have been described as "givens" if I had gained access any later. When I began my fieldwork, participants' recollections were fresh, their stories vivid, and their accounts full of details that have likely faded over time. Rereading my interview transcripts, I remain impressed with the incredible attention subjects gave to the particularities of their experiences, such as mundane everyday gestures, the pace of a conversation, where they stood and with whom, and the feel of the weather. Moreover, I began studying this group before there were any concrete successes or failures. There were many unknowns about who the group was, what participants would be able to do, and what they would ultimately become. Would WOS achieve its goals? Would it succeed in building a diverse group? How would it deal with hostile or supportive publics? Would it survive or fall apart?

Over the past decade, plenty has been written about WOS by both supporters and critics.[30] Most observers tend to describe WOS using static terms that highlight only attributes and characteristics rather than its processes. The group has done this, too, by creating narrative accounts of what it wanted to be and how it wanted to be perceived. These labels, whether internal or external, flatten out complex social processes. In my comprehensive review of material published about WOS, I found that commentary and interpretations of the group tend to fall into two broad polarities. On the one hand, public supporters, especially the New Orleans media, have showered WOS with praise, and sometimes even awards and honors. In particular, these positive interpretations often adopt WOS's official stance, which portrays itself as diverse, and present it as embodying the values of liberal multiculturalism. For example, on the forty-year anniversary of Dr. Martin Luther King Jr.'s assassination, James Perry, executive director of the Greater New Orleans Fair Housing Action Center, wrote that WOS served as an exemplary illustration of how "post-Katrina advocacy coalitions have almost uniformly transcended race and ethnicity." After naming several group efforts to "better our community," including the work of WOS, Perry wrote, "Examine the ranks . . . and you will find that diversity is the norm."[31] Observers in this camp tend to overstate the group's heterogeneity; more importantly, they overlook ongoing processes involved in attempts to bring about and sustain a diverse group membership.

On the other hand, more skeptical observers of WOS have called into question the group's diversity altogether. Critics focus instead on what is perceived as homogeneity and the reproduction of social power in the interest of dominant groups.[32] Some foreground WOS's whiteness while others suggest that the women were merely acting under the influence of powerful men. In this book I challenge both claims. The first group of critics effectively overlooks WOS's heterogeneity.[33] For example, Greg Palast, an investigative journalist, described WOS as a "circle of genteel rich white ladies who, after the flood, came out of their plantation houses to wipe the brows of the fleeing Black folk. The Women got awards and praise from Congress but never spent a night sleeping in a FEMA trailer."[34] (Palast continued, "Am I being unnecessarily nasty about ladies doing their best to be helpful?") In this journalist's account, which to me seems quite mean-spirited and misogynistic in addition to being inaccurate, the attributes of some members—whiteness, affluence—became attributed to all members, implying that the group as a whole was not only rich and white but also racist. There are numerous failures in this logic. Whiteness becomes equated with affluence, thus positioning these subjects in opposition to blackness and poverty. Any other configuration of race, class, and gender becomes invisible. Furthermore, this account ignores the many contributions of women of color, both elite and non-elite, to WOS's history, as well as the experiences of non-elite white women and some white WOS members who did in fact live in FEMA trailers after Katrina.

For a second group of critics, WOS is framed as a women's auxiliary group, merely supporting the political and economic agendas of the husbands of those in the group's inner ring. This interpretation leaves no room for understanding women's autonomy and independent thinking, and it fails to address the women's experiences on their own terms. When women's voices are included in such accounts, if at all, they are often trivialized. The ease with which these critics have dismissed WOS is symptomatic of larger cultural beliefs and stereotypes that portray women of means, and women in general, as frivolous and inconsequential.

While there is a wide spectrum in these popular interpretations of WOS, existing perspectives tend to employ static labels based on seemingly unchanging group descriptors, such as race, socioeconomic class, neighborhood of residence, or the women's perceived derivative status in relation to men. But to return once again to insights from Blee's work, "labels are misleadingly static, a way of *not* seeing as well as seeing."[35] Much of what has been written about WOS over the past decade greatly obscures the social processes involved in its emergence and subsequent group life. This labeling "implies that such characteristics are essential and durable. The description freezes in time what is actually in flux, treating variable states of activism as fixed attributes."[36] Blee offers this caution: "Labeling an activist group by using only its outward appearance thus risks the error of 'misplaced concreteness,' equating a model of reality with actual reality. In fact, groups can be much more dynamic than their public appearance suggests."[37] In each case, "what *is* (its attributes) creates a misleading sense of *how it came to be* (the cause)."[38] Focusing on *how* WOS came to be, I draw on Blee's work to take a another approach to understanding this group, its shifting composition, and its life course.

Drawing upon theories of group emergence, I posit that WOS's story is much more complex than any of these observers have indicated. It is only through a detailed description of the group that these social processes become evident. In contrast to those who have written about these women with little, if any, contact with them, I argue that one major issue under question—that of group diversity—needs to be considered differently. Rather than being defined by attributes that remain constant, I argue that WOS's composition varied considerably over time and across space. Empirical data show that the attribute often described as "diversity" was nearly always in flux—that is, the group's composition changed from moment to moment and from setting to setting. Diversity, as a central feature of WOS's "organizational character" or its sense of itself, was frequently an explicit issue of concern.[39]

Moreover, different questions about the social functions of diversity discourse could be asked. Drawing on Sara Ahmed, one could ask, "What does diversity do? What are we doing when we use the language of diversity?"[40] For example, in her study of educational organizations, a site where the deployment of "diversity" can be used to conceal systemic inequalities, Ahmed examines how "the languages of diversity are mobilized in various ways by different actors."[41] To use this approach in an analysis of WOS, or any group in which diversity is an issue, requires reframing questions about diversity so as to treat it not as fixed, but rather as a set of processes. Diversity is managed by actors to achieve certain ends for individuals, for groups, for institutions, and perhaps for entire societies. Mobilizing diversity is an activity that creates certain opportunities and forecloses others.

It is thus necessary to examine the meanings that participants gave to their actions and group arrangements, including gaps between what they were at any given moment and what they sought to become. Such an approach "captures activism as a process, the dynamics by which groups make choices, develop routines, advance alternatives, and lose them. It avoids attributing a solidity to activist groups that happens when we assume that they have a constant purpose, membership, agenda, and dynamics over time. It also moves away from relying on taxonomies of activism (as identity based or ideological, for instance) to explain how groups work."[42]

This process-oriented reading of WOS requires specific analytic tools. In addition to drawing on sociological scholarship on group emergence, my approach to questioning the treatment of group life as static is also guided by feminist intersectional theoretical perspectives, which requires looking at how social differences such as race, class, and gender intersect and interact in the individual lives, group dynamics, and structural conditions under examination.[43] Feminist intersectional approaches analyze how forms of difference and inequality are mutually reinforcing.[44] Analytically, intersectional theories help unravel group dynamics among participants who are differently situated in a society still structured by class-based, race-based, and gender-based inequalities.[45]

As readers will observe, WOS's composition fluctuated greatly. I do not argue that it evolved in a linear fashion, but rather that it was constantly in flux. By looking at WOS's fluctuations and dynamics, this book highlights the conditions under which the group became homogeneous or heterogeneous and examines how participants arranged themselves, formally and informally, according to ideas about—and ideals of—diversity and other material outcomes.

This book also seeks to document WOS's broad contributions to the Gulf Coast recovery. Many accounts of Katrina discuss the allocation of federal funds without considering the lobbying efforts or deliberations that shaped recovery policies. In doing so, they fail to discuss processes by which congressional decisions were made and how members of civil society groups, including WOS, might have influenced lawmakers. To talk about the billions of dollars allocated by Congress for the recovery without talking about WOS's efforts effectively writes these actors out of history. One of my goals is to make sure that WOS's work is part of the historical record.[46]

As such, this book is concerned with these women's yet untold stories of the Katrina recovery. I believe it is important to tell WOS's story, for it has already begun to fade from memory. In 2015, while visiting New Orleans as I worked on the final draft of this book, I visited the Historic New Orleans Collection's Williams Research

Center to see if I could find any additional material about WOS. The research assistant I spoke with had never heard of WOS, which surprised me given the group's immense influence on history and politics. Somewhat frustrated, I left without a single piece of new information—that is, until I realized that my interaction with the staff member was nonetheless instructive of the broader patterns of historical amnesia that this book serves to correct.

"Studying Up" on Katrina

Hurricane Katrina enlivened academic, activist, and political debates about social inequality in the United States.[47] As is often the case, those debates have focused on the disadvantaged and the marginalized, leaving the lives of the privileged unexamined.[48] But to truly understand the social reproduction of inequality in contemporary American society, we must also examine how forms of privilege function in the making of what sociologist Shamus Rahman Khan calls "democratic inequality."[49] In the twenty-first century, scholarship on elites reveals that some of their practices, identities, and relations are being reconfigured. "The new elite," writes Khan, "are acting differently than most of the elite before them." Khan found a paradox at the heart of new inequalities in the twenty-first century—namely, that elite institutions have become increasingly diverse, incorporating members from previously excluded groups such as racial minorities and women, even as overall inequalities during the same period of time have increased.[50] Understanding this paradox of "democratic inequality" requires unraveling the nature of power and access to resources, not merely studying the impoverished. This investigation of WOS provides case study evidence of the shifting composition of elites and their group activities in contemporary contexts.

To better understand issues of power and inequality, it is helpful to talk with elites about their lives and social worlds. This approach can be characterized as "studying power and inequality—from above."[51] Ethnographic research has periodically employed this strategy of "studying up," shifting sociological attention to privileged groups as part of a strategy to increase the "democratic relevance" of social science research by using it to show how citizens might better access state, legal, and economic resources.[52] For example, scholars now routinely examine whiteness in studies of race, masculinity in research on gender, and heterosexuality in work on sexuality.

"Studying up" is a type of empirical investigation with its own methodological challenges, given the gatekeeping by elite subjects that makes elites notoriously difficult to access in social science research. Even when the elite grant ethnographic interviews, I'm aware that their talk is not always congruent with their actions; yet their words can provide certain insights into how they construct meaning and make sense of their positions in the world.[53] My goal is not to offer these subjects a space for defense or for redemption, nor to champion their causes or to excuse their actions. Nor is it to unfairly criticize them. Rather, I hope to understand, in as balanced a way as possible, the wide range of motives, emotions, values, and meanings that actors attach to their actions under quite extraordinary circumstances. As Cynthia Enloe states, "The motivation to take all women's lives seriously lies deeper than admiration" or "hero worship," for such a scholarly endeavor is "motivated by a determination to discover exactly how this world works."[54]

In this study, I also draw upon the works of Kathleen D. McCarthy, Diana Kendall, and other social scientists who explore upper-class women's cultures of charity and volunteerism.[55] Existing studies of elite white women and elite women of color argue that their good deeds and philanthropy contribute to the social reproduction of power. Yet the focus is usually on established women's organizations in non-crisis times. By contrast, this book takes advantage of a rare opportunity to investigate the formation of a women's group, emerging out of crisis, with elite members from varied racial and ethnic backgrounds.

Although women of means have figured prominently in historical studies of social reform, very little is known about elite women's activities within contemporary disaster contexts.[56] According to a recent review essay, "in-depth class analysis is still relatively rare in gender-focused disaster research," and when socioeconomic class is addressed, it usually highlights vulnerable populations.[57] Disaster research on gender and class tends to focus on impoverished women's experiences, with the exception of a few studies that examine how middle-class women experience distress, anxiety, and downward mobility following disaster, especially after becoming recipients of charity and state-sponsored aid.[58]

I spoke with forty-one women who were part of WOS at the time of being interviewed. They ranged in age from thirty-two to seventy-eight years old; the mean age was fifty-two. The racial composition included high proportions of white interviewees, followed in frequency by black and then Asian women: thirty women self-identified as white/Caucasian, six as black/African American, three as Asian/Vietnamese, and two as Other. On average, they were highly educated. All but one had completed college; the exception was only one semester short of completing the bachelor's degree requirements. Eighteen of the forty-one had earned masters degrees, and two held JDs. I am aware of at least five WOS participants who held a PhD, four of whom were African American. Information on marital status was also solicited. Thirty-three of the women were married, six were single, and two were divorced. The political party affiliation breakdown is as follows: twenty Republicans, ten Democrats, and three Independents, with eight interviewees providing qualified answers or avoiding answering the question about party affiliation entirely; among the eight with qualified answers, two said they were Republicans but switching to Independent, and one described herself as an ex-Republican. (In addition to the forty-one WOS members, I interviewed nine women from other post-Katrina women's groups; the demographic breakdown just given does not include them. These additional interviews contributed to my understanding of the general context; I discuss this further in "Notes on Method.")

Most women I interviewed enjoyed privileged backgrounds and social networks. But I use the term "elite" with some caution. How can "elite" be defined in a way that allows for multiple positionalities? My conceptualization of elites, as people with various forms of privilege, is relative rather than absolute, open-ended rather than closed. Following Khan, I understand elites as "those who have vastly dispropor-tionate control over or access to a resource."[59] Khan notes that resources—whether political, economic, social, cultural, or knowledge capital—must somehow have "transferable value"; that is, "understanding elites means not just making sense of the resource they control or have access to; it also means considering the conversion of that resource into other forms of capital."[60] This definition focuses less on the content of the resources, since this can vary quite widely in transferability according to social context. Drawing on Khan's insights, I call attention to the "social process by which some [resources] become valuable and others do not."[61]

A number of WOS participants hailed from the most prominent families in New Orleans and in Louisiana, some of whom were also part of national elite networks. While many were part of the economic and political elite, status was determined by much more than income, wealth, or political connections. For instance, group members Carol Bebelle, director of the Ashé Cultural Arts Center, and Leah Chase, the famous chef known as the "Queen of Creole Cuisine," are arguably at the center of the New Orleans black cultural elite, although not necessarily part of the highest economic tiers of New Orleans society. Other participants, such as the Vietnamese Catholic nuns from New Orleans East, may have had little personal wealth, because their assets are pooled collectively; they nonetheless have a great deal of status within particular ethnic and religious contexts. Not all the elite women of WOS are wealthy. In this way, WOS functioned as a Weberian status group, one demarcated by a combination of esteem and respect, power and prestige, rather than by narrow indicators such as income or wealth.[62]

In general, WOS participants were highly active in civic and community life. Many had served on charitable organizations' boards and fund-raising commit-tees. For the most part, WOS participants returned home soon after the storm, a period when New Orleans had become, as described by one observer, a "city of men."[63] Many, though not all, lived in unflooded New Orleans neighborhoods such as Uptown or the Garden District, areas on high ground near the Mississippi River that came to be known in post-Katrina vernacular as the "sliver by the river." Typically, their homes were spared, which allowed for their early reentry and swift political mobilization.

But some WOS participants did in fact experience storm losses, including eight of the forty-one women I interviewed. And some women, usually in the group's rank-and-file positions, were drawn from non-elite communities to share their experiences with lawmakers. The homes of some of these women flooded as well. For months, and in some cases years, they lived in temporary housing—apartments, hotels, and FEMA trailers—while gutting their homes. They navigated the bureaucratic maze of the insurance industry. They began rehabilitating their abandoned neighborhoods, some of which remained without lights, water, or basic services for months after the storm. WOS members believed their group's credibility would be strengthened by including participants who could tell members of Congress stories of loss. Participants, however, were unlikely to be drawn from the thousands of displaced residents dispersed across the nation in the 2005 Katrina diaspora, the largest internal forced displacement in the United States since the Dustbowl migrations of the 1930s.[64]

Aware of their relative privilege and the magnitude of this event, the women felt an urgent moral responsibility to speak on behalf of others and to engage in what sociologists Paul Lichterman and Nina Eliasoph describe as "civic action," in which "participants are coordinating action to improve some aspect of common life in society, as they imagine it."[65] Their work involved "self-organizing action" that was aimed at helping "'steer' society, even in a small way."[66] Because the women's civic actions were clearly imbued with meaning, this book examines the significance that group members gave to their individual and collective activities, however routine or extraordinary they might have been. This study draws upon the symbolic interactionist tradition, which suggests that understanding the social world requires an examination of the meanings that social agents attribute to their own actions, and it treats these meanings as embedded and negotiated at the individual, group, and institutional levels.[67] For many participants, a newfound agency replaced feelings of helplessness, and they felt a renewed sense of purpose and belonging. Simply put, they felt that they were "doing something" to help.

But why did they need to "do something" in the first place? What led them to mobilize themselves and to act on behalf of others? What challenges arose in the process of crafting spaces for participation? And how was this work part of an attempt to construct "good character" and to do what was right? This book seeks to answer those questions, and in doing so, it brings the exigencies of identity formation and morality to the foreground. It shows how the women's collective efforts to rebuild after disaster were also attempts to reconstruct their moral selves, to craft lives with direction and purpose, and, in Émile Durkheim's language, to establish and maintain more meaningful moral bonds with others.[68] I hope to convey the sense of urgency, despair, and hope in the wake of Katrina, a context that gave rise, I would argue, to one of the most influential groups of women in Louisiana's history and in the post-Katrina era.

Narrative, Tactical Humanism, and Public Sociology

To make this investigation of WOS accessible to as wide an audience as possible, to engage in what Michael Burawoy calls "public sociology," I have written this book as a narrative rather than as a traditional social science study.[69] To do this, I draw upon what ethnographer Lila Abu-Lughod, in *Writing Women's Worlds*, calls "tactical humanism," an approach that adopts "techniques of humanistic writing."[70]

Abu-Lughod is part of an ethnographic tradition that calls into question the analytical language of the social sciences and the concomitant imperatives to search for generalizations that sustain a "professional discourse of objectivity and expertise."[71] There are challenges, Abu-Lughod writes, for ethnographers in this search for generalizations—namely, that "in the process of generalizing from experiences and conversations with a number of specific people in a community, the anthropologist may flatten out their differences and homogenize them."[72]

With this "tactical humanism" in mind, I occasionally situate myself in the text, with the intent, as Abu-Lughod puts it, of "leaving traces of myself throughout," but overall I aim to keep the focus on the women's lives. I also examine the lives of individuals, a technique that "encourages familiarity rather than distance and helps break down 'otherness,' for it not only corresponds to the way we ordinarily think about those close to us in our everyday world, but also actively facilitates identification with and sympathy towards others."[73] The chapters weave individual experiences into the group story to encourage some sense of familiarity and avoid the pitfall of treating WOS as homogeneous. Finally, I adopt a narrative form. As Abu-Lughod writes in her ethnography of women's everyday life in a small community in Egypt: "I could have distinguished between the women's words and my own commentary, or interjected reminders of the ways I was using their narratives to produce certain effects. The latter technique might have made for more honesty but would have drawn attention away from the stories. The former would have set up the usual hierarchy between 'informant's words' and expert's explanations, a construct that, even when unintended, is hard to resist because of habits of reading and the structures of authority."[74] With Abu-Lughod's words in mind, I seek to minimize the reproduction of these hierarchies, although at times I do provide commentary and observations.

Abu-Lughod is part of a long history of narrative accounts of ethnographic work, including feminist social reformer Jane Addams's 1910 book, *Twenty Years at Hull-House; with Autobiographical Notes*, and, more recently, João Biehl's *Vita: Life in a Zone of Social Abandonment* and Chad Broughton's *Boom, Bust, Exodus: The Rust Belt, the Maquilas, and a Tale of Two Cities*.[75] In the growing body of Katrina literature, some of the most memorable works draw upon the tools of narrative nonfiction; in particular, I've been inspired by Dan Baum's *Nine Lives: Mystery, Magic, Death, and Life in New Orleans*, Tom Wooten's *We Shall Not Be Moved: Rebuilding Home in the Wake of Katrina*, and Rebecca Solnit's *A Paradise Built in Hell: The Extraordinary Communities That Arise in Disaster*.[76]

The narratives included here are meant to portray what really happened—as a collection of individual stories and experiences rather than as an assemblage of fictionalized accounts. In researching this group, I drew heavily on archival sources, including newspaper articles, photographs, video footage, natural documents, and social movement ephemera. News stories of key events provide the architectural scaffolding, and I use multiple sources of data to fill in the details, including archival and documentary materials, my ethnographic observations and field notes, and my in-depth interviews with WOS members. Unless otherwise noted, direct quotations throughout this book come from my interviews with participants. Weaving these data sources together, the book chronicles WOS's formation and subsequent collective actions. That said, this book is not intended to be *the* definitive group history; it is a partial view based on my observations and the narrative reconstruction of events by participants who recollected some details and not others. I have used many sources to reconstruct just one possible picture of what transpired.

Overview of the Book

Women of the Storm chronicles the group's struggles and accomplishments over many years, beginning with the women's collective efforts to convince Washington lawmakers to see Katrina's destruction firsthand and ending with WOS's campaign to restore the Gulf Coast after the BP oil spill. The chapters unfold in a loosely chronological order, focusing on key events, turning points, and processes that shaped group action. The chapters begin with WOS's emergence, a period during which its goals, structure, and composition were under construction. Readers are introduced to WOS's founder, Anne Milling, and the core leadership, and they learn about the recruitment process and the rapid-fire labor involved in preparing for WOS's first collective action. Next comes a description of WOS's first trip to Washington, D.C., in January 2006, highlighting the subjective experiences of participants with one another and with elected officials. Readers then learn about the immense amount of follow-up work that occurred through the first year after Katrina and Rita as the women continued their efforts to bring members of Congress to New Orleans and the Gulf Coast, a campaign that culminated in a second trip to Washington, in September 2006. The book goes on to examine how WOS expanded its membership and campaigns in the years thereafter.

The narrative makes brief detours to examine the lives of a few individuals, both at WOS's center and at its edges, whose profiles show that the group was far from homogenous, that each participant brought a unique perspective, that each had a story to tell.[77] Readers will meet upper-class white women and women of color, some of whom are considered among the most esteemed and powerful in contemporary Louisiana, as well as women of middle-class backgrounds, at least one of whom weathered the storm in the Superdome after being rescued during the flood. And readers will meet community workers who have dedicated their lives—pre- and post-Katrina—to helping others. The text occasionally turns from the narrative to sociological analysis and commentary, but more often than not the analysis is implied by the material on the page, leaving room for readers to weigh information, consider the participants' experiences, and arrive at their own conclusions.

Disasters provide a lens through which we can see everyday social inequalities in the United States. The vast majority of work on Katrina and Rita, even a decade later, has examined the experiences of the disadvantaged, and with good reason, given that marginalized groups experienced by far the most negative consequences of the storms. But what new understandings might be gained from "studying up" on disaster? I invite readers to pause and to consider a difficult question: "What would you do if you had the power and resources available to help a city like New Orleans recover from catastrophe?" It is my hope that readers will see that decisions about what actions to take, and with whom, are rarely easy.

CHAPTER 1

Emergence

*In which it occurs to a New Orleans philanthropist,
in the wake of disaster, to form a group*

Women of the Storm emerged in the wake of hurricanes Katrina and Rita, cata-strophic events followed by a slowed and flawed recovery.[1] Consider for a moment the bleak conditions in New Orleans in January 2006. While post-Katrina repopula-tion estimates varied widely, officials estimated that the population of Orleans Parish on January 1 was about 134,000, or about 71 percent below the pre-Katrina level of 462,269.[2] In neighboring St. Bernard Parish, the population was down by 88 percent, with a population estimate of 8,000 compared to the pre-Katrina figure of 65,554.[3] The infrastructure of New Orleans was in shambles; 45 percent of the city's street-cars and 53 percent of its buses had been destroyed. The number of public transit routes in operation dropped from 57 prior to Katrina to just 28, and there were only approximately 11,709 public transit riders per week, compared to 124,000 before the storm.[4] Fewer than half of the city's 450 traffic lights were working. Officials at the time estimated that it would take another six months to complete the remaining repairs.[5] Only 35 percent of retail food establishments had reopened; only 32 percent of major hospitals were back in operation. Less than 15 percent of public schools in Orleans Parish had reopened, compared to 100 percent in Jefferson Parish and only 7 percent in neighboring St. Bernard Parish.[6] Much of the city felt like a ghost town. Thousands of homes sat vacant, and bodies were still being found.

Anyone who witnessed this ruined landscape would have wondered about how to speed up the recovery. New Orleans philanthropist Anne Milling had been thinking about it for months. Around Thanksgiving 2005, Milling thought that if members of Congress visited the devastation, they would be more likely to direct additional federal funding to the Gulf Coast. Her idea was simple: gather a group of women, charter a plane to Washington, and personally invite lawmakers to see the area for themselves. The proposal was ambitious. But as a wealthy New Orleans woman deeply involved in philanthropic causes, Milling had mastered the art of civic organizing. This "invisible career" (sociologist Arlene Kaplan Daniels's term that captures the social significance of women's volunteer work) had prepared her well.[7] Her involvement with women's organizations had taught her to think up big ideas and bring them to fruition. She drew upon a long history of women's clubs and institutions that provided women of her race and class background with opportunities to participate in public life. Her biography is part of this long tradition and became important background for WOS; for this reason it is worth considering her personal history before delving into the history of the group.

Anne Catherine McDonald was born in New Orleans on September 26, 1940, to a young, socially connected couple, Hugh Gibson McDonald and Hilda Wasserman McDonald.[8] Anne McDonald spent much of her early childhood in New Orleans, attending elementary school at Academy of the Sacred Heart, an all-girls Catholic school, where she recalled the nuns being quite "rigid," instilling discipline and respect for elders. At age nine she and her family moved to Monroe, a small city in northeast Louisiana, where Hugh McDonald served as vice president and manager of Krafco Container Company, an industrial plant that produced paper and corrugated boxes. Before bringing the family to Monroe, he had attended Loyola University for two years, but in the hard times of the Depression, he was unable to complete the degree requirements. Hilda Marie Wasserman, on the other hand, earned a bachelor's degree in music from Newcomb College (Tulane University's women's college, which merged with Tulane after Katrina) on June 9, 1931, and was recognized that same year with the Kaiser Medal for Excellence in Music.[9]

The young Anne McDonald enrolled in public school in Monroe, where she was exposed to classmates from varied socioeconomic backgrounds, an early life experience that in many ways set her apart from those whose parochial educations in New Orleans went uninterrupted. She was by all accounts an outstanding student and one of the community's most popular young women. During her years at Neville High School, she moved on from her childhood dream to become a water ballet swimmer like Esther Williams and accumulated a long list of honors, participating in many activities—the French club, the Latin club, and Thespians—and she was the secretary treasurer of her class. She also had athletic ability. Playing the position of forward, she was an all-state basketball player and helped the girls' team win the 1958 state championship. She was part of the Tigerettes, a Neville High "spirit group." A photo in her high school yearbook shows her with five other girls in the cheerleading club encircling a Bengal tiger statue, each girl with a hand on the tiger's back. This all culminated in her senior year when she was crowned homecoming queen.[10]

From Monroe, she returned to New Orleans and enrolled in Newcomb College, just as her mother had done some years earlier.[11] During her time at Newcomb, she pledged in a sorority, Pi Beta Phi, later becoming its president, and she served as president of her senior class. Although popular and active at Newcomb, McDonald did not conquer it as thoroughly as she had her small high school. In her college yearbook, the *Jambalaya*, McDonald is pictured with her sorority and in her cap and gown with the rest of the senior class; these appearances were buried deep in the yearbook compared to some of the first few pages dedicated to more glamorous portraits of the participants in the *Jambalaya* beauty contest. Her name did appear frequently in the city's society pages as attending teas, debutante parties, and weddings, though it might very well be that her outsider status as a non–New Orleanian, a young woman from Monroe, made access to some of the city's most important social circles, like the old-line Mardi Gras krewes, more difficult. Young society women are invited to be maids and queens of krewes that hold parades and balls, and the debutante season in New Orleans is calibrated with the Carnival season. During the 1960 Carnival season, Anne McDonald was selected as a maid in the court of Athenians and was presented as a debutante at the ball of the Society of the War of 1812, which was held at the New Orleans Country Club. Many of her classmates at Newcomb were having elaborate coming-of-age parties after being selected as maid, lady-in-waiting, or queen at the lavish krewe balls of the top-rank societies: Comus, Rex, Momus, Proteus, Atlanteans, Oberon, Mithras, and Twelfth Night Revelers.[12] And while the Athenians and the Society of the War of 1812 are not the most prestigious of society organizations, they still qualify as elite organizations. The cultural machinations of New Orleans high society can appear byzantine to outsiders, but they may just make explicit the familiar in-group/out-group dynamics at play throughout the United States, including the fact that status hierarchies exist even among the elite. And they reveal that while McDonald was talented, driven, and well-connected, her chances of becoming a leader of New Orleans social life were not assured—that is, her rise to influence was not a foregone conclusion.

Her academic career at Newcomb culminated in her graduation in 1962, and she earned a Woodrow Wilson Fellowship, which she used to attend Yale University in 1963.[13] An East Coast school like Yale, her parents decided, was more stable during the turbulent 1960s than going out west to Stanford or Berkeley, where she had also been accepted for graduate school. She recalled that going away to graduate school was something quite novel, even odd, for New Orleans women at the time, and she found the experience to be incredibly stimulating. She lived in the dorms and ate her meals at the Yale Law School, where she would discuss the issues of the day with students who had attended elite colleges such as Harvard, Princeton, and Yale. Her New Orleans education, she recalled, stacked up against theirs and set the stage for her to earn a master's degree in history.

After earning her degree at Yale, McDonald returned to New Orleans and taught history for two years to seventh-, eighth-, and ninth-graders at Louise S. McGehee School, a prestigious, all-girl preparatory school in the Garden District that has "long catered to the daughters of upper-crust New Orleans," and that today still has ties to many WOS participants and their families.[14] G. William Domhoff, scholar of the power elite in the United States, lists association with the McGehee School as one indicator of upper-class standing.[15] McDonald resigned from her teaching post to start a family with her attorney husband, Roswell King Milling, also born in 1940, who would eventually become president of Whitney National Bank, the famous repository for old money in New Orleans. The Millings, married in 1964, became parents to three sons. As a mother, Milling organized her early volunteer activities around her children's schedules, she told *Times-Picayune* reporters in 1983. She made great efforts to be home in the afternoon, and she served as a Cub Scout den mother as well as a room mother at the boys' school, Isidore Newman, where one of her sons would become a star quarterback.[16] While her volunteer work in those early years was enabled by having what she called "the luxury of time," she also remarked on how volunteerism pulled her away from the activities that characterized the lives of many wealthy white women of the era: "You can't fix soufflés and gorgeous dinners. Certain things do have to slide."[17]

Charity work was part of Milling's membership in women's social clubs. In 1966 she was invited to join the Junior League of New Orleans, and she accepted with "alacrity."[18] Her participation in the Junior League, she said, taught her "how to organize, have an agenda for every meeting, assess, evaluate, incorporate diversity. All the things that the Junior League teaches you, and you just seem to absorb it into your DNA."[19]

In March 1973 Milling was profiled in an advertisement in the *Times-Picayune* in conjunction with her recognition as one of "The Beautiful Activists," an annual designation by Germaine Monteil, a cosmetics company, and D. H. Holmes, the New Orleans department store.[20] The ad described Milling as "tall, slim, bright, clear eyed, cheerful, active, busy, unhung up and universally liked" and discussed her many "impressive" contributions to civic life and public service.[21] Also that year, Milling became the first woman appointed to the New Orleans Sewerage & Water Board (S&WB). One newspaper article recounts how upon her arrival at her first board meeting, the S&WB president pro tem "showed her to a seat in the audience and said how pleased he was that she came to watch the panel at work."[22] Little did this man know that Milling would be actively participating in that day's meeting and would remain a working board member for the next twelve years, the last two of which were spent in the elected position of president pro tem. By the early 1980s an unnamed "City Hall insider" told *Times-Picayune* reporters that "Anne is refreshingly active in a pursuit that is not trendy or chic. She's into drainage and sewerage and duking it out with the mayor, instead of running around in pursuit of Chagalls."[23] Whereas some critics described Milling as "very naïve" or out of touch with grassroots politics, as one unnamed leader of a black political organization told reporters, others, "including several city councilmen, say anyone who thinks Milling is not politically astute is only fooled by her blond and breezy facade. Her

FIGURE 1. Original caption (1983): "Anne Milling, recently elected president pro tem of the Sewerage & Water Board of New Orleans, is a former president of the Junior League and a past queen of the Mystic Club. The mother of three sons is a ten-year veteran of the S&WB and its only female member at present." *Times-Picayune* staff photo/G. E. Arnold.

indifference to politics and personal political agendas, they say, only make her a better advocate."[24] New Orleans councilman Mike Early told the *Times-Picayune* that Milling possessed a "rare combination of charm and professionalism. She is difficult to say no to."[25]

Fund-raising is a valuable activity and area of specialization for women volunteers, like Milling, involved in philanthropic work. As Arlene Kaplan Daniels writes, "Women who know their city learn how to collect from it so they can redistribute some of the wealth."[26] From 1977 to 1978, Milling served as president of the Junior League of New Orleans, helping to establish the Parenting Center at Children's Hospital.[27] In 1982 she helped raise ninety-five thousand dollars for the Arts Council of New Orleans, and a year later she helped coordinate a black-tie gala fund-raiser,

"Seldom Seen: Art from Private Collections."[28] Milling would reign as Queen of the Mystic Club during the 1982 Carnival season, over a decade before her husband was Rex, King of Carnival, in 1993.[29]

Milling was also involved with a number of efforts to feed the hungry, including the Second Harvest Food Bank of Greater New Orleans and Acadiana (an affiliated corporation of the Catholic Charities Archdiocese of New Orleans) and Feeding America, in addition to working with United Way. Bishop Roger P. Morin of New Orleans said, "Anne was a terrific advocate in terms of acquiring resources—food for poor people, for folks who are unemployed, people falling on hard times."[30] She was also active in supporting residential care facilities for people living with HIV/AIDS. In the late 1980s, Milling helped raise eighty-eight thousand dollars for Project Lazarus, which had been established by the Archdiocese of New Orleans in 1985 to offer hospice care to persons living with AIDS.[31] Once limited to cramped quarters in an old convent, the residence house at Project Lazarus was able to expand with these funds. Not only did Milling raise funds for Project Lazarus, but she also spent time there weekly, mopping floors and driving residents to their medical appointments.[32] Unlike civic activities that put her in touch with politicians or the city's cultural elite, volunteer work at Project Lazarus put her in direct contact with one of the most stigmatized groups of that era. Milling remembered being part of the care facility's early history: "I was on the front lines back in the mid-'80s when Lazarus formed and there were only six (hospital) rooms for people with AIDS."[33] This was a period, as Milling described, "back in the '80s when no one was willing to do that."[34] Another New Orleanian, Mark C. Romig, one of the city's most visible civic leaders, made similar observations: "At the time of the disease, it [Project Lazarus] was somewhat, sort of the untouchable organization. Nobody wanted to get involved. And I think Anne Milling showed the way for many, many people to step up and be part of something that was so necessary in our community."[35] Longtime *Times-Picayune* publisher Ashton Phelps Jr., who led the newspaper during Hurricane Katrina, said, "I've never seen anyone who could lead the biggest events in town and then could also be so one-to-one personal, visiting with a dying person at Lazarus House, or taking care of and consoling somebody when they've just lost a family member."[36] For this work, Milling received Project Lazarus's Guardian Angel Award in 1998, and in 2016 she received the Pawell-Desrosiers Award, given to those who have demonstrated a significant commitment to the organization.[37]

In 1987 she served on the Papal Visit Executive Committee, which organized Pope John Paul II's visit to New Orleans, the first trip made to the city by any pope. Milling chaired the hospitality committee for the papal visit, which was responsible for mounting a "formidable welcome campaign for the ultimate houseguest."[38] Her committee responsibilities included planning details of the pope's visit, handling hospitality at all sites during his stay, and staffing a "pope hotline" in the basement of the Notre Dame Seminary, where volunteers answered questions from callers.[39]

Committee members were even responsible for choosing the chair the pope would sit in while dining at Archbishop Philip Hannan's New Orleans residence and for selecting silverware and place settings at the dinner table. Upon arrival at Archbishop Hannan's residence, Milling recounted, she was "dismayed to find a hodgepodge of old, mismatched furnishings—the home of a long-time bachelor indifferent to decor."[40] In one account of her event planning for the formal lunch to be served for the pope and nearly twenty bishops, Milling discovered that there were only eleven full place settings in Archbishop Hannan's cupboard.[41] Milling reflected on what she did next: "I found a telephone number and went for the best."[42] She contacted Lenox China and managed to secure a donation of two dozen custom-made place settings embossed with the papal and archdiocesan coat of arms. When the plates arrived in New Orleans just before the papal visit, Milling contacted Lenox China to thank them—and to make another request, as Archbishop Hannon later told the *Times-Picayune*: "She called them again and said, 'But we don't have any crystal.' So they gave a whole setting of crystal—24 places." With hospitality as her forte, Milling also held the position as head of protocol for the papal visit. In this capacity, she served as contact person for etiquette, providing *Times-Picayune* readers with advice about how to act and what to wear should they meet the pope in person.[43]

Throughout the 1980s and 1990s, Milling organized fund-raising events for some of the most prominent political actors in New Orleans.[44] Her record included serving on governing boards of the New Orleans Museum of Art, Loyola University (where she took a course every semester between 1979 and 1983), and the Bureau of Governmental Research.[45] The Junior League of New Orleans named Milling the 1990 Sustainer of the Year, and in 1995 she received the prestigious *Times-Picayune* Loving Cup, an award given annually by the newspaper since 1901 to recognize "local residents who have worked unselfishly for the community without expectation of public acclaim or material reward."[46]

Milling had benefited from her education at Newcomb College, and those concerned with keeping that institution's history alive were keen on highlighting these connections. In *Newcomb College, 1886–2006: Higher Education for Women in New Orleans*, Susan Tucker, who oversaw the Newcomb Archives and Special Collections, and Beth Willinger, a feminist scholar and the founding director of the women's studies program at Tulane, noted that of the twenty-nine women who had received the Loving Cup since 1901, ten were Newcomb alumnae, including women like Coca-Cola heiress Rosa Keller, a Newcomb student in the late 1920s, who would later become the first woman appointed to the New Orleans Public Library Board in the 1950s. The awarding of the Loving Cup recognized Milling's place in the ranks of influential New Orleans women.[47]

Milling's long career taught her how to raise money, maneuver through difficult political terrain, and make bold requests. Consequently, she and many others with similar experience in philanthropic social circles of New Orleans felt quite comfortable with the idea of calling on lawmakers—or knocking on their doors with hand-delivered invitations—and asking them, politely but firmly, to drop what they were doing in Washington and visit the hurricane-ravaged Gulf Coast.

A common question asked of New Orleanians after Katrina was whether they stayed or evacuated. Milling did neither. She was vacationing in Canada when Katrina made landfall, according to a conversation she had with *Washington Post* journalist Melinda Henneberger, who wrote about Milling's unique ability to navigate politics. "Anne is no Cindy Sheehan," Henneberger wrote, drawing comparisons to the antiwar activist who camped out for weeks in front of President George W. Bush's sixteen-hundred-acre ranch in Crawford, Texas, after her son was killed in Iraq in 2004. "But that's the point. Because when a mover like Anne Milling gets mad, it's harder to write her off as some kind of liberal lunatic."[48] Watching the Katrina crisis, Milling, like many others, wanted to do something. She decided that witnessing the disaster firsthand would speak for itself, so why not issue an invitation?

Milling first pitched this idea over a Thanksgiving dinner at her home just off St. Charles Avenue near Audubon Park, one of New Orleans's most affluent neighborhoods.[49] While about 40 percent of the Audubon/University neighborhood flooded, Milling's home was spared.[50] Her friends at the table that day, some of whom had lost their homes to Katrina's floodwaters, received the idea with great enthusiasm. During the last few weeks of 2005, Milling continued to discuss her idea at holiday parties throughout the depopulated city. But it wasn't until January 10, when Milling invited a carefully selected handful of people to her Uptown home, that she gained the support needed to activate her proposal.

This core group became known as the "executive committee," a recognizable organizational title that signals a "hierarchy of authority," the kind of structure they would have been familiar with through past work in women's civic organizations.[51] According to early media reports, the original "core leadership" included Anne Milling, Peggy Laborde, Beverly Church, Pam Bryan, Nancy Marsiglia, and Liz Sloss. Their civic participation was often enabled by the fact that they hailed from prominent families or were married to some of the city's most influential civic and business leaders, some of whom had long-standing ties to Louisiana's offshore oil and gas industry.[52]

Like Milling, members of the executive committee were highly active in women's clubs, charitable organizations, and philanthropy. Peggy Laborde, for example, served as president of the governing board of Longue Vue House and Gardens in suburban Metairie, a historic estate open to the public that showcases a neoclassical house built in the late 1930s and early 1940s for Edgar and Edith Rosenwald Stern, daughter of Julius Rosenwald, one of the owners of Sears, Roebuck, and Company. The Sterns were considered at the time to be pillars of the New Orleans community, in part because of their participation in progressive causes, such as improving education for the city's African American youth, that often required them to "[step] out of line with the color caste system."[53] Another core member was Beverly Church, New Orleans's version of Martha Stewart. Known for her stylish event planning,

Church had transformed her skills into a series of glossy, how-to entertainment books, a nationwide speaking career, and the founding and editorship of the life-style monthly *St. Charles Avenue Magazine*. She was also a powerhouse fund-raiser, volunteer, and teacher, whose causes ranged from teaching at public schools like McDonogh No. 1 to restoring Storyland, a fairy-tale-themed playground in New Orleans City Park.[54] Pam Bryan was a marketing director for several New Orleans nonprofit organizations, while Nancy Marsiglia had developed a community health clinic at Lawless High School in the Lower Ninth Ward. Liz Sloss organized events such as Audubon Zoo's annual fund-raising benefit, the Zoo-To-Do.[55]

These elite white women, like many others from the city's philanthropic community, described the months after Hurricane Katrina as a period of helplessness. Their pre-storm lives were made meaningful through charity, volunteerism, and social work, but the disaster disrupted their daily activities. Many people try to reestablish everyday life activities in the wake of disaster, and these women needed to create new avenues for their energies.[56] As with other women-led emergent groups such as Katrina Krewe, which swept storm debris from the city's main thoroughfares, and Citizens for One Greater New Orleans, which engaged in local and state-level political reform, including the post-Katrina consolidation of the city's levee boards, Milling's call to action resonated with these women. They felt a profound moral responsibility to act on behalf of the less fortunate.[57] Recalling WOS's formation, a white woman in her fifties described the desire to help: "When we were away, we desperately wanted to do something. We're the type that have all chaired a million things in the city, and we felt helpless. I'm [out of state] and not able to do anything to help the city. There wasn't a venue to do it." Milling's idea gave the women a sense of purpose: "We were like, 'Oh! [claps hands once] We're on it! This is our job.' All the things that you used to do, you weren't doing. So we had plenty of time to be able to put whatever we needed together. So when Anne said, 'Do you think it'll work?' We all went, 'Yes! It will work!'"

In many ways, though, this new endeavor was a departure from their pre-storm philanthropy. Milling described the differences to me: "There were so many unknowns. In other organizations or fund-raising endeavors I've done, there's pretty much a formula, a way of doing things, whether you're doing a capital campaign for the university or for the museum. There's a process that we can almost give to you. It's totally different from anything I've ever done." Instead, their post-Katrina project required improvisation and the ability to depart from rigid rules and procedures. WOS quickly became what disaster sociologists Tricia Wachtendorf and James Kendra call a "learning organization," one with the "collective ability to think about the environment; to pick up signals; compare them with what is known, and then assess what is needed to fill in gaps in knowledge."[58]

There were of course also many continuities with the women's pre-storm work. In *The Power of Good Deeds: Privileged Women and the Social Reproduction of the Upper Class*, sociologist Diana Kendall (who is also a member of numerous elite women's

organizations in Texas) discusses the philanthropic diversity in elite women's volunteerism and breaks down women's volunteerism into five categories: arts and
cultural organizations; groups that benefit prestigious schools; health-related volunteerism in foundations, such as hospitals and medical schools; efforts to battle "the
diseases"; and causes that help the "less fortunate."[59] For the women in Kendall's
study, age, race and ethnic background, class, and "special circumstances" (such as
illness) served as important social factors that motivated some elite women to join
certain organizations and not others. For the women in my study, many of their
pre-storm activities fit neatly into Kendall's typology. But unlike volunteerism in
more settled times, this moment was a period of great upheaval, and the women felt
that because the entire city was at risk of being lost or abandoned, they, too, were
at risk of becoming displaced. In this way, some elite women's work after Katrina
expanded from engaging in causes that benefited the "less fortunate," since they,
too, felt like they were in need of help. A white woman in her fifties, whose adult
children's homes flooded, explained: "The difference is a sense of urgency and a
sense of survival. Before, they were always projects to enhance. They were projects
to certainly help people that needed it. Never have they been projects to help ourselves. We need help. Never in my life would I have considered myself a victim of
anything. I'm a victim. And I am in danger of losing the place I live in and the place
I love. So it is very, very [long pause]—it is vastly different."

Although the situation was unique, the women had acquired the necessary skills
over years, if not decades, of volunteer work to bring their plan to fruition. They
were well positioned, as one woman told me, to take on this work. The project they
developed in their first meetings was ambitious. WOS planned to make the case for
wetlands restoration, estimated to cost over $14 billion over the next three decades,
and to come up with a proposal to fund it. This is where politics and business values quietly entered the conversation. The plan involved a request that Washington
grant a 50 percent share of royalties generated from oil and gas revenues earned off
Louisiana's coasts, which would be placed into a trust fund for coastal restoration.
They believed this would break Louisiana's dependency on the federal government
for flood protection and environmental projects. It wasn't the first effort to obtain
a "fair share" of royalties generated by offshore oil and gas production. In 2004, for
example, Governor Blanco proposed a 10 percent share of royalties, far less than the
50 percent portion that goes to inland states where drilling occurs on federal land.[60]
Such proposals did not come without controversy. Critics expressed concern that a
cost-sharing agreement might lead to additional drilling in federal waters, and the
federal government appeared reluctant to lose a steady stream of revenue.

Linking the Gulf Coast recovery with long-term coastal restoration, the group
partnered with America's WETLAND Foundation (AWF), an organization formed
in 2002 with a $3 million donation from Shell Oil as part of an initiative by Governor
Mike Foster (R), who served from 1996 to 2004, to educate the public about coastal
restoration.[61] In addition to emphasizing links between energy development and

the environment, AWF argued that wetlands help protect coastal areas from hurricane storm surge; and they pointed out that wetlands are disappearing at a rate of over twenty-four square miles annually.[62] For WOS, this would be an important framing device for claims that wetland protection was tied not only to disaster risk reduction for New Orleans but also to economic investments in the entire region.

There was a personal connection to AWF as well. Anne Milling's husband, R. King Milling, was AWF's chairman of the board in addition to being chairman of the Governor's Advisory Commission on Coastal Protection, Restoration, and Conservation. Before becoming president of Whitney National Bank, he had worked for years as a "big oil and gas lawyer."[63]

After their first meetings, the group of women had a plan, but they still didn't have a name. What would they call themselves?[64] The group sought guidance from Marmillion + Company, a Washington-based public relations firm that also ran AWF campaigns. At one early brainstorming session, the women and the PR firm suggested several ideas for the group's name—including "Matriarchs of Louisiana" or "Sisters of the Storm"—but these didn't catch on. Then someone pitched "Women of the Storm," and Milling remembered saying, "That's it!" The core group proceeded to recruit women as Women of the Storm, and the PR firm helped develop the group's logo, showing that this self-described grassroots group was also carefully crafted—and branded—from its inception.

On January 11, the day after the group first met at Milling's home, the *Times-Picayune* printed a front-page story, "In Congress, Vast Majority Yet to See Ruins; Lawmakers Say Damage Tours Strengthen City's Case for Aid." In the article, Louisiana lawmakers, including Senator Mary Landrieu (D) and Representative William Jefferson (D), emphasized that members of Congress needed to see the effects of Katrina. The journalist quoted Senator Hillary Clinton (D-NY), who had made the trip to New Orleans in December: "It is one thing to read reports about levees and what went wrong. It is another to stand on top of them and have someone explain what happened."[65] Another visitor, Senator Bill Frist (R-TN), said of his visit in late 2005, just before Congress adjourned, "I had the opportunity to talk to people on stretchers who three days before had homes that they had been in for 30, 40, 50 years. Those homes were totally washed away and destroyed with all their belongings. Whole towns were washed away."[66]

The *Times-Picayune* printed a table with the names of lawmakers who had visited post-Katrina New Orleans, and with this article the counting of congressional visits had begun. According to staff research through January 10, thirty-six members of the House and twenty-three members of the Senate, not including the Louisiana delegation, had visited. This article quantified trips by out-of-state lawmakers, creating a baseline against which WOS could measure its success. These counts would soon become part of the synergy between WOS and local media. The *Times-Picayune* (where Anne Milling was on the advisory board) and other local media outlets routinely trumpeted the group's cause, becoming vital to nearly everything WOS would do. This supports sociologist Diana Kendall's observation that the "media may serve as public relations outlets for the wealthy."[67]

Things were coming together. The group had a goal and a name. A key part of the women's mission was to increase the number of congressional visits, but as a tiny group of less than a half dozen, they couldn't do it alone. Needing backup, they began enlisting women from devastated areas to join the cause. But who would they invite to participate?

CHAPTER 2

Bridgework

*On the calling upon of old friends and
new acquaintances to join together*

In WOS's earliest stages, the core leadership, all white women, carefully considered the group structure and composition, and they began recruiting women from New Orleans and south Louisiana to participate in their one-day trip to Washington, D.C., where they would deliver invitations to members of Congress to visit New Orleans and the Gulf Coast. Emerging activist groups often make great efforts to develop an "operational sense of size"—that is, a general sense of the number of people deemed necessary to make an action worthwhile.[1] For many budding groups, this definition can be fairly imprecise. But for the WOS core, the number of participants was dictated by an external factor: the number of seats (140) on the plane they planned to charter. Given their desire to mobilize local media to help publicize WOS's cause, some of those seats were given to the press. In the end, only about 130 women could go to Washington.[2]

The limited number of seats created moral dilemmas of inclusion and exclusion that were not unlike the dynamics that play out when exclusive clubs create "membership caps."[3] While space limitations reflect what Diana Kendall calls "objective criteria" for shaping membership caps and categories, the women also needed to develop "subjective criteria" for deciding who would be invited.[4] A key consideration was racial and ethnic diversity, which the core leadership deemed necessary for WOS's success. A white woman in her forties explained the stakes: "We really felt that it was important that this was a grassroots initiative, that it was as diversified as we could possibly make it, that that would make our voice that much louder and make us that much more credible. That was one of the number-one requirements, that this was not going to go anywhere unless you had a broad-based coalition."

Racial politics in the predominantly black city of New Orleans had been divisive long before the storm, and these white women were attuned to the social, political, and moral implications of WOS's racial composition. Core members developed shared ideas about a broader moral order of inclusion, one shaped further by "imagined external standards."[5] When I interviewed her in early 2006, Milling explained, "We felt very strongly that we were representing metropolitan New Orleans, which is a very diverse area, south Louisiana, I mean. You've got African Americans, Caucasians, Hispanics, Vietnamese. That's what makes our area so unique. And just to go there with a group of Uptown white swells is not New Orleans, and not metropolitan New Orleans, and not Louisiana. We were trying to project an image that was very inclusive. I think everybody felt the same way. We want diversity. We want to promote that."[6]

Many WOS participants spoke in similar terms. By considering how they would be seen from the vantage point of others, WOS engaged in self-critical assessments of membership and belonging. As Blee writes, "By taking account of how others might see them, activist groups engage in a collective form of reflexivity."[7] How groups see themselves, and thus the images they project, helps construct self-definitions that shape subsequent action. Thus, WOS core leadership tried to diversify the group nearly from its inception.

Diversity first meant crossing a black-white racial divide, and recruiting black women was prioritized. One interviewee, a white woman, explained the early efforts to include participants from black women's civic organizations, especially those that were parallel in structure and stature to exclusive white women's organizations, which meant that ideas about race intersected implicitly with ideas about class and status: "You ever heard of the group Links? I think it is L-i-n-k-s," she said as I wrote down the organization's name. "It is a black ladies' civic organization. There is another one called Jack and Jill. Go figure. Anyway. [An African American woman] said that you need to get Links involved."[8] With the help of a few black women who served as key contacts, some of whom were members of both elite white women's groups such as the Junior League and elite black women's groups like The Links, the core began recruiting women of color from black elite circles of New Orleans.[9] In its beginnings, WOS quickly became more racially diverse than economically diverse, which could be attributed to the initially all-white executive committee's decision to begin to recruit primarily from socially and economically privileged groups of black women.

The Links Incorporated, a prestigious, invitation-only civic organization for elite black women, was founded in November 1946 by two women from Philadelphia: Margaret Hawkins and Sarah Scott.[10] In 1952 there were 56 chapters across the United States.[11] By 2015, Links membership had grown to nearly fourteen thousand in over 280 chapters nationwide; they collectively log more than five hundred thousand hours of community service each year, reflecting a long-standing tradition of African American philanthropy that is guided in part by notions of racial uplift.[12] In *Our Kind of People: Inside America's Black Upper Class*, a study of the private boarding schools, social clubs, vacation spots, and rituals of the black elite, Lawrence Otis Graham notes that although The Links is not the oldest elite black women's group in the United States, it is "by far the largest and most influential."[13] Graham states that for those in the know, mention of The Links needs no explanation: "As my mother and every other woman in her crowd would have told you, getting accepted into the Links was a big deal, and it was not something you'd ever need to explain if you were in the company of the right kind of people. In this case, some would say the right kind of people didn't include whites or blue-collar blacks."[14]

Membership in each Links chapter is limited, and admission is "extremely competitive"; positions become available only when a "current member vacates her position by death, by a move to another city, or through resignation (the latter being extremely rare)."[15] Most are invited to join in their forties and fifties and only after many years of showing up at the right events, wearing the right attire, and volunteering for the right causes. Like many aspects of in-group/out-group dynamics, criteria are rarely explicit. In addition to carrying oneself in particular ways, refraining from certain types of talk, and going to as many Links events as possible, aspiring nominees are also expected to distinguish themselves from other candidates. They are expected to own large homes, fancy cars, and even vacation residences for entertaining fellow members. In a meeting that Graham was given permission to observe during the organization's annual convention in New Orleans in the 1990s, one Links member in her late fifties said to an aspiring candidate, a CPA in her early thirties: "And sweetheart, don't take this the wrong way, but you might want to go and get yourself some more education—like a master's degree. . . . A graduate degree will help your chances, especially if you're going to be going after one of the older chapters. They really want to see as many degrees as possible."[16] Another Links member told Graham that it took her over a decade of "strategizing, party-giving and brownnosing to get into this group. . . . My mother didn't have the connections to get in when she was trying thirty years ago, and she never got over being left out."[17]

The Links provides access to elite networks of people with shared values. One Links member from the San Francisco chapter told Graham, "You can generally be sure the most important, best-connected, most affluent, and most socially acceptable black women in any city belong to the local Links chapter." She went on to say, "Maybe it sounds a little pretentious, but I simply can't waste time getting to know women who aren't Links. It's an automatic screen that lets me know if this person comes from the right background and has the same values. I'm almost fifty and I live a busy life. I don't have time for people who don't have the right stuff. Rich, educated white women don't hang around with middle-class college dropouts, so why should I?"[18]

At the time of Katrina, there were 140 Links members in three New Orleans chapters: the New Orleans chapter, the Crescent City chapter, and the Pontchartrain chapter.[19] By recruiting women from these chapters, the WOS core benefited from the "automatic screen" that ensured that these black women harbored similar values tied to class, status, and social standing. This starting point snowballed, making it unlikely that those who were lower on the economic ladder would be contacted.

Additional subjective criteria were used in recruitment. A white woman spoke to me about the desire to include African American women who were, among other things, civic minded: "We just got on the phone and we'd say, 'Who do you know? Who would be good to go on the trip?' Now, a lot of them, the people that we contacted, are community activists, which is very important, especially in the African American community, because we needed people who were *articulate*, who understood the deal, who'd been affected. And many of them were." The subtleties of racialized language should be noted. Many scholars of color-blind racism see the word "articulate" as a loaded word "that implies unspoken racialized meanings."[20] A few remarks were far more explicit. Consider the following comment from one white woman about seeking "high-falutin' African American women" that "you know, we are always trying to find": "Every time I get on a board it is like, 'OK, we need an African American on the board. Who can we ask to do it?' Some of them are wonderful, and you can't say that they are all not. But they are hard to find. The ones that really want to work. God, I really shouldn't even be saying that on your—[pause] on your recorder there. But I really enjoyed meeting all these very cool women."

Post-Katrina racial politics were contentious, and most white interviewees knew they would be held accountable for any hint of racism in their interviews. While this white interviewee seemed to express a genuine desire to work with black women's civic organizations and to engage in "bridgework" across the city's racial divides, she still appeared to hold some unconscious ideas about African American women.[21] Aware that she vocalized these sentiments, she sought to save face, not just to protect herself, but to protect the group image at large.[22] While rehearsing the trope of diversity, the interviewee's statements also laid bare negative assumptions about the work ethics of women of color and simultaneously issued an image of a morally neutral work ethic of elite white women. In stark contrast to her disapproving comments, the sudden turn to referring to "these very cool women" seemed to be an effort to restore the discourse of inclusion.

Another white woman recounted a story about including women of color in WOS. After she named several high-profile black women who met a complex set of standards, I asked why the women just mentioned had been contacted. She explained, "They were just very dynamic, and they showed a huge interest. And they interviewed very well. Because, there again, whenever we did interviews, particularly on television, we wanted the face of New Orleans to be there, and they interviewed extraordinarily well." Racial inclusion was shaped by classed standards and required strict adherence to certain features, such as a particular kind of camera presence, interview skills, and polished, television-ready speech.

Such responses show how the group's diversification efforts included a tension with respect to race. The group wanted to include diverse populations yet exclude those who might have resembled the widely disseminated images of the black under-class that had been broadcast during the height of the disaster. Recruiting women of color from the "right" backgrounds helped ensure that racial and ethnic differences were represented, but the faces of widespread urban inequality were largely excluded. Those stories or images, if shared at all, were filtered through polished women of color from the city's social and cultural elite. Women of color of a certain socioeconomic class, then, became a powerful mechanism through which disparities between wealthy whites and low-income people of color were mediated. Among some of the white women I interviewed, there were often implicit meanings about the type of black community activists suitable for inclusion, indicating that they made distinctions within racial categories rather than treating women of color as a monolithic group. In this context the term "activist" more often referred to a volunteer on a charitable board or foundation rather than a street activist or community organizer, which again points to class dimensions of membership criteria. These meanings were shaped by unspoken assumptions about socioeconomic class as well as political values. I did not get the impression that the core would have considered including community activists with overtly radical or oppositional politics. And radical activist women of color might not have wanted to participate in WOS even if given the chance.

The wide range of black community activists organizing in New Orleans both before and after Hurricane Katrina provide a reference group against which elite black women could be compared. For example, there is Shana Griffin, a radical black feminist and member of the New Orleans chapter of INCITE! Women of Color Against Violence, which on September 11, 2005, circulated Griffin's account of displacement along with a statement that characterized the federal government's response as a series of inactions based on "a racist assessment of the value of 150,000 mostly Black and poor people—a disproportionate number of whom are women—left behind in New Orleans." INCITE! also linked Katrina to U.S. government policies on global warming, the war in Iraq, and tax cuts for the wealthy. Janelle White, also of INCITE!, in November 2005 published a moving account that linked the personal with the political, sharing a story about a friend who had died two days after the storm and recounted how her friend's lesbian life partner was not allowed to be with her at the hospital.[23] Tanya Harris, a community organizer for ACORN (Association of Community Organizations for Reform Now), born and raised in the Lower Ninth Ward, told a U.S. senate hearing how she ended up in an evacuation shelter outside Baton Rouge, where she began engaging in what she would later describe as "a different type of organizing, not door to door, but bed to bed in shelters."[24]

And there is Dyan French Cole, also known as "Mama D," a longtime community organizer from New Orleans's Seventh Ward, who stayed through the storm. On December 6, 2005, Mama D testified in front of the Select Bipartisan Committee to Investigate the Preparation for and Response to Hurricane Katrina hearing "Hurricane Katrina: Voices from Inside the Storm." When U.S. representative Cynthia McKinney (D-GA) asked about the flooding of some parts of the city, as well as the breaching of the levees, Mama D responded, "Can you define that word for me, baby? What does breached mean? Bombed? I was on my front porch. I have witnesses that they bombed the walls of the levee. And the debris that is in front of my door will testify to that. So what do we mean breached?"[25] She believed that Katrina was part of a racist, capitalist plot working to drive African Americans from the city, to close public housing, and to develop properties for white investors.[26] In response, Rep. Christopher Shays (R-CT) said, "When I hear that you were on your porch and you saw that the levee was blown up and bombed, I can't let that pass. I don't know if that was theater or the truth." The questioning escalated into a heated exchange, culminating in Shays saying, "Ma'am, we don't need to speak in tongues. We just need to speak in honest answers." Mama D replied, "That is an honest answer. I have no reason to lie to you. Who are you Mr. Shays? . . . Why would I have to sit here and lie to you, first of all?"[27]

Some observers considered Mama D's testimony damaging in the efforts to earn federal support. In *A Breach of Faith*, Jed Horne wrote that Mama D "set back Louisiana's efforts to win the sympathies—and loosen the purse strings—of Congress when her rambling appearance before the House committee investigating Katrina included a full-throated testimonial to her belief that the levees had been dynamited as part of a plot to drive blacks from the city."[28]

The upper ranks of WOS would become slightly more diverse. Two women of color, first Madeline West and then Dolly Simpson, both Links members, were soon invited to serve on WOS's steering committee. Madeline West, a New Orleans attorney with a law degree from Tulane University and a former all-American basketball player for Louisiana State University, had evacuated with her eleven-year-old daughter, Simone, while her husband, Rod, stayed through the storm in the Hyatt hotel as director of electrical distribution operations for Entergy, one of New Orleans's primary utility companies.[29] For West the privileged had a moral obligation to contribute to the city's recovery, a Katrina-era reincarnation of noblesse oblige, the idea that the well-off should engage in benevolent acts of kindness and generosity.[30] In a filmed interview years later, she said, "Because we were so fortunate, more was expected of us. And it was up to us to help others in the community along and advocate for them."[31]

Another New Orleans Links member, Dolly Simpson, whose everyday work was also guided by the idea of noblesse oblige, would soon join the executive committee.

Simpson had a master's degree in health administration from Tulane, worked as chief of clinical operations at Daughters of Charity Health Center, and served in the mid-1990s as president of the Crescent City chapter of The Links.[32] By the end of the recruitment process, there were about two dozen black women in WOS, at least nine of whom were Links members.[33]

In addition to recruiting black women, Milling and the core group also sought to diversify beyond the black/white binary. To do so they began recruiting participants from the Asian and Hispanic communities of New Orleans, although these groups made up only 2.3 and 3.1 percent of the city's population respectively.[34] Milling drew on a contact in the Catholic Vietnamese community, Father Vien Nguyen, a priest at the Mary Queen of Vietnam Church in New Orleans East.[35] Father Nguyen, Milling recalled, put her in touch with several Vietnamese women, including Kim Dung Nguyen, volunteer coordinator and case manager at the church, and two nuns, Sister Anne Marie Kim-Khuong and Sister An Nguyen.[36] There were fewer women representing the Hispanic and Latino communities, in part because these communities made up a much smaller percentage of New Orleans's population. But they nonetheless had a presence, including participation by Ana Gershanik, who was born in Argentina and had lived in New Orleans since 1979.[37]

Inclusion meant different things for women of color who were invited because of their racial or ethnic background and class status. One African American Links member reflected on the process: "I got a call, the attempt of the group to have some diversity. They thought they needed some minorities in the group. So no matter how you slice it, that's always the bottom line, unfortunately [laughs]." I asked what she meant by the "bottom line." She replied, "The whole diversity piece." Just as the white women in the group commented on routinely trying to find women of color to participate in their organizations, the women of color talked about being the ones who were routinely asked.

Who else was invited to participate, and how were these invitations extended? The WOS core leadership didn't always extend the invitations. Newly invited women also began recruiting others in their own networks. In this way the invitations spiraled outward through a web of association.[38] This required giving up some control over recruitment and trusting those involved in particular social circles, including women of color, to pick suitable people. One white woman noted that there weren't any set criteria or particular people making all the decisions. "We would call a point person, as I call them, [and say,] 'You pick the people. How are we to know?' And that's how we did it. And with some of the African American ladies, sure, we knew a lot of them, but there were many whom we didn't know. We'd call somebody and say, 'Help me, tell me who would be good and who would want to participate and represent us.'"

In addition to drawing participants from existing women's organizations, the newly forming WOS drew participants from other groups that emerged after Hurricane Katrina. Notable among these women-led groups were Citizens for One

Greater New Orleans and Katrina Krewe.[39] WOS also drew upon at least one other group in the making, whose group members later became absorbed into Milling's efforts. I learned about this group during interviews with several WOS participants, including a white woman in her late thirties who, shortly after returning from her evacuation, like Milling, had intended to organize a diverse group of women from different neighborhoods and social backgrounds. She said she was inspired by the efforts of the widows of 9/11 to hold Congress accountable for organizing an independent investigation of the 2001 terrorist attacks.[40] I learned that in mid-December 2005, a month before Milling convened the small group at her home, another small group of women, most of whom were many years younger than Milling, gathered at a Garden District home to discuss recovery issues facing New Orleans at the time. These women dreamed up a plan to form a group of twenty-five women from New Orleans and neighboring St. Bernard Parish to present a "united front to act on behalf of all citizens."[41] They imagined recording video testimonials, getting national press, and, if all things came together, making a trip to Washington.

As we sat outside a coffee shop on Magazine Street, this interviewee, an attorney by education but now a self-described homemaker, talked about her incipient group. "For the past few weeks, I had been talking to a different group of women, and it wasn't just my friends," she said. "I mean, we were trying to find people from every corner of this city and not just white people, not just black people—just people. We wanted women that were basically the same age, trying to raise families, you know—many working, some not working, but, you know, juggling, trying to live away for several months and then come back here and rebuild our lives."

Around the time of the unnamed emergent group's second meeting, on January 17, this woman received a phone call from the WOS core leadership. After learning about their similar goals, they combined efforts, with several members of the small, 9/11 widows–inspired group quickly being absorbed into Milling's group, just days before WOS's Washington trip, since Milling clearly had more status, resources, and connections at her disposal.[42]

As the size of WOS increased, the organizers quickly produced new structural arrangements to help with the division of labor and to navigate political institutions. As a group under construction, WOS's emergent organizational structure aligned with the institutional structures with which it sought to engage. WOS's organization had three tiers: the core membership, the team captains, and what I call the base or rank-and-file membership. Core members at the top delegated logistical tasks to a second tier known as the WOS "captains."[43] The eight captains served as liaisons between the core membership and members at the base, whose participation was more limited or who attended only the larger collective actions, like those in Washington. This multilevel structure is typical of arrangements found in other disaster-related emergent groups: an "active core," "supporting circle," and "nominal supporters."[44]

WOS was not completely segregated by gender, despite what its name might suggest. Two white men, Christian T. Brown and Charles Stern, served as WOS coordinators, conducting backstage logistical activities.[45] Often referred to in casual conversation as "Men of the Storm," these two friends of the Millings traveled with WOS to Washington and advised on group decisions while remaining out of the spotlight.[46] The press did not highlight the men's participation, nor did WOS advertise the men's behind-the-scenes labor.[47] Instead, the public focus remained on the women's unified efforts to rebuild, a tactic to mobilize support for their cause.

In addition to racial inclusion, the group recognized that economic diversification would be necessary if it wanted to present itself as inclusive. To facilitate this, participation in the one-day trip was free, except for the cost of lunch in Washington. Because expenses were minimized, one white woman told me that it "removes any economic barrier, too." WOS organizers anticipated that some would drop out or refuse to participate if they were required to fly to Washington on their own dime. A white woman in her sixties described questions about cost: "So when we started calling people, they were so excited. The first thing they said was, 'How much does it cost?' We go, 'Nothing. You just get to go. It's free. You don't have to pay to get on the jet, you don't have to pack, you get up in the morning, you go on the jet, you come back that night.' So basically it was a pretty easy sell, especially if you weren't asking them for a thousand dollars to get on the jet." She said the trip would have failed if invitees had been required to pay. "There are people struggling in this community," she said, "and even people who have what you would call 'money' are in trouble. That was really Anne's vision, to make sure that no one had to pay to go on this trip."

While the flight was free for participants, attending may not have been possible for many working women. Even a day away from one's job could have had financial consequences, especially in light of research findings released a few years after the storm that documented women's post-Katrina economic downward mobility.[48] Although there seemed to be less energy given to recruiting low-income women, including renters and those living in public housing, class dynamics were still discussed during early conversations about membership.

The money, including seventy thousand dollars for the cost of the plane, was raised in a very short amount of time. Many participants were unaware of the funding source, and the private donors remained anonymous.[49] However, several participants did wonder about it. A white woman in her thirties speculated that one of her male relatives might have been financially involved and that this could have spurred organizers to invite her to participate. She considered the following scenario: "I'm highly suspicious that my [relative] was one of the donors, but I don't know. He's not the type to tell me, and I haven't asked him. I know that money was raised to get that trip to go. I don't know who the donors were, because nobody ever released them. I actually don't care, but I'm suspicious—I'm pretty confident that he would be part of that group, because the core group that put it together is all buddies of his. They have the excess cash to help something move forward like that."

Even those WOS participants with close ties to presumable donors could not confirm the funding source. In contrast to the "excess cash" of private donors, other women mentioned possible financial links to large corporations, suggesting that the trip was bankrolled, in part, by the oil and gas industry. Another white woman wondered: "How they raised the money to fund the trip, I have no idea. Just so you know that. It's sort of been hush-hush. So I'm not . . . [pause] not [hush-hush] in a bad way. But I guess that wasn't what was important. It was just the fact that they made it happen. Was it Shell Oil? Or was it an anonymous person who just wanted to remain low-profile. Or a combination of both? I don't know." One woman who seemed to know the funding source, told me that "big corporations donated the money for the jet," without specifying which corporations.

The ethnographic and interview data told me very little about WOS funding sources. But archival records reveal part of the story of the group's finances. Many years later I learned that Anne Milling had recently donated her WOS papers to the archives at Newcomb. I immediately booked a flight to New Orleans to consult the WOS records. On my last visit to the archive, I unearthed the group's general ledger, which included all financial transactions from January 2006 to July 2008. From this document I learned more about the individual and corporate giving that helped fund WOS activities. For example, the ledger notes that the January 2006 US Air jet rental was paid for with contributions from the Samuel Newhouse Foundation, the Helis Foundation, the Selley Foundation, and Freeport-McMoRan, a mining and oil and gas company.[50] I also learned from the archival materials that in 2006 the group had established a financial relationship with the Greater New Orleans Foundation (GNOF), a 501(c)(3) nonprofit organization, which allowed it to receive tax-exempt charitable gifts that could be given to the GNOF earmarked for the "Women of the Storm Fund."[51]

The women involved didn't view the feat of the quick fund-raising as unusual. One interviewee explained that many of the women were embedded in the local charity cultures, and that the fund-raising involved for WOS's trip was similar to charitable spending at philanthropic events. She told me about a fund-raiser called Sentimental Journeys, an event that raises a "fortune," held at the Longue Vue House and Gardens. She explained, "They ask people from all over the country and the world to donate their homes. They get planes. The whole idea of the plane [for WOS] wasn't so far-fetched."

But why was the issue of funding so obscured? From a sociological perspective, it is important to note that this financial information was kept quiet among those in the know and that many participants were not even aware of the sources. Although there was transparency in the membership roster, in part because it allowed the group to highlight what it considered to be a racially diverse membership, the women's capital and financial assets remained hidden. Other than vague remarks about using their own resources or receiving private donations, WOS's funding sources were rarely publicly disclosed.

Given the fact that black and poor residents were disproportionately affected during Katrina, the women's activities created a dilemma of representation, which they carefully managed individually and collectively. As self-appointed representatives, WOS sought to speak on behalf of those most affected by Katrina. As core member Peggy Laborde explained to reporters, "We'll try to be the voice of those who cannot be with us, the displaced, those with their homes destroyed."[52]

And it wasn't just white women who sought to speak on behalf of others. One African American participant, a member of The Links whose home had flooded, told me, "Everybody was hit. Katrina didn't discriminate. She hit everybody. There were no winners per se. So while there were sometimes positive effects of Katrina, everybody lost. It was just the degree of loss. So when people started sometimes apologizing and saying, 'I still have my home,' I said, 'Look what you lost. You lost your prior life. You lost what it was.' We all lost. It's just the degree of what people really lost and how you look at it. But we all lost." She went on to describe being the voice for others: "So people at work start saying, 'You're going, please speak on behalf of us.' It was amazing how many people said, 'You can just speak for us, on behalf of us.' Because we had several people that worked in St. Bernard Parish, we had a large amount that lived in New Orleans East. We had a large amount of people that lost their homes. And they said, 'If you could just speak on behalf of us, we should appreciate it.'" This responsibility was on many women's minds as they prepared for the trip.

CHAPTER 3

Making Plans, Going Public

On the crafting of a mission statement,
descriptive of how the group's roster is revealed,
and then how the phones begin ringing

With much to do leading up to the group's day in Washington, D.C., the newly formed WOS set to work immediately. In addition to participant recruitment, at least two important tasks needed attention: developing a statement of purpose and deciding how best to deliver the message.[1] In looking at WOS's internal dynamics, it is clear that core participants played a central role in crafting the group's narrative. Their mission was to invite members of Congress to see the destruction firsthand, and they knew that coastland restoration was part of a larger recovery plan. But what would be their overall goal? And how would they present it?

A set of talking points was distributed to WOS members on January 23, beginning with this paragraph that outlined the group's immediate goal:

> In the aftermath of Hurricane Katrina, an area in and around New Orleans which is seven times the size of Manhattan was devastated. Countless businesses, homes and livelihoods were destroyed. Today, we extend a personal invitation to every member of Congress to visit New Orleans and our southern coast and experience first-hand the devastation and scope of this national tragedy. Once they see block by block, mile by mile the magnitude of this destruction . . . we urge them to return to Congress and support the following initiatives.[2]

After emphasizing the importance of these visits, outlining the problem, and conveying the scale of Katrina's destruction, the talking points centered on four main goals: (1) a 50 percent share of revenues generated by offshore drilling, (2) enhanced levee protection, (3) coastal restoration, and (4) passage of the Baker Bill, a housing recovery plan pending in Congress.

WOS's first priority was to "allow Louisiana to receive 50% annually of the revenue generated by our offshore drilling that currently goes into the national coffers."[3]

Offshore drilling might appear unrelated to the Katrina recovery, but the women, as well as many Louisiana politicians, reasoned that this recaptured revenue would provide a steady stream of funding to finance coastal wetlands restoration projects and levee protection. To better understand the group's push for a revenue sharing agreement, it is necessary to discuss the legislative context of early 2006, particularly with respect to offshore oil and gas industries in Louisiana and related debates about federal leases and revenue sharing from energy production.

The offshore oil and gas industry in the Gulf of Mexico can be traced back to the late 1930s when petroleum companies began adapting their drilling and production techniques to marine conditions along the bays and wetlands of south Louisiana, where "salt dome" discoveries were numerous in the marshes and swamps throughout the 1920s and 1930s.[4] In the 1940s and 1950s, similar discoveries were made in shallow waters offshore, leading to mid-century developments of open-water drilling techniques. But seismic technology available at the time for locating oil prospects was imprecise. Consequently, notes Tyler Priest, who has written extensively about the history of Shell Oil Company and the petroleum industry in Louisiana, "oil companies desired large and cheap leases to allow for wider-ranging drilling programs—a spatial fix to compensate for imperfect seismic technology and the relatively high costs of operating in the wetlands environment."[5] Priest argues that "Louisiana officials were happy to oblige," and in the 1920s and 1930s oil companies began striking deals that allowed them to lease millions of acres of land, thereby "stimulat[ing] oil development in marine locations onshore and in the open sea."[6] Local, state, and federal interests chased the lucrative profits produced by offshore petro-economies, and questions arose over legal jurisdiction in waters off the coast.

In 1949 President Harry Truman proposed to give Louisiana a 37.5 percent share of revenues generated from offshore oil and gas production, but Plaquemines Parish president Leander Perez convinced Louisiana governor Earl Long to reject the offer, despite strong support from other Louisiana politicians, and its demand that Louisiana's offshore legal jurisdiction be extended from three miles to as far as thirty-seven miles.[7] Perez (1891–1969) was legendary in Louisiana for his heavy-handed rule of Plaquemines Parish and his unapologetic approach to political power. A frustrated Truman withdrew the initial proposal, a decision that resulted in giving Louisiana and other Gulf Coast states nothing at all, costing Louisiana tens of billions of dollars in lost revenue over the decades.[8]

Contentious legal battles about these issues, popularly referred to as the "Tidelands Controversy," went to the U.S. Supreme Court, where a series of decisions between 1947 and 1960 resulted in federal jurisdiction of areas beyond three miles of the coast.[9] In the late 1990s, newly elected senator Mary Landrieu revived revenue sharing initiatives with the introduction of her bill in Congress known as the Conservation and Reinvestment Act (CARA). According to Jason Theriot, in his book *American Energy, Imperiled Coast: Oil and Gas Development in Louisiana's Wetlands,* Landrieu drew attention to a geographic disconnect in federal energy policies,

noting that inland states received a 50 percent share of revenues generated from
energy extraction activities, such as mining and drilling, whereas coastal states did
not.[10] Proponents of the legislation argued that the annual share of revenue produced
off the coast would be spent on coastal wetlands restoration projects. Although
the bill was not signed into law, the debates over Gulf Coast energy production
and coastal restoration "laid the groundwork for redefining the problem as an economic one," Theriot writes.[11] Hurricane Katrina seemed to provide an opportunity
for Louisiana politicians like Landrieu and groups like the newly formed WOS to
revisit this legislation.

Oil and gas revenue sharing legislation was framed by WOS as central to rebuilding flood protection and coastal wetlands, the second and third priority issues listed
in WOS's talking points. The second priority issue was enhanced levee protection,
which the group saw as necessary to ensure displaced residents felt safe to return
and rebuild their lives. The third issue was coastal restoration, supported by statistics
claiming that Louisiana accounts for more than 30 percent of the nation's wetlands,
an area twice the size of the Everglades. In addition to emphasizing that wetlands
are home to endangered species and millions of migratory birds, the talking points
stressed that the wetlands provide storm protection for the ports and waterways for
"21% of waterborne commerce in the U.S." and the "infrastructure that transports
30% of oil and gas consumed in the U.S"; the commercial fishing industry was
also mentioned.[12] With this framing, WOS argued that coastal restoration was an
economic issue that tied local industries to regional and national interests, just as
Landrieu had in her pre-Katrina offshore revenue sharing initiatives.

WOS's final priority issue was the passage of the Baker Bill, a housing recovery
plan proposed shortly after Katrina by Richard H. Baker, a Republican representative from a mostly white suburban district in Baton Rouge. Rather than leaving
the housing recovery to private enterprise and the free market, an approach that
many feared would lead to spotty and uneven redevelopment—"islets of rebuilding
in a sea of destruction"[13]—the Baker Bill proposed to create a federal agency, the
Louisiana Recovery Corporation (LRC), to buy out vast numbers of home owners whose properties had been flooded. As a "big-government fix-it plan" for the
post-Katrina housing crisis affecting home owners, insured and uninsured alike,
who were having difficulty making mortgage payments on their flooded properties, the proposed LRC would have spent a projected $80 billion, financed by the
federal government's sale of U.S. Treasury bonds, to purchase large tracts of land,
paying off home owners and lenders at a percentage of the home's pre-storm value,
rehabilitating the properties, and selling them to developers, who would then work
with local authorities on redevelopment plans.[14] Under the plan, home owners
would have had the option to be bought out at 60 percent of the equity, and lenders would have received 60 percent of what was owed to them.[15] "As free market as
I am," Baker told the *New York Times*, the disaster in New Orleans would require
"a precedent-setting remedy," one that necessitated large-scale federal intervention

akin to the congressional bailouts of the savings and loan industries in the late 1980s.[16]

The Baker Bill garnered support of all nine members of Louisiana's congressional delegation, along with Governor Blanco and Mayor Ray Nagin. Despite being approved by the House of Representatives' Financial Service Committee in December 2005, the bill sank when Congress adjourned at the end of the year.[17] Concerned about exorbitant costs, the lack of an upper spending limit, and perhaps Louisiana's long-standing reputation for corruption, Rep. Jeb Hensarling (R-TX) stated what may have been on the minds of many Congress members when he told the *New York Times*, "It is irresponsible for Congress to write a blank check, drawn on the account of American taxpayers, bound only by the imagination of politicians. We need to ensure that taxpayers are not asked again two or three years from now to pay for the same disaster."[18] The Baker Bill was taken up again, in slightly modified form, when Congress reconvened in 2006. But even if Louisiana's delegation had been able to convince Hensarling and other conservative lawmakers in Congress that this remedy was warranted, the bill also would have needed White House support. Thus, strategizing about message and audience, WOS planned to meet not only with those in Congress but with top White House officials as well.

While much was in flux for WOS, there was one constant about their Washington trip: the number of senators and representatives. If each of the 130 women visited four lawmakers, then almost all 535 members of Congress would receive an invitation to tour the disaster area. But visiting in pairs had a strategic advantage.

Everything about these visits had to be carefully planned, and here, too, diversity played a key role. Given that the Katrina catastrophe was racialized in the popular imagination, core members decided that the invitations would need to be delivered by teams of women rather than individuals and that, as much as possible, these teams would be racially diverse, especially those teams who were assigned to visit key decision makers such as senior members of Congress sitting on important committees. As one white woman in her fifties recalled, "And the team-matching, what we tried to do was to pair people who were different. No best friends. We tried as much as possible to put African American women with white women or Spanish-speaking women with non-Spanish-speaking women. Of course, there were more of us than there were of the minorities, but we tried to be just about half and half, so that our teams didn't look like they were cookie-cutter teams." When asked about the rationale for these cross-race pairings, she replied, "I think [the intent was] to put a face on it that we were the community and not just a group of do-good women. . . . We wanted it to look like the face of New Orleans."

The core organizers spent hours preparing packets for the broader membership. Inside each packet, participants found the talking points, a sheet with the partner's name, and the names of four lawmakers to whom they were assigned. An introductory letter included in the packet opened with this line: "We're delighted that you will be joining us on our Washington, D.C. adventure on Monday, January 30th." It asked the pairs to begin making afternoon appointments by phone and to familiarize themselves with their assigned lawmakers. They were asked to study talking points to ensure that participants would "speak with one voice." The letter concluded by highlighting WOS's gendered unity: "Thank you for giving a day to our city, region and state. Passionate, committed ladies WILL succeed where our elected officials have failed!!!"[19]

On the morning of January 23, participants received an e-mail asking them to pick up the packet of printed materials at Milling's home, which Tulane University president Scott Cowen would later describe as a "gracious uptown manor house in the same Audubon Park neighborhood as Tulane—it's one of those imposing piles with three-story pillars, wide flagstone porches, and gabled roofs."[20] This seemingly small detail—where to pick up the packets—raised moral dilemmas. Some members were concerned about the possible messages it sent to participants. In an interview with me, one white woman reflected on concerns about the location: "I'll tell you one of my [concerns]—and I addressed this with the core members. I said, 'I don't think we should pick up our packets at Anne Milling's beautiful home. I just don't think you should. I think that's intimidating for some of these people.'" According to this interviewee, meeting at Milling's "sent the wrong message right out the get-go." She said, "I told them that. But the little nuns from New Orleans East, some of these black ladies that went? Now, some of them, as you know, are the wives of serious black leaders here, but I don't know that all of them were. I just didn't think that was the right thing to do." This participant understood the meeting place in moral terms. Driving Uptown to pick up packets was seen as problematic because it would highlight racial and economic disparities between group members. Despite concerns being voiced, convenience and routine for those at the group's center seems to have won out.

During this preparatory period, each pair of women made appointments with four members of Congress and their aides, researched the biographies of each lawmaker, and read up on the personal and economic impact of hurricanes Katrina and Rita. Their political education consisted of hours of studying; some participants even made spreadsheets that outlined the demographics, rankings, and voting records of their assigned lawmakers. One participant I interviewed did this work at the end of the day, well after 10 P.M. on weeknights after her children were asleep. Many began to acquire an encyclopedic knowledge of Congress, including the composition of each subcommittee. Shattering the image of ladies who merely lunch, many WOS participants strove to become political strategists.

On Tuesday, January 24, participants received additional material in an e-mail from the core leadership to help them secure appointments with elected officials, including a form letter that gave them more prescribed language to work with when requesting appointments. Members simply had to write the lawmaker's name in the

"To" field and sign their names in the "From" section and then e-mail or fax the form to scheduling assistants. Because the proposed trip for lawmakers included round-trip airfare from Washington to New Orleans, hotel accommodations, meals, and tours of the area, WOS's letter emphasized the ease for lawmakers. It read, "All that is necessary from members of Congress is to block the necessary 36 hours for such a visit to one of the nation's most historic cities and vital regions of our country." The letter continued, "Certainly this is little to ask when so many are suffering."[21]

In addition to extending requests through formal letters, participants scheduled appointments by phone. Some made cold calls to lawmakers or their aides, efforts that resulted in only limited success. In other, more successful cases, the women drew upon their extended social networks. In one case, sixty-year-old attorney and WOS member Adriel Graham Arceneaux made use of her connection with First Lady Laura Bush, her college roommate from Southern Methodist University in the 1960s. Drawing on Arceneaux's entree, Peggy Laborde was able to set up appointments with Mrs. Bush's chief of staff.[22] Arceneaux, widely known as "Sparky," was a resident of Lacombe and was temporarily living in Covington, a town forty miles north of New Orleans, as she prepared to rebuild her three-generation family home in Bayou Lacombe, which had been destroyed during Katrina. She was a passionate environmentalist known for fighting industrial pollution caused by the ship-cleaning business in Bayou Lacombe and was instrumental in developing the Big Branch Wildlife Refuge in Lacombe.[23]

As group members scrambled to prepare for the Washington trip, the Baker Bill, as Jed Horne would later say, was on "life support."[24] The day after WOS participants began picking up their packets at Milling's home, another New Orleans native, Walter Isaacson, was taking the Baker Bill fight to the heart of Washington. Isaacson, from a prominent Jewish family, grew up on Napoleon Avenue in the Broadmoor neighborhood. He was well known in the corridors of power, having long served as a political reporter, then managing editor of *Time* magazine, and more recently as CEO of CNN, a position he held from 2001 to 2003. Isaacson left CNN to become president and CEO of the Aspen Institute, which one reporter describes as the "Ben Franklin of think tanks: well connected, intellectually broad, and consistently practical minded."[25] In September 2005 Isaacson was appointed vice chairman of Blanco's newly formed Louisiana Recovery Authority (LRA), a state board tasked with coordinating short- and long-term rebuilding plans, and he would remain on the LRA for the next three years.[26] Isaacson met with White House officials, including Allan B. Hubbard, director of the National Economic Council and the chief economic advisor for President Bush, in a last-ditch effort to get the Bush administration to support the legislation.[27] During the meeting it became clear that the bill was going to fail.

On Wednesday, January 25, two days after WOS began distributing its talking points to members, the White House announced that it would not support Baker's proposed reconstruction plan. Donald Powell, former chair of the Federal Deposit

Insurance Corporation and the federal coordinator of the Gulf Coast recovery, published an op-ed in the *Washington Post* describing three primary objections to the Baker Bill that had contributed to the proposed program being voted down. The first concern centered on the federal government; Powell argued, "State and local leaders—not those in Washington—must develop the recovery plan." The second issue for Powell had to do with the creation of a federal bureaucratic agency that would have "weak congressional oversight and thus little accountability." Finally, Powell and the Bush administration opposed the Baker Bill because "markets must be able to work properly without interference from the government."[28] Powell went on to say, "If the heavy hand of government impedes the private sector's proven ability to speed the recovery, it will take longer and cost more." Furthermore, he argued, it would "destroy free-market mechanisms."[29]

Consequently, one of WOS's priority issues was effectively off the table even before group members had the chance to make their case in Washington. This was a turning point that changed the group's trajectory. WOS has been portrayed by popular critics as serving the white elite of New Orleans. But given this information about support for the Baker Bill drawn from my interviews and internal group documents, it appears that charges about elite self-interests were somewhat misguided. The group initially endorsed programs that called for more state intervention in the recovery process rather than relying entirely on the private sector's market-driven recovery.[30] WOS's position on the housing recovery showed that they were in support of a large-scale government initiative that could have wound up, as the *New York Times* put it, "largely benefiting African Americans in New Orleans."[31]

On Saturday, January 28, all eleven elected officials in the House from Louisiana and Mississippi signed a letter urging House Speaker Dennis Hastert (R-IL) and House Minority Leader Nancy Pelosi (D-CA), neither of whom had been to the area after the storm, to lead a bipartisan delegation of members who had not visited the devastated communities along the Gulf Coast. The letter stated, "From the air you will witness the blue tarps on broken roofs stretching toward the horizon. You will hear stories from our community leaders and constituents who continue to battle the FEMA bureaucracy. On the coast you will see firsthand the vulnerability of America's energy infrastructure to future storms and the immediate threat posed to our energy security." Mirroring WOS's goals, the letter said, "To fully appreciate the historic challenges faced by Louisiana and Mississippi and the urgent need for additional congressional action, we urge you to visit the region personally and encourage other members to join you."[32]

On the same day, final plans were sent by e-mail to the group. The core leadership conducted follow-up phone calls to make sure the women received some last-minute instructions, including a note about appearance: "Dress for the day is business attire, either skirts or pants. Keep jewelry to a minimum."[33] Participants were instructed to dress up for the occasion, but they were also instructed to dress down, limiting the accessories worn on the trip. These instructions reveal that dressing up and dressing down are always strategically and situationally enacted, as Diana Kendall found in her sociological study of elite women, who at charity garage sales purposefully dressed down by wearing jeans and tennis shoes in an effort to address "the disparity between their own lifestyle and that of the average shopper."[34] This self-presentation can also be seen as part of a long history of reforming individual behaviors and attitudes by members of the black Baptist women's movement who emphasized manners and morals in what Evelyn Brooks Higginbotham describes as a "politics of respectability," which was a "goal in itself and as a strategy for reform of the entire structural system of American race relations."[35] WOS participants' attention to dressing for the occasion reveals the cultural construction of class as a dynamic, everyday process that involved careful attention to outward appearance.[36] They dressed down so as not to stand out for their class, and they dressed up to show they were professional and to differentiate themselves from racialized and classed images of Katrina victims broadcast from the Superdome and the Ernest N. Morial Convention Center.

As Higginbotham notes, "The discourse of respectability disclosed class and status differentiation."[37] On the trip, the women did not want to be at the center of attention while the city's survival was at stake.[38] They wanted their message to outweigh their appearance, especially in the company of less affluent women, and in the broader context of a highly stratified society that Katrina made evident. The instructions for attire left little room for flair. Sartorial conformity was the rule of the day. As one Vietnamese nun said, the women resembled a group of "penguins," uniform and professional, with only slight variations among them.

On Thursday, January 26, just four days before WOS's trip, the *Times-Picayune* published a front-page story about this newly formed group.[39] The article, "Storming D.C.," was accompanied by the subtitle, "Local activists think every member of Congress needs to see Katrina's devastation firsthand. They plan to invite them, in person."[40] The newspaper also printed a vivid color photograph of three group members, including Lauren Anderson, an African American woman who served as CEO of Neighborhood Housing Services (NHS) of New Orleans, a nonprofit organization promoting home ownership among low- and moderate-income residents. Anderson, who at the time was operating NHS out of a temporary office in Covington, Louisiana, after the Freret Street headquarters flooded with three feet of water, was joined by Peggy Laborde and Liz Sloss, both white women on the executive committee.[41] The three were pictured in Anne Milling's elegant dining room hard at work assembling packets for WOS participants. They sat under an impressive chandelier of wrought iron and crystal; on the table were layers upon layers of paper, a can of Diet Coke, and a cheese plate. In the background, floor-to-ceiling curtains were gathered at each side of the patio doors, letting in bright light and revealing a well-manicured garden untouched by the flood.

As the article continued, readers encountered, for the first time, the list of women scheduled to fly to Washington. The list included many well-known movers and

FIGURE 2. Lauren Anderson, Peggy Laborde, and Liz Sloss (*left to right*). Women of the Storm members arranging packets of information in preparation for the group's January 30, 2006, trip to Washington. *Times-Picayune* staff photo/Jennifer Zydon.

shakers, and anyone from New Orleans's elite circles would have recognized names. The core had managed to get numerous local luminaries to sign on to their cause, particularly those with political clout in Washington, including Verna Landrieu, mother of Mary Landrieu, and Lindy Boggs, a former member of the U.S. House of Representatives and U.S. ambassador to the Vatican. Also on the list was Gloria S. Kabacoff, who, along with her husband, Lester Kabacoff, was described by cultural geographer Richard Campanella as "one of the most influential couples in local business and philanthropic circles" in the second half of the twentieth century.[42] Other notable participants included Carol Bebelle, director of the Ashé Cultural Arts Center in Central City, and Olivia Manning, mother of professional NFL football stars Peyton and Eli Manning and wife of Archie Manning, a retired quarterback for the New Orleans Saints.[43] Another participant was Blanche Francis, whose husband, Dr. Norman Francis, president of Xavier University of Louisiana, was also appointed by Blanco as LRA co-chairman; Francis had moved into her son's home after the first floor of her home was flooded by the London Avenue Canal levee breach, just a few blocks away.[44] At press time 123 women had already been assigned seats on the plane.

One white woman I interviewed reflected on what happened next. "Once that list came out," she said, "everybody's phones started ringing off the hook with people who wanted to be on the plane." Many of these calls came from women in the participants' immediate and often homogeneous social circles who wondered why they had not been asked to participate. Core participants reported difficulties managing relationships with friends and acquaintances while maintaining a commitment to diversity. They aimed to be inclusive but consequently had to exclude many people. The women described or hinted at hurt feelings, difficult conversations, and attempts to save face.

Until this point, the women's kitchen-table organizing took place behind the scenes—through calls, e-mails, house visits, and so on. But the *Times-Picayune* article catapulted WOS into the media spotlight, exposing it to public critique. Addressing how the list came together, Milling told reporters: "There was no formal process. . . . We were tossing out names, people who we work with, people we know. One name would lead to another. Or, one person we would talk to would say, 'So-and-so would love to do this.' It just evolved. It wasn't like, oh, we're going to have someone from the Chamber of Commerce, we're going to have someone from Tulane, we're going to have someone from Xavier. It just happened rapidly."[45]

An organizational document used in WOS's planning and later donated to the Newcomb Archives reveals some of the ways the list did come together, including a central focus on racial and geographic diversity. The core had identified close to ninety, mostly white, potential WOS participants from Orleans, St. Tammany, Jefferson, St. Bernard, and Plaquemines parishes. Another part of the typed document showed space on the trip set aside for a dozen women from south Louisiana, including the Lake Charles area. A third section of the document was titled "African American Women of the Storm" and listed the names of sixteen women. Handwritten in the margins were the names of eight more women, bringing the total number of African American participants on the list to twenty-four. And in a handwritten section titled "Vietnamese," the number "4" was scribbled over the number "2."[46]

The list of names, referred to by participants simply as "the list," was a frequent topic of conversation during my interviews. A white woman, for example, reflected on criticisms about who was or was not invited: "It really was not a popularity contest, but, you know, people [long pause]. I think at the end of the day it was great for us to put the list in the paper, because there it is, it's public and you can see that it is not a list of white, Anglo-Saxon, Protestants—you know." Using the term "popularity contest" signaled that many women wanted to be part of the "in crowd." Yet this woman and other group members had different considerations in mind, imagining that WOS's success hinged on not being a list of affluent, white invitees drawn only from New Orleans's high society. The appearance of diversity mattered.

These were hard choices for WOS members, straining relationships with close friends who had not been invited. Another white participant I interviewed remarked on that subject: "We know we hurt a lot of feelings of friends, and we didn't mean to. But it wasn't gonna be a planeload of friends. It was just not gonna be that way. That's not the city." This woman, like many others, felt a moral responsibility to represent the social differences of New Orleans and south Louisiana. But this didn't stop informal conversations about who was invited to participate.

One WOS participant, a white woman in her forties, commented on the in-group/out-group dynamics. After describing her in-laws as "very civic minded," she said to me, "What's funny is that my mother-in-law was not asked, but I think it's because they didn't want just Caucasian Uptown women. They wanted an age spectrum." Another participant, a white woman in her thirties whose home had flooded, conveyed a similar story: "I have a good friend who has a very high-profile community job right now, and they didn't ask her. She's still miffed about it. I've heard there was lots of 'Mnn-mnn-mnn.' . . . I mean, this friend of mine, she's president of a very important organization right now, and she wasn't asked. It might have been pure oversight, or maybe someone really doesn't want to work with her. I don't know, and I don't want to know."

In the days after the list went public, WOS was gathering support, and a few local residents weighed in positively. On January 29, the day before the trip, two letters to the editor supporting the group appeared in the *Times-Picayune* alongside a photo of WOS group members at a kitchen table covered with stacks of paper. The image, taken a few days earlier, featured Lauren Anderson and Brenda Brown, both African American women; Kim Nguyen, a Vietnamese woman; and Peggy Laborde and Liz Sloss, two white women. By printing this image alongside the letters, the local press helped WOS mobilize images of a diverse kitchen-table organization.

In a letter to the editor titled "Taking Activism to Washington," Mandy Cho-cheles, a resident from Metairie, a suburb of New Orleans, wrote, "Good luck to the Women of the Storm!"[47] She said that she had no personal connections to the women on the list though she did recognize the names of numerous "community activists." She ended the letter by expressing her hope that the WOS trip would provide "incentive" for members of Congress to visit the Gulf Coast. In "Let's Hear It for Women's Work," another observer, Evelyn Bryan, from Algiers, an unflooded area on the West Bank of New Orleans, wrote that the idea of women going to Washington showed the strength of women and brought a smile to her face. She concluded by making ties between history, civic action, and WOS's endeavor to help rebuild New Orleans. She said, "Over the years, women historically have joined together to support causes close to their hearts. I applaud these dedicated women."[48]

CHAPTER 4

The Flight

*Comprising a brief description of a journey to
Washington and a few accounts of surviving the storm*

On the morning of January 30, the day of WOS's trip to Washington, one participant I spoke with, a black woman in her forties, woke up "before the crack of dawn" in the FEMA trailer stationed outside her flooded home. Five months after Katrina, electricity in her neighborhood had yet to be restored. She got into her car and picked up two women who were also part of WOS, and together they drove to Louis Armstrong International Airport. Like many participants, she remembered even the smallest of details. "It was so foggy, you could barely see," she said. As early as 5:45 A.M., a full hour before sunrise, she and other participants began arriving at the airport, which had served not only as an evacuation departure point during Katrina but also as a makeshift hospital. It was there, in the days after Katrina, that patients from flooded hospitals were taken, some sick and others dying. The *New York Times* reported that "one corpse in a wheelchair, not far from the Delta counter, lay covered by a blue blanket."[1] The airport resumed commercial operations in mid-September 2005, but months later, things were far from normal. In January 2006 a heavy sense of absence could still be felt, a quiet reminder of the horrors that had transpired there when New Orleans was still underwater. Sean Payton, coach of the New Orleans Saints, remembered the airport's strange feel that January: "When I got off the plane, the airport was eerily quiet, almost empty, motionless. It was different from any airport I'd ever seen. You know what it felt like? It felt like they had only one flight a day here, the one I'd just gotten off of. The airport was whatever the opposite of bustling is."[2]

One could imagine a similarly eery quiet in the concourse early that morning before WOS members began arriving. First a handful appeared. Then a few dozen.

Then over one hundred. That is when the scene became loud and boisterous. Core member Peggy Laborde circulated through the crowd, distributing WOS pins from a wicker basket, while other core participants and team captains handed out boarding passes. Many participants were meeting each other for the first time, and they were all asked to wear handwritten name tags to facilitate interaction.[3] Most wore professional attire—blazers, scarves, and skirt-suits—deemed appropriate for meetings with lawmakers. A few wore more informal outfits chosen to highlight the group's efforts; one had donned a black top with a gold fleur-de-lis; another sported a shirt emblazoned with a macabre post-Katrina message—"Drove my Chevy to the levee, but the levee was gone."

Amid the morning meet and greet, something was weighing on core member Pam Bryan, who was paired with Anne Milling for the day's Capitol Hill visits. Bryan had been tasked with setting up appointments with Nancy Pelosi, Dennis Hastert, and Republican representative Don Young from Alaska, prioritized because of his membership on committees that focused on energy and natural resources. In the twenty days leading up to the trip, many in WOS had already confirmed appointments, but Bryan had yet to secure a single meeting. She was running out of time.

Bryan recalled the immense challenges she faced when trying to schedule meetings by phone. "Well, 'I'm Pam Bryan, from New Orleans, and I'd like to have an appointment with Speaker Hastert,' wasn't getting me very far," she recalled. Concerned that the pair would get to Washington without anything scheduled, she approached Milling on the concourse, pulled her aside, and said to her, "I just can't get an appointment with them and they won't call me back. I keep leaving messages and they keep passing my name to someone else. I can't nail this appointment." At this point, Milling got on her cell phone and made a call to a friend at WWL-TV Channel 4, a CBS affiliate news station in New Orleans, in a last-ditch effort to pull some strings. Recounting the phone conversation, Bryan remembered Milling saying to someone on the phone, "Listen, I know that you know a lot of people in Washington. We need appointments with Hastert, Pelosi, and Young." Then the WWL contact went to work, Bryan said, making calls on WOS's behalf. The two got back in line with those on the concourse, and once on the plane, turned off their phones, hoping for good news when they landed.[4]

By 6:30 the women had boarded the chartered plane, and many ignored the seat assignments listed on their boarding passes, often sitting with team partners. Once in the air, they were served coffee, juice, and king cake, a festive and sugary Carnival confection.[5] As they flew to Washington, the group received a quick lesson from those women with experience in lobbying. One woman recalled the situation like this: "Here we've got 130 people on a plane and nobody really knows exactly what to do. Some people did, but other people really didn't." When the core members gave those on the plane an overview, she remembered a very clear message: "You go in. You're very polite. You don't tell them in-your-face anything. You are a Southern lady who is very grateful. You're giving them an invitation."

They were also instructed what not to do. They were reminded to monitor their behavior in front of the press, some of whom were on the plane, and during meetings with elected officials. While many participants were angry about government responses to the catastrophe, they were encouraged not to reveal these negative emotions in public. One woman scribbled notes to herself on her packet, which she later showed to me: "(1) * stay on message, (2) do not get in an argument with anyone."[6]

Participants were instructed to be pleasant and polite rather than oppositional. The women did not want to present themselves as making demands, because this might hurt their cause, not to mention that it might seem unladylike. By contrast, they sought to extend invitations and use Southern niceties as their ultimate political tactic. *Times-Picayune* commentator Jarvis DeBerry would later describe WOS as waging "an amazingly successful charm offensive, sweet-talking members of Congress into coming to New Orleans so they can see that our requests for aid are legitimate."[7]

After the crash course in lobbying, the women continued looking over the biographies of elected officials and reviewing the talking points included in their packets. One woman shared with me a table that she made for the trip, which she had arranged carefully in a notebook. There were columns for each of the pair's four lawmakers and eleven rows that included the following information: representatives' state, party (all Democrats), age (ranging from 66 to 74), race (all white), religion (two Lutherans, a Baptist, and a Catholic), term (ranging from 13th to 17th), marital status (three married, one widowed), profession (two attorneys, one small-businessperson, one public official), committee (all on Appropriations Committee), office location, and phone number. They sought to memorize every detail possible.

But this was not a quiet study session. Excitement filled the plane. Many stood in the aisle. Others hopped from seat to seat. A white woman in her fifties described the scene:

> Oh! Well, the energy! I don't think I've ever been on a plane in your entire life where you can't hear yourself talk. Because the noise is so loud and very few people are sitting down. It was like hitting a beehive, OK? We got hit. A hive got hit. We are just buzzing around everywhere. It was unbelievable. It was exciting. It was exhilarating. It helped bring us together and realize that as different as we are, we at least know we have one thing in common, and that is to bring our city back.

Despite the excitement, the trip also created role conflicts for many of the participants, especially among women with school-age children or those in the process of rebuilding their homes. For one day everything in the women's lives was suspended: attending their children's extracurricular activities, repairing flooded homes, dealing with contractors, making insurance claims. A white woman in her forties explained, "You have to understand, this is something so out of character. I would never get on a plane and leave my kids for a day." After describing herself as a homemaker, she said, "You know, I'm just a mom with three kids. I never had any political, any activist side to me at all. This is something that just evolved because of all the hurt I would see around the city."

Sitting in an aisle seat that morning was Barbara Blackwell, an African American participant, who told a CNN reporter on the plane the message they hoped to convey to lawmakers: "You can't see it from the air. You have to be in the neighborhood. Walk block-by-block, mile-by-mile."[8] At the time of Katrina's landfall, Blackwell was an administrative assistant in the judicial administrator's office in the Louisiana Supreme Court Building, and after the storm she would become highly active in rebuilding efforts as the community liaison for the Gentilly Sugar Hill Neighborhood Association. The words she spoke on camera were informed by talking points in the group's packets but also by her lived experience. She and her family had survived a harrowing ordeal during Katrina.[9]

When Katrina came ashore on Monday, August 29, Blackwell and her family rode out the storm in their home in Gentilly, a middle-class neighborhood with large numbers of African American professionals who in the 1940s began moving to this area adjacent to Dillard University, one of New Orleans's historically black colleges and universities.[10] After the nearby London Avenue Canal breached and floodwaters began rising in their home, Blackwell and her family dialed 911 and then climbed up into the attic, where they would stay for nearly eight hours before making their way to the rooftop to wait for help.[11] The New Orleans Fire Department eventually rescued Blackwell and her family by boat, navigating their flooded neighborhood in search of higher ground. The boat eventually dropped the family off on the elevated portion of the I-610 highway just a few submerged blocks away.[12] From there, they made their way to the New Orleans Superdome. On Sunday, just a day before Katrina's landfall, the city had opened the Superdome as a refuge of last resort, and by Sunday evening nearly ten thousand people had already sought refuge there. The Blackwells were among the additional tens of thousands of people who converged on the Superdome in the days that followed as the city began filling with water, bringing the total number in the large sports venue to between twenty and thirty thousand.[13]

After entering the Superdome, the Blackwells were not allowed out for days. The doors had been kept closed by a significant security presence, which included the New Orleans Police Department (NOPD) and troops from the Louisiana National Guard. The Louisiana Office of Homeland Security and Emergency Preparedness and the Texas and Florida National Guards were also called in for support as the crowds swelled. Rumors about theft, crime, and general unrest circulated. It was there that the family, sleeping in fifteen-minute shifts so that someone would be awake to watch their belongings, would spend three nights cooped up in the bleachers with thousands of evacuees. The structure had lost electricity by Monday morning, leaving the crowd without air conditioning, and by Tuesday the plumbing had failed, causing toilets to back up and overflow.[14] Late on Tuesday, security at the Superdome opened its doors for the first time, letting in fresh air and allowing those inside to see for themselves that the facility was surrounded by water, posing a challenge for any sort of land evacuation.[15] But where were the buses that were supposed to bring the people to safety? On Monday, FEMA's director, Michael Brown, told Blanco that the buses were en route and would be there within hours; yet it was later revealed that FEMA didn't direct the U.S. Department of Transportation to deploy the buses until Wednesday.[16] It wasn't until 10 A.M. on Thursday, September 1, that the bus evacuation of those at the Superdome would begin, a disorganized response that would not be complete until the afternoon of Saturday, September 3.[17]

After four long days inside the Superdome, Blackwell and her family were brought outside to board buses that were to take evacuees out of the swamped city. Blackwell described the scene outside the Superdome as "like being on Bourbon Street on a very crowded Mardi Gras day."[18] The family became separated amid the crushing crowds outside, and they boarded buses that would disperse them across the country, like thousands of other Katrina evacuees, with little or no record of who was taken where. Blackwell found herself aboard a bus that ended up taking her to an evacuation shelter in Arlington, Texas. Her sister, Jean, was on a bus bound for Houston, where she would end up in a relief center in the Astrodome. Other family members were taken to shelters in McKinley, Texas.[19]

Blackwell's home was flooded with over five feet of water, and as she began rebuilding, she became more active in Gentilly civic groups and neighborhood associations. It was this civic involvement in neighborhood rebuilding efforts that led to her receiving a call from Norma Jean Sabiston, a WOS member employed at Marmillion + Company, who invited her on the trip. And so she found herself sitting on the plane, like many others, prepared to share her storm stories with lawmakers. Her dramatic story was not unlike the struggles experienced by many others across the Gulf Coast who could attest that Katrina's effects were ongoing and that help was still needed; for many it was a disaster without end. At the time of WOS's trip to Washington, five months after the storm, Blackwell was one of over seventy-five thousand displaced people still living in hotels.[20]

A few rows behind Barbara Blackwell, near the back of the plane, sat Cecile Tebo, a forty-five-year-old white woman and licensed clinical social worker with a master's degree from Tulane University. She, like Blackwell, had plenty of stories to tell about her life in New Orleans and her struggles after the storm. Five years earlier, at age forty, this fourth-generation New Orleanian and "ex-debutante" had become a reserve officer in the NOPD, and by October 2004, the year before Katrina, she was hired as the crisis unit coordinator for the department, where she spent her workdays on patrol dealing with mental health cases.[21] Given the deeply personal battles that she would encounter immediately after Katrina, she began to describe herself as a reformer, finding her voice, speaking up, and taking on the insurance industry, the crumbling health care system, and a slow-to-act Congress.

On Sunday, August 28, 2005, Mayor Nagin had ordered a mandatory evacuation of New Orleans, and thousands of residents left town in a massive exodus as Hurricane Katrina barreled toward the city. Early that morning, Tebo and her husband, Balad, had gathered their three children and evacuated first to the Florida panhandle and then to Charlotte, North Carolina. The following day, Katrina made landfall. Tebo touched base with friends who had stayed in New Orleans throughout the storm, one of whom reported to her, "It's the funniest thing. Someone said, 'your street is wet.'"[22] Their home was soon underwater. Tebo and her family learned that the levees had failed, and they watched the flooding of New Orleans from Charlotte, where they would remain until November.

When Tebo and her husband returned to New Orleans in Katrina's immediate aftermath to inspect their two-story home for the first time, during a short visit on September 24, 2005, just a few days after Hurricane Rita, they were accompanied by a reporter and film crew for CBS 3, a local news station in Charlotte. The video captured the couple's reaction to seeing their destroyed home and nearly abandoned Broadmoor neighborhood. Although the home was perched several feet above ground, the first floor had still flooded with over two feet of water. A dirty, charcoal-tinted watermark stretched uniformly across their home's pastel yellow exterior indicating the floodwaters at their highest point. Next to the front door, hastily sprayed search-and-rescue marks scarred the home's façade. Upon entering their flooded home, the Tebos assessed the damage—moldy drywall, overturned furniture, a destroyed baby grand piano. Somehow, sheet music remained on the piano stand, indicating that rising floodwaters, rather than a wind event, had caused the damage inside the home.[23] As she looked in disbelief at the damage within her home, Tebo told the CBS reporter, "I don't even understand how you begin with something like this."

Outside, the street remained covered with storm debris and broken tree limbs. A lone, white pickup truck sat parked in the street, a water line across the windshield. A neighbor or two on the block had already begun the cleanup process, as evidenced by ugly piles of destroyed belongings hauled to the curb from their flooded homes.

Tebo called out the names of her two cats, Felicity and Parish, hoping that their pets, just two of the estimated 727,500 animals affected by Katrina in the city alone, had survived during the family's weeks-long evacuation.[24] When the Tebos evacuated the day before Katrina hit, viewers would learn from the newscaster's voiceover, they had planned to be gone for just a few days, and they left their two cats, thinking they would quickly return as they had after numerous other hurricane evacuations. But like thousands of New Orleanians, the Tebos were gone much longer than ever imaginable. Rather than being gone a day or two, they ended up being displaced for three and a half weeks, and still they were among the earliest Katrina evacuees to return. Standing outside, Tebo threw her arms up in despair. She looked away and began to sob. "We had so much fun in this house," she said through tears.

Minutes later, Felicity, an orange, short-haired cat, emerged from the rubble, tail up, good-spirited, and, as the reporter described, "a little thinner, but okay." Embracing her cat outside, Tebo said, "If we could get the other one, I've got a whole rainbow over me." Then came a surprise. "Oh my God! It's Parish! It's Parish!" she said from the elevated porch. She darted down to the street to greet a second orange cat, one with slightly longer and somewhat matted fur, that had made its way into the sunlight. Tebo knelt on the pavement with happiness, overjoyed that both cats survived the storm. A friendly Parish circled Tebo, rubbing up against her and the reporter who knelt nearby.

In the months thereafter, Tebo's stories would move from local to national stations as she became an outspoken critic of the pace of the recovery. Over the subsequent months, she and her family moved four times. She found herself living in a rental apartment as she continued to rebuild her home and while waiting for the delivery of a FEMA trailer to her property. For Tebo and many others, the recovery seemed stalled. Many residents hadn't returned to the city, and those who had were living a fragile existence, struggling to operate in a world that had been torn apart. Tebo's close friend James Kent Treadway, a native New Orleanian and her children's pediatrician, took his own life, hanging himself in his storm-damaged home.[25] Upon learning of his death, Tebo nearly cracked under the pressure. She dealt with the stress by going to bed, where she stayed for the next seven days.[26]

On December 2, 2005, a week after her friend's death, Tebo received a phone call from an out-of-town friend. The chipper voice on the phone commented on images of the recovery she had seen on television and assumed that everything was okay for Tebo and her family. Tebo fumed. In the middle of the night, jolted out of bed by thoughts about an outside world that just didn't understand what felt like perpetual crisis, she found herself at the computer, typing away. That night, Tebo composed a letter titled "We Are Not OK!," which CNN invited her to read on air. Highlighting her private battles with depression and with insurance companies over the slow disbursement of claims owed to her under her homeowner and flood insurance, she read the letter from her home, still being rebuilt:

> So, my friend calls me from North Carolina and says, "Wow, I was just watching the news and it looks as though the city is doing great. The French Quarter looks wonderful and I see that the zoo is back. You must be so much better."
>
> My response, "No, we are not better at all. We have received no assistance from either our homeowners or flood insurance, despite the fact that we met with adjusters in September. The home we are renting will no longer be available in three weeks.
>
> Our trailer has not arrived. We have never met with a FEMA adjuster. We are broke and we will be homeless again in three weeks. No, we are not OK."

I know I speak for thousands and thousands of people who have called New Orleans their home. The attention received in [the] early days of this tragedy was relentless. Our pain and suffering touched every home in this country, in this nation, on a daily and sometimes hourly basis. But now, as thousands continue to suffer and drown in grief and despair, the cameras have stopped, the attention has left us to suffer alone in fear and broken promises.

I sat today with hundreds at the FEMA station. The looks in everyone's eyes display the heartache and sadness of what has happened to them.

The insurance companies have robbed us of future hopes and are responsible for the now ongoing mental anguish of uncertainty, fear, and inability for many of us to even take a step in the rebuilding process.

My job is to work the streets with our heroic police officers, trying to assist them in response to calls of a mental health nature. The calls these days are generally from those who have given up. They have lost everything and are completely devastated.

A precious, dear friend of mine took his life not long ago. The agony of what lay ahead was simply too great to bear. Others are making this same choice because the agony, hopelessness and helplessness are greater than one's own ability to cope.

Why is the media, who tends to love the horror stories, not sharing this news? We are living the ultimate nightmare.

No, we are not OK and we cry for your help.[27]

After Tebo read the letter from her living room, with empty dresser drawers stacked behind her, with ruined drywall ripped out leaving only the studs, CNN cut to a live interview with her outside her home, where she drew attention to private interests and the government: "The people have done their part but the insurance companies and the government are not doing their part, and it needs to happen now because we are drowning. The floodwaters have gone, but inside, emotionally, mentally, we are drowning."

Later that day, Tebo appeared again on CNN to speak with Anderson Cooper, who had just told viewers that "the fact remains that for the tens of thousands of people in the Gulf, progress is an illusion." He then shifted attention to Tebo, who said that within thirty minutes of her earlier interview, in which she had named her insurance company—Fidelity—her husband received a phone call from a Fidelity vice president. Two hours later the Tebos were meeting with an adjuster who had been told to expedite their claim, and the following morning their check arrived via FedEx. Tebo insisted that sharing her plight on national television was not only about getting their individual insurance check: "The point of my story really wasn't the Tebos; it was three hundred thousand people here that are struggling with this. Although I am very grateful, it's just given me more time and energy to focus on others." She went on to discuss harnessing the media to get things accomplished: "It's obvious that the power of the media gets people moving and that's what we have to do. And we have struggled to find any avenue to get people moving. If this is the way we do it, I'll tell you what, I will line them up by the thousands. Because when I came on, it wasn't just about the Tebos, it was about my community."

On Wednesday, January 11, a day after Milling held her impromptu meeting with the tiny group of women who would form the backbone of the soon to be named WOS, Mayor Nagin's seventeen-member Bring New Orleans Back (BNOB) Commission unveiled its final rebuilding report and called for a moratorium on rebuilding in areas that experienced severe flooding, giving residents in flooded neighborhoods four months to make a case for their viability. Six neighborhoods, including Broadmoor, were at risk of becoming parks; the *Times-Picayune* and local news stations showed a city map with six green dots. Tebo's home was under one of these dots. A few days later, standing in her once-flooded neighborhood wearing a T-shirt that read "Battle of New Orleans," Tebo told local reporters, "I've clawed my way through insurance. I've clawed my way through FEMA. I've clawed my way home. And then I wake up on a beautiful morning. I'm drinking my coffee and I open the paper, and I'm a proposed park."[28] Tebo was not the only one in her neighborhood to experience anger at the proposed green space. Virginia Saussy, a thirty-nine-year-old white woman whose house not far away on Napoleon Avenue was flooded with seven feet of water, stepped up and began organizing friends and neighbors to rally against the BNOB recommendation.[29]

Three days later, on January 14, Saussy mobilized hundreds of neighborhood residents—some sources estimate one hundred showed up, others say three hundred—to gather at a 4 P.M. rally on the neutral ground of Napoleon Avenue, a main thoroughfare cutting across Broadmoor, a neighborhood that nearly seven thousand residents called home.[30] A diverse group gathered: blacks and whites, elderly, couples and their dogs, and at least one person in a wheelchair. Saussy, described as a neighborhood organizer by WWL-TV, told reporters, "When we heard the Bring Back New Orleans Commission issue a challenge, we responded. This is not a park. This is the center of New Orleans."

Saussy soon contacted the Broadmoor Improvement Association (BIA) president, LaToya Cantrell, a thirty-four-year old African American woman, who had evacuated to Houston.[31] Cantrell had moved to New Orleans from California and purchased a home on Louisiana Avenue with her husband in 2000. She was in the process of planning the first post-Katrina meeting of the BIA when she heard that Saussy and others were organizing.[32] Cantrell, whose home flooded with five feet of water, together with Saussy and other BIA members, was able to mobilize almost five hundred people to attend a meeting four days later, on January 18.[33] It was at this meeting that the BIA began developing a community-driven rebuilding plan, complete with subcommittees, including the Repopulation Committee, which was co-chaired by Saussy and Kelli Wright, a local realtor.[34] From January to July 2006, hundreds of community meetings were held, resulting in a 335-page document outlining the neighborhood's vision for rebuilding, including a six-point implementation strategy involving citizen input, developers, and support from universities, faith groups, government, and the private sector.[35] Because of the participatory nature of Broadmoor's revitalization efforts, many looked to the neighborhood as a "model for disaster recovery."[36] Both Saussy and Cantrell would also join WOS.

When WOS made its Washington trip, the lives of the women discussed in this chapter were still uprooted. Virginia Saussy had returned to her Broadmoor home in November 2005, spending three months living on the second floor without gas or phone service; she and her husband were the only people on the block well into February 2006.[37] As she repaired her home and waited for a FEMA trailer, LaToya Cantrell was living in a Marriott. Barbara Blackwell was also staying in a hotel.[38] Cecile Tebo was living in a FEMA trailer parked in the driveway of her once-flooded home. She had even staked an American flag on her lawn and a sign that read "House NOT For Sale." None of them planned to leave New Orleans.

These were the types of personal stories of post-Katrina life that nearly 130 others on the plane hoped to share with lawmakers. Just as Tebo had used the media to pressure the insurance industry, the women on the plane knew very well that a media presence would help hold those in power accountable. This ethos of working on behalf of a larger collectivity was part of what motivated WOS participants to take their cause to Washington in the first place. WOS members saw themselves as interconnected, and they understood their activities as part of a moral responsibility to work on behalf of others. Later, in an interview on the plane with CNN correspondents, Tebo distanced herself from politics: "You know what is so cool. We are not a commission. We are not sponsored by any government program. This is literally New Orleanian women." She continued, "You have to feel [for] the people who have lost everything."[39]

Just like the weather in New Orleans a few hours earlier, there was a dense fog over Washington that January morning. The flight was running late, and WOS members were worried about making it to the 11 A.M. press conference on Capitol Hill. The group learned from the US Airways flight crew that the plane was being diverted from Reagan National Airport to Dulles International Airport because of the fog. The core membership had carefully orchestrated the trip, detailing the itinerary with precision almost down to the minute. Reagan National Airport was a short fifteen-minute drive from Capitol Hill. But the drive from Dulles would take three times as long. Not only would the change cause them to miss the press conference, but the ground transportation picking them up at Reagan National would need to move to Dulles International. The group was in a fix, and the core group scrambled. One interviewee told me that Norma Jane Sabiston got on her phone and began making calls despite regulations that prohibited it. She managed to tell someone to send the buses and press vehicles stationed at Reagan to Dulles. Minutes later, soon after she completed the call, the flight crew announced that a slot had just opened up at Reagan. The plane was diverted yet again, and Sabiston got back on the phone to turn the buses around.

Upon arriving at Washington under clear skies, some saw the shift in weather as a sign. "We got there, and it was just as God had ordained: a beautiful sunny day. The fog had lifted," said one African American participant. "When we landed, it's like the heavens smiled upon our visit. And we had the support from the heavens above."

CHAPTER 5

The Press Conference

On political drama, performative utterances,
and blue-tarp umbrellas on Capitol Hill

When WOS's plane landed at Reagan National Airport, Pam Bryan turned on her cell phone and discovered two voicemails.[1] She immediately listened to the messages, turned to her partner, Anne Milling, and exclaimed, "I did my job!" The voicemails were from the WWL-TV contact in New Orleans who had been making calls while WOS was in flight and had secured appointments for the pair with Rep. Nancy Pelosi and Rep. Don Young; a response from the offices of Rep. Dennis Hastert was pending.

After landing, Bryan and fellow core member Madeline West were taken by limousine for live interviews with CNN. Three Grayline buses were waiting for the rest of the group outside the US Airways baggage claim. Once aboard the buses, some women continued to make a last round of calls, finalizing plans for their meetings later that afternoon. CNN showed footage of Cecile Tebo calling an office from the bus to announce their arrival in Washington.[2]

As the buses neared Capitol Hill, team captains gave instructions about their first public unfurling of the group's blue-tarp umbrellas, embossed with WOS's logo, which had been placed on each plane seat for participants.[3] The idea of the umbrellas had been suggested during the brainstorming sessions by WOS core member Beverly Church, described by Anne Milling as the group's "entertainer, party planner guru."[4] Church, a Junior Leaguer and member of the Garden Club of America who has appeared on *Good Morning America* and Home and Garden Television, said the umbrellas were intended to make WOS visually striking, not unlike the everyday acts of hosting and entertaining described in her how-to books *Entertaining Celebrations: Celebrate Each Month with Pizzazz*, *The Joys of Entertaining*, and *Seasonal Celebrations*.[5] Her books include step-by-step instructions for creating dramatic tablescapes for themed parties, with attention-grabbing items such as flower-edged tablecloths, chair-back bouquets, gold-stamped napkins, and cocktail tables wrapped in grass skirts. Decorative umbrellas were often the focal point for her themed parties. For example, in *Seasonal Celebrations*, the "Graduation Party" plan included instructions for a hand-painted umbrella adorned in acrylic; the "Red Hot Rose Soirée" themed event, held to mark the Kentucky Derby, called for a rose-adorned umbrella with rosebuds pinned or hot-glued along the perimeter; and the "Posh Polo Party" featured umbrellas draped in fabric and accented with tassels.

But unlike these whimsical decorations, the blue-tarp umbrellas were meant to play a political role. Created specifically for the press conference, the umbrellas were to be the same distinctive shade as the FEMA-issued blue tarps that covered thousands of homes across the region, a particular hue that had entered the region's post-disaster visual vocabulary. The executive committee found a company that made custom umbrellas, and as they went through the color swatches, the employee told them, "We have navy blue. We have red." But neither color would have had the intended effect. "No," recalled one woman as she sorted out the umbrella order. "It's got to be the blue-tarp blue." They continued looking through the color options and landed on the perfect shade.

The blue-tarp umbrellas were used to garner media attention, and the women were given very specific instructions: "Hold umbrella so that the logo faces forward." Like most of WOS's activities, even the prop's positioning was orchestrated for maximum effect. Details mattered.

Around 11 A.M. the buses arrived at the corner of Louisiana Avenue and Constitution Avenue NW. As the women exited the buses, they unfurled their umbrellas one by one and ascended Capitol Hill to the press conference at Upper Senate Park on Constitution between Delaware Avenue and New Jersey Avenue, a site chosen because the U.S. Capitol building loomed large in the background.[6] Video footage and press photos show the women carrying the umbrellas; as close-up shots focused on their shoes, one could hear their heels on the sidewalk. One woman looked at the camera and said, "We're here!" Another chimed in, "Yes, we're here! We're here to make a difference!"[7]

The collective action was designed for broadcast and imbued with social drama, resembling what scholars have described as "political theater" or "performance protest."[8] It included all the defining features of what sociologist Jeffrey Alexander calls "cultural performance," or "the social process by which actors, individually or in concert, display for others the meaning of their social situation."[9] Alexander writes, "In order to perform a cultural text before an audience, actors need access to mundane material things that allow symbolic projections to be made. They need objects that can serve as iconic representations to help them dramatize and make vivid the invisible motives and morals they are trying to represent."[10] For WOS the blue-tarp umbrellas became those iconic representations.

FIGURE 3. Marvalene Hughes (*left*) and Tania Tetlow walk to Women of the Storm's news conference on Capitol Hill, Monday, January 30, 2006. AP photo/Susan Walsh.

Lasting only minutes, this collective action marked a special moment of solidarity for participants, who recalled the event in vivid detail. A white woman in her thirties, who described herself as a mother and an activist, remembered, "Women who have been on fiercely opposing sides for years and years politically in town were all on the same bus, with the same message, with the same blue umbrella." Another white woman described the onlookers: "A sea of people [were] watching these women with blue umbrellas and it was incredible. In my life I have never seen so many press people. Never. I've been a part of many things. But I've never been a part of anything that felt so right at the right time."

Overflowing with excitement, a white participant explained the symbolism: "It was blue tarp. I mean it's [the color of] a blue roof. Three buses of women and we all opened our umbrellas as soon as we got off of the bus. It was very visual. We walked for about a block and a half, and I was on the third bus, and you see these blue umbrellas going up and then you see them coming up the hill. I think it was very impressive." She was not alone. A white woman in her sixties suggested that the blue-tarp umbrellas referenced not only the actual tarps that covered homes but also the catastrophe's human dimensions: "It was unbelievable, those umbrellas, the impact. Just simply because it's blue tarps. That's what it represents, the people that are still struggling to get their lives together and their houses, everything."[11]

WOS's collective actions were highly gendered. To the women, the umbrellas invoked a gentle, nonthreatening symbol. They were not placards with aggressive slogans, and their unfurling was not intended to appear oppositional. Even as they talked about the powerful, place-based symbols, some participants also recognized how the layers of meaning may have been lost for those in Washington.[12] Despite this potential "performative failure," group members still believed the umbrellas succeeded in catching people's attention.[13]

The performance activism of WOS evoked not only FEMA's ubiquitous blue tarps but also the rich New Orleans parading tradition. Walking parades called "second lines" are woven into the fabric of the city. Led by a brass band, revelers dance and strut along the parade route, some carrying decorated umbrellas and waving handkerchiefs. It might be fair to say that no public event in New Orleans is considered complete without a second line: weddings, family reunions, school events, the opening of new businesses, and, of course, funerals. Widely referred to as "jazz funerals," the tradition has roots in nineteenth-century funeral customs whereby a brass band leads the funeral cortege to the cemetery. By the early twentieth century, this tradition had taken a specific form among the city's working-class African American community. Leaving the church, the brass band leads the solemn procession, playing somber hymns like "Preservation Dirge," "A Closer Walk with Thee," or "Joe Avery's Blues." The hearse, often an elaborate horse-drawn wagon, comes next, followed by the "second line" of marchers, the band being the first. There is a transitional moment in the ritual referred to as "cutting the body loose" whereby "the deceased parts company with the procession in his honor" and the mourners turn back as uplifting music, joyous shouts, and laughter fill the air.[14] The stylized parades, heavily orchestrated activities consisting of matching outfits, improvised dancing solos, and the unfurling, popping, and twirling of umbrellas, have crossed over from the African American community, becoming yet another form of New Orleans entertainment that draws large crowds, including many whites and tourists.[15] Helen Regis, a cultural anthropologist at Louisiana State University, has argued that such rituals became more visible throughout the region as they were appropriated by other segments of society, including the city's elites and the tourism industry.[16]

For WOS participants, the umbrellas evoked this long, complex history even as they also referenced the immediate post-Katrina context. One white participant described the delicate process of managing these multiple meanings. She said some group members were worried that the umbrellas would be interpreted as lighthearted: "Because usually when we do umbrellas, it's a second line, people are dancing, whatever. And I said, 'I agree that this should be serious. It's got to be totally solemn.'" Another white participant gave a similar response: "We wanted to make sure that no one thought that this was not a serious trip. This wasn't Mardi

Gras. This wasn't Bourbon Street. This wasn't second-lining in Washington D.C. This was women saying 'pay attention to us.'"

The women quickly filed into the Upper Senate Park with their blue-tarp umbrellas unfurled and then assembled behind an open-air podium placed on a small wooden platform erected over dormant grass. Some participants held their open umbrellas in the air while those in the front row held their umbrellas in some other position, usually facing forward, which created a multitiered layering of blue for the media cameras. The women faced reporters with the Capitol dome behind them, placing themselves in a national political context.

Rather than protesting with chants or giving impromptu speeches, tactics typical of oppositional movement groups, WOS's press conference was executed with skillful restraint, including prepared remarks by three speakers: Anne Milling, Cheryl Teamer, and Mary Landrieu. This carefully orchestrated event provided WOS with an opportunity to accomplish a number of objectives. It helped establish a sense of group credibility and publicly define the "scope of the problem" for external audiences.[17] And it provided yet another occasion to mobilize images of diversity, in the racial composition of the speakers who would be seen at the event and whose images, meant to be representative of the group, would circulate through media venues long after the press conference concluded.[18]

The Lakeview home of Cheryl Teamer, a forty-two-year-old African American attorney, had been flooded with nearly ten feet of water during Katrina.[19] Teamer gave a face to the Katrina catastrophe that differed greatly from many of the images of black suffering at the Superdome or the New Orleans Convention Center. She came from a prominent, well-to-do family in Southern black society.[20] She graduated from Spelman College, where in the mid-1980s she would join her father, Charles C. Teamer, then general president of the Alpha Phi Alpha fraternity, on the activist front lines of the Free South Africa march and rally.[21] After moving to New Orleans, she went on to earn a JD from Tulane Law School, becoming an attorney for the Louisiana House of Representatives Committee on Municipal, Parochial, and Cultural Affairs, and teaching at the University of New Orleans as an adjunct professor of public policy and urban affairs. On September 20, less than a month after Katrina, Teamer was invited to serve on the advisory board of Lt. Gov. Mitch Landrieu's National Advisory Board for Culture, Recreation, and Tourism, a group co-chaired by Ed Lewis of *Essence Magazine* and jazz musician Wynton Marsalis.[22] At the time of WOS's trip, she was regional vice president of government relations at Harrah's Entertainment, whose New Orleans casino was set to reopen on February 17.[23] This long list of achievements demonstrated her credentials, and as a member of both the Junior League and The Links, Teamer served as a symbolic bridge between elite white women and elite women of color in New Orleans. Like Barbara Blackwell and Cecile Tebo, Teamer could also speak as a Katrina survivor who lost her home. Like others who experienced direct losses, the credibility that Teamer brought to WOS reflects what Kathleen Blee calls "credibility-by-connection," which is "bestowed on members for who they are rather than what they do."[24] Blee writes that activist groups focus a great deal of energy recruiting these members, because they help establish a direct connection to the problems the group is seeking to address; in doing so they often receive "some measure of credibility," because they have "members who experience these issues firsthand."[25]

Very little of Teamer's speech was recorded, and only snippets remain in the public record, showing that she was given much less air time by broadcast media than her white counterparts, Anne Milling and Mary Landrieu, whose credibility came not from experiencing direct loss, but by past action. This type of credibility, Blee notes, is "more often attached to those from higher status social groups."[26] Nevertheless, some of Teamer's words made it onto the news broadcasts. "I'm very proud to be here," Teamer said from the podium in a small, seconds-long clip of her speech. "We will return and we will rebuild," she continued. She would later tell CNN correspondent Kathleen Koch, "It's now five months since the levees were breached, and we really want to see progress. I mean, people now are making the decision to rebuild. It's a hard decision, and we're going back, so once you make that decision, you're ready to jump in and get started."[27]

The most airtime was given to Anne Milling, who was quoted as saying, "Only 12 and a half percent of Congress has come to witness the devastation, and less than a third of our Senate has come. This is a major national catastrophe, but we don't think they understand the magnitude of it. And that's been a big disappointment."[28] In addition to linking the Gulf Coast to the nation, Milling expressed the need to learn lessons from Katrina: "To fail to act, and thus to neglect the needs of this vital region of this country, set an unimaginable precedent for responses to future catastrophes in our nation."[29] She added, "It was a storm that was felt around the world. Yet, who would dream that 87 percent of the House of Representatives and 70 percent of the Senate haven't found time to visit the site of the largest catastrophe in the history of America?"[30]

The press conference also included a short speech by Landrieu, who said, "I want to thank Anne Milling for her extraordinary leadership. I've known her for many years. I've watched her family, her husband, herself, and her children serve our community, time and time again. And she stepped up again to lead this great effort, with Cheryl Teamer and others. I've watched my mother, I've watched Blanche Francis, who between them, have raised sixteen children and now are raising probably over fifty grandchildren. And they do a hell of a job." Landrieu continued:

> So we're here today with a simple message, but it's a message of urgency for the Congress to act. As the Women of the Storm have said, "Until you see it, you can't believe it." So these women, as they have done for literally hundreds of years, their mothers and grandmothers before them, have put up their own money and their own energy to encourage the members of Congress to come down and walk the streets, not just in the broad daylight and on beautiful days like this, but as the sun goes down, to hear the silence, to experience the suffering, and to see what

this great nation [could do], if it could pull its will together, to rebuild again a great region, a great city. I most certainly hope that we can do it. My work will be tireless in this endeavor. Because not only do I have our two children to raise, along with my husband, Frank, but I'm committed to the millions of children that call Louisiana their home.[31]

Landrieu emphasized the importance of the city for the women and their families. Her voice was trembling as she said, "It is a place that we have all raised our children, and dreamed the dreams that people dream all over this country."[32] In line with WOS's requests, Landrieu highlighted Louisiana's relationship to the nation by requesting "a fair share of the billions of dollars that our state generates right off of our shores to keep the Treasury of the United States full, and the lights on from New York to California to Chicago."[33]

Beyond the speaker list, diversity was mobilized in more subtle ways during the press conference. An examination of how the women arranged themselves behind the main speakers is revealing of attempts to present a certain image of the group to audiences. Photographs show that those standing in the front row were from different racial backgrounds. White women such as Peggy Laborde, Tania Tetlow, Joyce Pulitzer, and Nancy Marsiglia were standing shoulder to shoulder with women of color, including Barbara Blackwell, Jeanette Bell, and Blanche Francis. This was probably not done by chance.

Standing directly behind the podium where Teamer, Milling, and Landrieu spoke was Dr. Marvalene Hughes. In July 2005 Dr. Hughes became president of historically black Dillard University. Katrina inundated Dillard's campus with seven to ten feet of floodwater; it flooded again during Rita.[34] Originally from Alabama, Hughes left her previous job as president of California State University–Stanislaus and started at Dillard just fifty-nine days before Katrina. The day before Katrina's landfall, Hughes helped evacuate students, escorting more than 225 of them onto buses intended to take them out of harm's way. She evacuated to her sister's home in Alabama, where she received a call that one bus had encountered a mechanical problem, catching fire en route to Shreveport, where arrangements had been made with Centenary College to house the evacuated students. Hughes then drove four hundred miles to console the 37 students who had escaped the fire-engulfed bus without harm but whose belongings had been destroyed.[35] In the months thereafter, Dillard students were taken in at more than two hundred colleges across the country, becoming part of a nationwide diaspora of nearly 50,000 college students from the storm-affected areas.[36] By January, with the Dillard campus still closed, classes began at the Hilton New Orleans Riverside Hotel, where just about half of the 2,200 students enrolled pre-Katrina returned for the spring semester.[37] Despite all that Hughes needed to do to ensure that the university could reopen that month, she still traveled to Washington to stand with WOS in order to call attention to the needs of the Gulf Coast.

As the press conference aired live on CNN, Madeline West and Pam Bryan, a racially mixed pair from WOS's executive committee, were interviewed in CNN's studios by news anchor Daryn Kagan. While the women conversed, the networks showed aerial shots of a flooded New Orleans along with ground-level shots of abandoned homes, their front doors wide open after being searched by rescue crews. Kagan asked, "Why now? Why is the time right more than five months after the storm?" West replied, "I think it is a critical point, because most of the locals are becoming tired and weary and not seeing the results that we should be seeing." Addressing Bryan, Kagan said, "You say that this group is nonpartisan and nonpolitical. That seems almost impossible on a topic that seems all about finger pointing." Bryan responded: "Oh, quite the opposite, Daryn. This is a group of diverse women. We're speaking with one voice. Because we are all committed to our city. We care so deeply for our city that we have come together and we know now that we want coastal restoration and we want enhancement of our flood protection. We want people to feel safe in the city of New Orleans. And we desperately need better housing."[38]

The details presented thus far demonstrate how diversity efforts were at the core of nearly everything the group did. At the press conference and at the broadcast studios, diversity was mobilized through the deliberate choices about who would speak for the group. At the press conference, a white female senator and WOS's founder both spoke beside an African American woman. At the CNN studios, a racially mixed pair appeared on national television to further WOS's cause. Decisions about where to stand and with whom helped communicate to audiences what

FIGURE 4. Sister Anne Marie Kim-Khuong of New Orleans looks on during a press conference near the U.S. Capitol in Washington, January 30, 2006. Catholic News Service photo/Bob Roller.

the group valued. Beyond what was said by the speakers at the press conferences, the processes by which they organized themselves to portray diversity is revealing. Besides being an ethical and political necessity, as Milling said, diversity also played a vital role in the group's public relations strategy.[39]

The invitation extended to Congress was central to nearly everything WOS set out to accomplish. It is worth pausing to reflect on the invitation as a material object, a vital resource in making group claims. Again, every detail mattered. Measuring 5½″ by 8½″ and printed on noticeably heavy card stock, WOS's oversize invitations had several parts: an outer envelope, a top-fold invitation, an inner envelope, and an RSVP card. The front of the invitation was imprinted with the WOS logo, which was an adaptation of the hurricane-tracking symbol used by the National Weather Service. Upon opening the invitation, one would find a summary of Katrina's and Rita's effects:

> Just five months ago, the world watched with shock and sadness as 80 percent of New Orleans was flooded by storm surge brought on by Hurricane Katrina. More than 1,000 Louisianans died; 350,000 Louisiana citizens were displaced to 44 states; more than 217,000 homes were destroyed; and 81,000 businesses were severely impacted. Just a few weeks later, Hurricane Rita struck, devastating the southwest portion of the state.
>
> As the media reported the worst natural disaster in our nation's history, people around the world mourned the tragedy with us. However, there is nothing more powerful than witnessing the devastation first-hand and experiencing the hardship and triumph that accompany recovery and rebirth of the state.
>
> Women of the Storm is a non-partisan, non-political alliance of more than 100 women from Metropolitan New Orleans and South Louisiana whose lives were disrupted by Hurricanes Katrina and Rita. They formed with the mission to persuade Members of Congress to visit South Louisiana and to see first-hand the devastation wrought by these deadly storms, while bringing attention to the need for coastal protection as a key to rebuilding and revitalizing the Gulf Coast.[40]

Below the fold, the following text appeared:

WOMEN OF THE STORM

Cordially invite you to join us on a
Ground and aerial tour of the New Orleans area
and Louisiana's coastal wetlands
So that you may realize the full extent of the impact Hurricanes Katrina
and Rita had on the land and people of South Louisiana.

Four trips are being conducted on the following dates:
February 10–11, 2006   February 12–13, 2006
February 17–18, 2006   February 19–20, 2006

Accompanying the invitation was a formal response card, which fit into a smaller self-addressed stamped envelope; it read, "To reserve your spot on one of the Women of the Storm's tours of New Orleans and coastal Louisiana, please complete this card and return it to the America's WETLAND Campaign at the address printed on the envelope." The fill-in response card provided space for lawmakers to pencil in their names, along with the names of a staff scheduling contact and a staff press contact. Lawmakers could also circle one of the four tour dates to visit New Orleans.

Since it seemed like such a crucial strategy for the group, I asked Anne Milling how she came up with the idea to extend invitations to members of Congress. She said, "When you want someone to see something or experience something, you extend an invitation, written or verbal. You invite them to your home if you want to discuss something. Probably subconsciously, I realized that members of the Congress were not coming, and it occurred to me, OK, if they won't come on their own volition, then maybe perhaps if a group of us went there and invited them, it would make a difference." She recalled that their public relations firm had planned to print the invitation on plain white, 8½" by 11" paper: "I remember saying, 'Wait a minute—no, you're missing this. It's an invitation. We want an invitation, like if I were inviting you to a dinner party. I don't want just a piece of paper that they can just toss in the wastepaper basket. We want to make a statement.'" Her insistence on form reveals that its imagined efficacy depended on how it much it resembled formal correspondence. Milling's account reveals the regional importance of the invitation.[41] "I bet you outsiders would say it was a Southern approach," she said. "This is something very natural for us here in New Orleans, very natural, to have an invitation with an RSVP card. That's how I would do it if I were inviting you to my home for something formal—I mean, not just to come to dinner, but to a party. I would have an RSVP card, and that's what we did."

Invitations, whether written or verbal, can be considered "speech acts," which philosopher J. L. Austin contrasts with constative statements, the mere reporting of activities or conditions. An invitation, according to this logic, is a "performative utterance," an act, a social practice, that actually does something instead of just stating or describing facts.[42] The words "Women of the Storm Cordially invite you to join us" set up relations of mutual obligation between the women and lawmakers. On the one hand, it obligated members of Congress, at least those who follow established codes of conduct, to respond properly with the RSVP card. On the other, the speech act committed the women to host members of Congress who accepted their invitations. An Asian woman in her fifties put it this way: "When we arrived to their offices, we were welcomed very warmly. We had the invitation, and we handed the invitation to them personally. Not just through words, but through invitation. Physically." As this participant's words reveal, the invitation helped to establish the conditions of a relation that was somehow binding. In this way, WOS's invitation served as a performative utterance whereby we "commit ourselves in various ways by saying something."[43] But this commitment can only occur in contexts where codes of conduct are widely understood. As Austin argues, the "felicity" of the performative utterance requires that the "convention invoked must exist and be accepted," and it requires that specific conditions are met: "The circumstances in which we purport to invoke this procedure must be appropriate for its invocation. If this is not observed, then the act that we purport to perform would not come off—it will be, one might say, a misfire."[44] Aesthetic and interactional conditions for the invitation had to be observed for the performative utterance to have its intended effect. It needed all the right components (a formal and explicit invitation, RSVP card, outer and inner envelopes). By passing through hands in a face-to-face encounter, the women imagined the invitation would create a moral obligation for U.S. lawmakers to respond. Personal delivery was perhaps the most important condition for WOS's invitation to have its intended effect. Thus, armed with disarming demeanors, this self-appointed group of women brought their invitations—and their plea for help—to the halls of Congress.

CHAPTER 6

Hill Visits

*Some accounts of invitations delivered to lawmakers;
certain interactions prove successful, others misfire*

After WOS's press conference, the women split up into groups of two and three, fanning out to make their prearranged Capitol Hill visits. They were there to deliver invitations offering a comprehensive itinerary scheduled on four specific dates in the weeks that followed, which would include land tours of decimated neighborhoods and air tours in Blackhawk helicopters over eroding wetlands, assisted by Brig. Gen. Hunt Downer of the Louisiana National Guard. The Greater New Orleans Hotel and Lodging Association also contributed to WOS's efforts by providing hotel rooms for the invited lawmakers.[1] In addition to extending invitations, the group planned to give each lawmaker a hardbound copy of *America's Wetlands: Louisiana's Vanishing Coast*, by Mike Dunne and Bevil Knapp, a book produced in cooperation with the AWF.[2]

Several news reporters followed the women throughout the day, and the women sought to use the media to make elected officials feel accountable. As Cecile Tebo and her partner, Gretchen Bjork, entered his office, Rep. Pete Stark (D-CA), a Tebo family friend, emerged from behind his closed office door and started to shake Tebo's hand. But she dodged his handshake and moved in for a warm embrace. Once seated on his office couches, Stark inquired about the meeting's purpose. Tebo answered with conviction, "You are coming to New Orleans." After Tebo explained WOS's requests and extended an invitation, Stark said, "If you get two or three Republicans, then maybe" he would visit.[3] Later reflecting on her visit with Stark, Tebo exclaimed, "Rep. Stark committed to coming if I was successful in getting three Republicans to commit. I told him to pack his bags—that our group would have many more than that!"[4] Outside his office, Tebo and her partner exchanged a high-five.

It might seem extraordinary to interact so informally with members of Congress, expressing a sense of familiarity and entitlement. Yet, by talking in certain ways and using normative ideas of womanhood, participants could frame their actions in a way that seemed to neutralize their political nature. For example, in the offices of one representative, Tebo told reporters, "I'm a mom. I have three kids. I do mommy stuff. But here I am in D.C., and I am fighting for the survival of my city."[5] She conveyed her personal storm experiences. "We want them to see the destruction, smell the toxicity, embrace the person who has lost everything and hear the silence—just to get a taste of what has happened to us," she said.[6]

The first appointment for Anne Milling and teammate Pam Bryan was with Don Young, a Republican representative from Alaska who chaired the House Transportation and Infrastructure Committee, and his congressional staffer, Benjamin "Bailey" Edwards, who reportedly had a sister in New Orleans. Bryan recalled that Young kept "raving about what a wonderful state Alaska was" and that she interjected by saying, "We're going to take you all to New Orleans. It's going to be Anne and I. We are going to personally take you all over the city of New Orleans." But it was staffer Bailey who would prove instrumental to the women's cause. Bryan said that when she and Milling left the meeting with Young, Bailey asked where they were going next. After they told him that their next appointment was with Dennis Hastert, she remembered Bailey saying, "I know the aide there. I'm calling him right now. I'm calling Pelosi's office too!"

With a congressional aide calling on their behalf, Milling and Bryan proceeded to the offices of House Minority Leader Nancy Pelosi. Bryan recalled that they were able to secure this meeting with Pelosi through Milling's cousin in California, whose husband was a friend of Pelosi's husband. Bryan recalled, "He was calling Pelosi's husband and saying, 'You listen to these women!'"

Their meeting with Pelosi and her staff was one of the trip's highest-profile meetings. "She gave us 30 minutes of her time," Bryan remembered. "And she was so empathetic and so sympathetic to listening to the stories we had to say."[7] During the meeting, Bryan slid a paper invitation across the conference table into Pelosi's hands and said, "It's something you cannot grasp until you experience it."[8] When Pelosi told them that she had already been to Houston, the women responded, "Yes, yes, yes, you've been to Houston, but we want New Orleans. We need you in New Orleans."[9] Pelosi then told the pair, "I'm dying to go," at which point an AP reporter observed that Pelosi bit her lower lip and held her hands in her lap.[10] Milling continued to press, saying, "I can feel your sympathy. But seeing is what will impact you, even more than hearing the stories."[11] By the time the two women left the lawmaker's office, they had given Pelosi a WOS button, which she immediately pinned on her jacket lapel, and they had elicited a commitment from the lawmaker to visit. "I'll be there. No one has forgotten you," Pelosi said.[12]

After meeting with Pelosi, Milling and Bryan learned that Young's aide had convinced an aide to Speaker of the House Dennis Hastert to return early from lunch and to meet with the women. With this news, the pair went on to their third meeting.[13] With the commitment from Pelosi in hand, the pair felt "armed" to meet Hastert, despite getting a lukewarm response from his aide, who Bryan remembers saying, "You'll never get him down there." During the private fifteen-minute meeting with Hastert, without cameras present, they made their pitch. According to one *Times-Picayune* reporter, Milling told Hastert "firmly and politely that if the speaker had the time to visit Thailand after the [2004] tsunami then he surely has the time to visit the scene of America's worst natural disaster."[14] When they left Hastert's office, Bryan recalled, they couldn't help but laugh, "because we just get so persuasive and we just get so aggressive, and we won't take 'no' for an answer." She remembered them saying to lawmakers and their aides, "This is your duty here. This is your duty to come down to the city. Because we are Americans. We are fellow Americans and you need to listen to us." Bryan remembered their conversations well: "Anne kept saying, 'Pam, you are just so assertive.' And I kept saying, 'Anne, well, you are too!'"[15]

Over lunch in the Senate dining room, Cheryl Teamer and Verna Landrieu, the seventy-three-year-old wife of former New Orleans mayor Maurice Edwin "Moon" Landrieu, and mother of Sen. Mary Landrieu and Lt. Gov. Mitch Landrieu, met with Senate Minority Leader Harry Reid (D-NV).[16] Teamer showed Reid before-and-after pictures of her home, pointing out that the water had been up to its roof. Reid asked Teamer, "Isn't that a beautiful home? Will you be able to salvage it?" At this point Verna Landrieu, interjected. "Senator, there are homes like this all over the city."[17] Landrieu's thoughts about the damage were also personal. After recounting how three of her nine children's homes had been flooded, she said, "I come home crying every day. It's devastating."[18]

While the focus was primarily on the devastation around New Orleans, some of the women tried to keep the focus more broadly on Louisiana. There were participants from parts of south and southwest Louisiana, areas hit hard during Hurricane Rita. Four participants from Terrebonne and Lafourche parishes hoped to educate not only members of Congress but also the women in New Orleans about the needs of residents living in areas outside the Crescent City. Sharon Bergeron, a banker and community activist in Houma, reported mixed results during her meetings with representatives Early Pomeroy (D-ND), Brad Miller (D-NC), Jim Matheson (D-UT), and Gregory Meeks (D-NY). In some cases congressional aides asked her to simply leave the packets of information at the front desk, she told reporters.[19] Another Houma resident, Alexis Duval, a former chairperson of the Houma-Terrebonne Chamber of Commerce board of directors, said, "We want to raise awareness that projects that are good for Terrebonne are good for them in the long run."[20] The two remaining participants from Terrebonne and Lafourche parishes were Jennifer Armand, owner of a Houma-based public relations and advertising firm, and Simone Theriot Maloz, who served as executive director of Restore or

Retreat, a "non-profit coastal advocacy group" based in Thibodaux, Louisiana.[21] On the day before the group's trip, Maloz told reporters at the *Courier*, a daily newspaper in Terrebonne Parish, "We should be throwing out a pretty wide net. One of the main things the group will do is let them know we're still out there. We still have some key issues they need to tackle in Washington."[22]

Dotti Church and Alva Chase, another interracial pair, felt well received, despite the fact that their appointments were with staffers and aides rather than elected officials. When the levees failed after Katrina, Chase's home in New Orleans East flooded, as did nearly all the homes of her neighbors in the Mark subdivision in the Read Boulevard East neighborhood, including a Chinese family next door and a Vietnamese family across the street.[23] She had lived there with her husband, Edgar, son of WOS member Leah Chase, for twenty-two years, and their home was mortgage free.[24] Unlike other parts of the city, home ownership was the norm in their neighborhood, one with 73 percent black or African American residents; nearly 89 percent of residents in her neighborhood lived in owner-occupied housing units.[25] She and her husband, past dean of business and soon to be vice president of master planning and facilities management at Dillard University, had moved to their home in 1983. But immediately after Katrina they were planning to move to high ground in Uptown, where they hoped to build a raised creole cottage.[26] Following their visit with a staffer for Rep. John Larson, a Democrat from Connecticut, Chase felt positive: "He accepted the invitation and I think he said that Congressman Larson plus some staffers are hoping to come in the future to visit New Orleans and see the devastation."[27]

In the Rayburn House Office Building, WOS participants Nan Galloway and Mary Christophe went to the offices of Rep. Rosa DeLauro, a Democrat from Connecticut, where they had a closed-door meeting with the state's head of Homeland Security. During the meeting, Galloway said, "If they are going to be voting on the future of Louisiana and the future of New Orleans, they need to come and see it to be able to make the right decisions and the right votes." Despite a noncommittal response, the women saw the possible visits as a sign of hope. On why lawmakers should visit, Christophe told reporters, "Because we are Americans, and there are lots of Americans that are very hurt in our city. And they should see it. They should want to see it."[28]

Not all of the meetings went well, but even the infelicitous encounters are revealing. During one meeting, Jeanette Bell said that she and her teammate, Patti Lapeyre, had scheduled an appointment with Republican senator Jim Bunning of Kentucky.[29] The pair arrived early for their noon meeting and waited patiently for the lawmaker to arrive. As the minutes passed, the women began to feel stood up. They used the half hour in Bunning's office to make their pitch to staffers and left them with the invitation. When they left the office, they encountered Bunning in the halls and reported that they were met with indifference and contempt. After saying that they "dilly-dallied a little bit at the end of the appointment," Bell described the encounter:

> As we were leaving, Senator Bunning came in and you got the feeling that he was like, "They're supposed to be gone by now. Here they are, still in my office." Luckily my partner recognized him from the internet and she said to him, "Senator Bunning." He looked at her and he said, "Yes?" She went on to tell him that we were there to extend an invitation to him to come to New Orleans. He said to us in a very, sort of, curt manner, "I've been to New Orleans many times." Then I said to him, "Then you'll recognize the difference when you come back!"
>
> We could not allow them to act as if we were just part of the furniture or the wallpaper. So when the opportunity presented itself, we were able to have him understand that we were not there just on a courtesy call. We had a mission. We were very clear on what we were there for. We seriously wanted them to come down and look so that they could make . . . informed decisions.

When I met with Bell in her rose garden a few weeks after the trip to Washington, she talked about the team's interactions with Senator Bunning:

> I was disappointed that he didn't invite us into his office for just two minutes. He was with an aide, but if you'd missed the appointment—and we had an appointment—I felt that the *courteous* thing to have done would be to say, "I'm sorry I missed the appointment, but if you'll just step inside the door, I have another meeting in a few minutes, but I'd just like to hear from you in person." I thought that would have been the thing to do. However, he didn't. He didn't even act as if he wanted to be courteous at all. Of course, we're not going to do anything, just say our little piece and move on.

This interaction between Bell, Lapeyre, and Bunning reveals how the women's subjectivities, their sense of being recognized as having something important to say about Katrina, depended largely upon what bell hooks calls a "culture of civility, of respect for others and acknowledgement of their presence."[30] When the lawmaker failed to invite the women into his office and initially even failed to speak to them face-to-face, they felt he violated implicit codes of civility, courtesy, and ultimately of mutual respect. They judged his words, actions, and body language to be impolite and rude, masculine forms of dismissal and aggression. The women's polite response did not emerge naturally simply because they were women. As one scholar of gender and language usage notes, "If others are likely to view assertiveness and other masculine forms as aggressive, women may well decide to strategically use more feminine speech forms in order to achieve their goals."[31] In this interaction there seemed to be a clear refusal of relation at a moment when the women sought connectedness and solidarity.[32] They hoped those in power would listen to their testimonies and acknowledge their presence—that is, see them as subjects. In the absence of recognition or courtesy, they responded with off-the-cuff wit. When Bunning remarked that he had already been to New Orleans, which seemed like an excuse not to accept the invitation, the women countered, inviting him to compare his pre-storm and post-storm impressions.

Bell and Lapeyre seemed to have won this battle of words—I suspect that is why this moment figured so prominently in their recollections. By naming him in the hallway, by shaming him for being impolite and dismissive, by engaging in a witty retort, and by telling me and others about the interaction, they sought to restore their sense of honor and dignity.

Like the umbrellas, the invitations were gendered, which helped diffuse concerns that WOS would be perceived as angry women. WOS members were keenly aware of what cultural historian John F. Kasson describes as the "high stakes in manners, the myriad ways that they go to the heart of southern politics and identity, their coercive uses and resistant possibilities."[33] Kasson points out that "Southerners, white and black, know and have always known, in ways that many Americans from other regions may have not, that, far from trivial, manners are political; indeed, they are often a matter of life and death."[34] These considerations were all part of the cultural and interactional context that helped structure the invitation's extension. The women didn't have to read Pierre Bourdieu to know that "concessions of *politeness* always contain *political* concessions."[35] In their political activities, WOS members deliberately used etiquette, respectability, and, above all, politesse; when these failed, they often turned to wit and humor.

WOS members used conventional notions of gender as a tactic. While portraying themselves as nonpolitical, members claimed that women were uniquely positioned to do this work. For instance, one black interviewee emphasized the "sincerity," "genuineness," and "passion that we bring to the table" and "no gains, no handshake deals, no good-old-boy syndrome." She also constructed women in relational terms. "If we met with women," she explained, "then you could relate woman-to-woman, because every woman knows what that role is. I don't care how much they're responsible for working, they're also responsible for taking care of a family. So that woman can empathize with you." She said, "If you met with a man, same thing. You look at somebody—'This could be my wife, this could be my sister. I'm responsible for being a physical provider and caretaker of her.' But now you look and say, 'Suppose that was my sister, suppose that was my wife, and I couldn't take care of her?'" The category "women" was imbued with traditional meanings, with ties to the family, gendered labor, and the domestic sphere. She continued on, saying, "Women sometimes are seen as more vulnerable, and now you're in a position of saying, 'Hey, look, we are vulnerable, we do need your help. But we have mustered whatever internal strength we needed to muster to come here and ask for help.' I think that Disney image of ladies doing what they needed to do to take care of their sisters and brothers back here was a powerful image." She thought of femininity as something to be deployed consciously for political ends, as something at once actual and constructed.

One white woman told me, "We had gotten word that they thought we were a group of angry women storming Washington." She continued, "We were going to come in and yell at people for some unknown reason. Then they realized what we were doing and everybody was very well informed. Nobody was ready to argue about anything." The notion of being angry women elicited amusement from another white woman, who told me a story about her visit to Capitol Hill: "I had to laugh. One of the aides that I spoke to was very young. He laughed because when we arrived, he said, 'Wow. I looked out our window and saw you all getting out of the buses, and one of us commented that, 'I wouldn't want to get my mother mad, either!' I said, 'Well, that's how this is. It's a lot of people that are very, very upset.'"

For many WOS participants, graciousness was a regional code of conduct that established and maintained identity and difference. "Etiquette is inseparably linked with conformity," philosopher Hazel Barnes writes, and yet "part of the function of etiquette is precisely to distinguish." This led Barnes to assert that "in all areas of etiquette we find this interplay between sameness and difference. Etiquette provides for the individual's need to belong to the group, but to this group rather than to that group; also it allows for limited self-expression within a group."[36] As such, political participation grounded in feminized etiquette affirmed the women's differences from men. An African American woman I interviewed described this process in gendered terms: "I think it's very difficult for people to tell women no. I think guys—I mean, they [lawmakers] were running from us because they didn't want to have to face us and say no. And they won't. No one will say no. I have actually called and said, 'I just want a yes or no.' And they won't give me a yes or a no."

In addition to reflecting on gender, participants reflected on the group's racial and class composition. A white woman said, "Well, it was definitely way, way overloaded with 'sliver ladies.' But once again, they're the ones that have the time to do it, the money to do it, and are not rebuilding their lives." She continued: "But there were enough other people involved. They paired off key people to see key congressional people with—they made sure certain people who were seeing the senators and congressmen we were really targeting that were key because of what committee they were on, or we thought we might have a shot at getting them down here, or because we had a contact to get in or for whatever reason—they paired those people with a Vietnamese or a black or something like that. So the key people saw diversity."

WOS also had to manage class difference in the context of a disaster event that revealed striking class disparities in American society. The women's negotiation of these differences was very nuanced. Just as a number of participants thought too much attention was paid to the racial disparities of Katrina, several women told me that the media were biased because they focused on how the poor suffered the biggest losses in the disaster. Some group members sought to challenge the prevailing representations of disaster victims as predominantly poor and black, and they made efforts to "expand the circle of the we" to include stories of the affluent whose lives were disrupted by the storm.[37] Several women said that when they were in Washington, they emphasized that homes in affluent areas were also affected. For these participants it was important that they could frame themselves, or someone in their own social circles or kinship networks with similar class standings, as having experienced loss as well. For example, a white interviewee discussed media representations of Katrina. She said, "I kind of feel like the media gave a slanted view of the fact that there were a lot of people affected from a lot of socioeconomic classes." She quickly added, "Granted, the people in the [New Orleans] convention center, I mean, that was horrible, but they kept focusing on that, to me more so than—I don't know, you didn't really see Lakeview and other areas. You kept seeing the Ninth Ward."

A white woman in her late thirties held similar views and wished that the damage in affluent areas, such as Lakeview or Old Metairie, had been given more media attention. She said, "Yes, there were apartments and hundred-thousand-dollar homes affected. But million-dollar homes were affected as well. And it ranged from everything in between. So it wasn't just one group of people that got affected by the storm." This interviewee, who didn't work in the paid labor force and reported that her husband made over three hundred thousand dollars a year, described family members who experienced loss. She said, "We didn't lose our home, but my brother's home was completely submerged. He couldn't find anywhere to rent, so he had to buy a home which he didn't want, but he needed a roof for his family's head." A white woman in her mid-sixties echoed this sentiment:

> I wanted them to know, because they hadn't been down there. I said, "I know you think it's just the projects, because only the black people were on TV. Nobody put my daughter on TV. Nobody put my friend on TV who's living in Houston now." I don't see any white people who were interviewed—"What happened to your house? What happened to your car?" It was a little biased, according to me. I never did see anybody that I knew interviewed on television talking about their loss, and there were a lot of them. That was really what I pointed out to them. I said, "Come see the mansions that were flooded, not just the projects."

Another white participant said, "People brought whatever they wanted to, but what we really brought were stories. My two children lost everything. And when I say 'everything,' I literally mean everything. To a congressional person, looking at someone like myself, they don't understand how anybody like me could lose everything. Well, my children did and now they live with me."

In listening to wealthy women talk about the need to focus on flooded mansions, I tried to understand what motivated their reframing of the catastrophe in these ways. Certainly, some thought that this reframing might elicit sympathy (and money) from people in positions of power who otherwise might have been unsympathetic to the plight of the black underclass. That was part of the story. But it was more than that. The women positioned themselves as speaking on behalf of a broader constituency, including those who occupied similar class locations and who also experienced loss.

This idea of "expanding the circle of loss" was not unique to WOS. An editorial printed in the *New York Times* on the morning of WOS's trip to Washington expressed similar sentiments: "Perhaps too much emphasis has been placed on the wreckage of poor, low-lying New Orleans neighborhoods like the Lower Ninth Ward. That has sparked the unproductive, blame-the-victim debate revolving around whether people should have lived there in the first place. The Ninth Ward provides a misleading picture of the city, as do the relatively unscathed tourist areas like the French Quarter and the Garden District. Huge swaths of the city have the empty quality of a ghost town." The editorial continued: "Now, Congress has a responsibility to follow its own lead rather than the president's. We were outraged once, shocked at the images on our television sets, at the poverty in our collective backyard and at the devastation of a great city. As the disaster threatens to become permanent, we have every reason to remain so."[38]

All told, the women deemed their trip a success. WOS had extended hundreds of invitations and was prepared to accommodate what they hoped would be a wave of congressional visits with fifteen planes on standby, according to one news broadcaster.[39] On the flight home, participants each wrote summaries of their meetings on "contact forms," commenting on the names of Congress members or staff persons with whom they met. For instance, Gloria Kabacoff, who was partnered with Verna Landrieu, reflected on their meeting with Sen. Barack Obama, with whom they met in the hallway outside the Senate Chamber. She wrote that Obama was receptive, but his schedule was very hectic; she told him that they would accommodate him. Kabacoff also noted that she also sat in on a meeting with Sen. Harry Reid, who suggested that WOS begin networking with women in Alabama to help influence Republican senator Richard Shelby of Alabama. Jennifer Fallon and Carol Leblanc, who also met with Rep. Pete Stark, said that he lamented the fact that Republicans hold the purse strings and that he was open to visiting, especially after Cecile Tebo had offered him a cot in her FEMA trailer. Some participants used the contact forms to reflect on the group and its leadership. Karen Wood, for example, wrote a note in the margins: "Such a great effort on your part. 'Anne for Mayor.'" Louise Saenz wrote, "Thank you for this wonderful experience!" In addition to giving praise, a few others offered subtle critiques. Esther Vincent of Lake Charles, Louisiana, added a personal comment about Katrina overshadowing Rita, that the word "storm" in the group's name could have been "storms," plural. She wrote, "I wish that Hurricane Rita devastation had been included. 'Women of the Storms.' However it was a great trip. Thank you for including us."[40]

They were provided box dinners and wine to celebrate the day's accomplishments. Spirits were high. An Asian woman in her forties confided, "I don't know whether it was the energy or a few bottles of wine, but everybody was in the aisles."

With excitement, a white woman in her forties talked about the plane ride back to New Orleans: "The momentum was just, che che che, you know. I think they told us, the flight attendants, 'OK, these women are going to be just dead [tired].' It was the opposite. No one would sit down, it was a little bumpy, and it was like a big party. Because everyone was really upbeat. It was very uplifting. How many times have I said that stupid word? If I could always feel that way, everyday life would be a bowl of cherries. It was like a natural high." Arriving in New Orleans shortly after 8 P.M., some women returned to pristine, undamaged Uptown mansions in unscathed neighborhoods spared from flooding. Others returned to FEMA trailers in deserted neighborhoods that still had not had power restored. On the trip, a common goal brought the women together and differences between members were minimized, though not erased. But when they went home that evening, many took divergent paths.[41]

CHAPTER 7

Noblesse Oblige

On thank-you notes and civic stewardship

The day after WOS's trip, a small group of "expatriates," New Orleans natives living in Washington, D.C., led by Miriam "Mimsy" Lindner, continued to deliver the remaining invitations to the almost 280 representatives in Washington who weren't on the WOS list for face-to-face visits.[1] Back in New Orleans, the women's euphoria after the one-day trip to Washington was subdued when they realized that a great deal of follow-up work would be necessary to bring lawmakers to New Orleans. As described by one white WOS participant: "When we got home, the reality hit. OK, we went up there and we got a lot of press, but our job has just begun. You've now got to get those people down here. That's when the hard work started, and it's also when the discouraging period first came. . . . Because I thought, you know, nice Southern women go and issue these invitations to come, and we've made it as easy as possible, transportation, food, lodging—who can turn that down? Well, everybody turned it down, initially!"

According to their code of conduct, WOS understood the invitation as an imperative to respond. While some lawmakers did accept the invitations, many requests were ignored. It is worth noting that a nonresponse on the part of lawmakers was seen as equivalent to the invitation being declined.[2]

Preparing for what would be the slow but steady trickle of congressional visits was WOS's next task. On Wednesday, February 1, core organizers contacted group members with instructions to thank elected officials and their staffers for their time, preferably by phone. In her correspondence with the group, Milling wrote, "We took Congress by storm on Monday but NOW is the time for serious follow-up."[3] The calls served a more pragmatic function than simply expressing gratitude.

During these calls, participants were to ask elected officials to commit to one of four thirty-six-hour time slots for their visits. If these dates didn't work for lawmakers, participants were to tell them that they "would be delighted to accommodate their schedules."[4] In meetings with elected officials and staffers, many participants were told that the four trips scheduled in February were inconvenient, so the core asked the women to invite lawmakers to visit anytime during the month of March. To encourage lawmakers to visit as soon as possible, WOS developed two itineraries for the congressional visits: a thirty-six-hour itinerary offered in the original invitation and a "day itinerary," a shortened, twenty-four-hour trip. This effort to accommodate lawmakers marked a shift in WOS's strategies. Because many elected officials could not make the designated dates with such short notice, the group needed to adapt. They soon distributed copies of the ethics rulings issued by the House and Senate that permitted members of Congress to accept the WOS's invitation so long as they traveled in pairs as part of an educational fact-finding trip.

Participants were asked to write thank-you notes, which also served as reminders of the women's point: members of Congress had a moral obligation to visit New Orleans. Handwritten notes are a gendered form of communication connected to what some view as women's traditional role of building and maintaining familial relationships and other social ties, and they correspond to classed notions of refined and polished femininities.[5] Once again, the instructions were specific: mention with whom you met and "urge" the members of Congress to accept the invitation. The sense of urgency necessitated immediate delivery, and not by standard mail. The letters were to be collected in a wicker basket outside Milling's residence no later than 5 P.M. on Friday, February 3. Some participants wrote letters to multiple elected officials; some of these letters included facts or statistics that had been requested by lawmakers during appointments. One participant even included copies of Tom Piazza's 2006 book, *Why New Orleans Matters*, with her thank-you notes. On Monday morning, after being sent by FedEx to WOS allies in Washington, the letters were hand-delivered by the "expatriates."

In a broader context, WOS's actions were directed to the nation, which still faced uneasy questions about how to handle post-Katrina New Orleans and the inadequate government response. Just two days after WOS's trip, Hillary Clinton spoke on the Senate floor about the need for an independent investigation of Katrina, suggesting they use the 9/11 Commission as a model. After mentioning a group of women known informally as the Jersey Four, which eventually transformed into the 9/11 Widows' and Victims' Families' Association, Clinton then referred to WOS's recent Washington visit: "I was heartened when I saw in the last several days a dedicated group of citizens from the impacted gulf coast region, called Women of the Storm, were up here demanding answers and actions. They deserve no less. These are our fellow Americans. . . . But if we do not establish this commission, I fear they will not ever get the information they deserve. Even worse, we may make the same mistakes again."[6]

On Monday, February 6, as thank-you notes were being hand-delivered in Washington, Kathleen Blanco prepared to open the Louisiana legislature in New Orleans, an occasion that marked the first time the state legislature had met outside Baton Rouge in 125 years.[7] Bus tours of the devastation, similar to those offered to members of Congress, were organized for the 144-member legislature of Louisiana, although it was reported that fewer than half took the tour.[8] Blanco mentioned WOS in her speech to the Louisiana legislature, which she delivered at the convention center: "I appreciate the efforts of the Women of the Storm and others to convince Congress to visit us. To understand the scope of this catastrophe is to see it. . . . The harsh reality is that for many people in Washington, Katrina is yesterday's problem, and Rita never happened."[9]

As WOS's significance began to be written into official speeches and documents, the core committee met again to prepare for the congressional visits. On February 8, Milling e-mailed group members, beginning with the salutation "Ladies" and reporting that each member of Congress had received the thank-you notes. Milling then wrote, "So . . . it's time to begin to badger in a big time way!!!" Encouraging what she called "a new wave of phone calls," she also told the group, "don't accept 'no' for an answer; (if you have already been rejected . . . try again as persistence pays)."[10]

WOS was not alone in pressing Congress to respond to Katrina. On February 8 and 9, ACORN led a four-hundred-person rally of Katrina survivors in Washington called Rally for the Return, an event attended by Harry Reid, Hillary Clinton, and Mary Landrieu. Like WOS, ACORN called upon Congress to provide additional rebuilding assistance. Also like WOS, ACORN fanned out in groups and "lobbied scores of members of Congress on their platform for return and rebuilding." But there were some differences as well: the ACORN Katrina survivors organized a march through the streets of Washington and picketed the White House; many of them carried pictures of their flood-damaged homes. According to the *Washington Post*, a caravan of buses carrying Katrina survivors arrived in Washington, where they soon marched up Independence Avenue, chanting, "Where is the money?" and collectively singing, "This little neighborhood of mine, I'm gonna let it shine."[11] Whereas WOS focused on issues of revenue streams from the oil and gas industry to fund coastal restoration projects, ACORN, led by Tanya Harris, who became the head organizer in New Orleans's Lower Ninth Ward, would press issues such as the importance of hiring local residents in rebuilding projects and health, safety, and wage projects.[12]

Back in New Orleans, the day after ACORN's coordinated events in Washington, Milling told reporters, "King Abdullah II of Jordan, Prince Charles and Camilla, the Netherlands' ambassador to the United States and others outside the country have all visited the New Orleans area. . . . There is no reason why every member of Congress cannot find a time to visit this region."[13] The core membership sought new ways to pressure Congress. Though 130 women swamped lawmakers with hundreds of follow-up e-mails, faxes, and handwritten thank-you notes, the core understood the need to increase the pressure by tapping into a broader constituency. This meant revisiting the issue of group size. The one-day trip was limited to 130 participants, thereby allowing core participants to focus their energies on issues of diversity rather than on increasing its membership exponentially. But immediately after the trip, the group began to revisit its definition of an "operational sense of size."[14] On February 12, Milling requested help from the broad membership base to contact national women's organizations such as the Junior League of New Orleans, the Council of Jewish Women, The Links, and the Garden Club of America to "assist us with this 'push' to get members of Congress here." She wrote, "Perhaps some of you know other national organizations who might be willing to assist with this endeavor. Remember, we are a non-political, non-partisan group. . . . Our goal is to get these elected officials to New Orleans and the region 'to see!'"[15]

For WOS participants the Washington trip renewed a sense of agency, hope, and solidarity at a time when many in New Orleans were experiencing Katrina fatigue. Immediately after the trip, participants reported feeling a sense of pride and accomplishment. One white woman recalled, "We were actually doing something. Because I think we all felt that there was a strong possibility that things would just move on and we would be forgotten."

In addition to considering the group's efficacy, participants self-consciously reflected on issues of group diversity. Most felt satisfied by their attempts to work across racial divides. This was certainly made easier by the fact that many were from the upper tiers of the economic ladder in their respective racial and ethnic groups. But these feelings were present even among the least affluent participants I interviewed. When I spoke with participants about their Washington experiences, commonality and togetherness were frequent themes, and women of different racial backgrounds expressed satisfaction with the diversity. A white woman said, "I mean a lot of those women—I'm from here—a lot of those women I didn't know. It was just great." Sitting in an Uptown coffee shop, a well-off woman in her forties, who was sought out to represent the Vietnamese community, also related that she felt pleased with the racial diversity: "It was a very good diverse group. From the Vietnamese community, I know there were some other community activists. There were two sisters from Mary Queen of Vietnam Church, and there were two other women." After saying it was a good "cross-section" of African American, Vietnamese, and Latino women, she said, "I went with not much expectation, because I've been involved in the political arena long enough to know, 'Promises, promises.' But I was very pleased." Then she described how WOS had cooperatively developed solutions to the recovery: "On the plane we were asked to put aside our personal agenda and focus on the talking points. We were asked to put aside everything and just focus on one thing." At that moment she pointed to a white woman in the coffee shop: "I think she was in the group. I know I saw her on the plane [laughs]. It's very fascinating, because you put 130-something powerhouse women, and they're all powerhouse in their own way, and somehow they worked very well together." Somewhat amused, she said, "I wonder if it would work the same with the men, though. If you put 130-something powerhouse men together, are they gonna be that together? [laughs]."[16]

One African American participant I interviewed, a well-connected member of the New Orleans black elite, said, "In the end, I was pleasantly surprised on the trip, because I knew a few women that were going, but when I got there, as far as—I mean, they had the Vietnamese, Hispanic—but as far as African Americans were concerned, they had more than I anticipated and more than I knew. I didn't even know some of them."

In addition to race, participants reflected on the "women" question. One said, "Why women? Why not?" There seemed to be generational differences in how the women related to contemporary feminism. The vast majority of older women distanced themselves from the feminist label, telling me that Southern women had other tactics for bringing about change. The youngest interviewee in my interview sample, an African American woman in her thirties, had this to say: "I think it was empowering. It made me believe that people can really do something, that you can really spark change. At the same time it was really emotional, because, like I said, you had people from all walks of life who had lost something or knew someone who lost something. But I think it was definitely empowering, especially I'm really big on girl power." She was not alone. Barbara Blackwell reported that she felt empowered by this journey and emphasized that WOS members were very "unselfish women whose sole purpose was to help everyone by the tragedy."[17]

Others were thankful for being invited to participate and share their stories. A black woman in her forties, whose home had been flooded and at the time of our interview was living in a FEMA trailer, said, "I cannot express my gratitude for them inviting me to be a part of the movement, because I will bring that perspective of what it means for me personally."

This brings me to a central finding of this study. On several occasions I have been asked if the women of color who participated in WOS felt used by the white women. Based on my interviews, this was not the case. Those asking seemed to have made up their minds before I could even respond; for them, the women of color *were* being used. But when I spoke with the women of color, they found their participation to be meaningful and empowering. And despite the uneven racial composition, the women I interviewed, almost across the board, reported that the diversification efforts were successful.

After the trip, the women also reflected on the media reports, some of which focused more on the group's fashion choices and Mardi Gras connections than on their lobbying mission. When reporters drew attention to expensive jewelry, handbags, and the lofty place of some members among the city's Carnival roy- alty, members decried these comments in part because participants had sought to appear as a unified voice focused on the immediate task at hand. Participants felt particularly betrayed by some of the journalists who traveled with them to Wash- ington, especially an Associated Press reporter who had just moved to the French Quarter. One white woman recounted, "She has a fascination with Mardi Gras and she wanted to bring that into the article. I said, 'Please don't do that; you will lose your footing with us if you want to do anymore interviews, because if you start putting in there that this is a bunch of Mardi Gras queens, trust me, it will not go over very well.'" When the article was published the day after the trip, many of the women were upset, particularly because things they asked not to be included in the article were in print. Trying to understand the coverage, one white participant talked about the media reports this way: "And the one from the AP who said we were all in pearls, her original thing when she was with us the whole time? Debutantes and pearls and designer bags? It's just a bunch of—why? But I mean, I guess that's what she saw. But when she says the people get on the plane, that's not what—but she had to turn that article in early. And meeting at Anne's house—you see, this is another thing. It's the perfect Uptown home, expensive art, expensive everything." She continued by describing the reporter's efforts on the plane to uncover details about high-status women in the city:

> The reporter asked someone, "Are there any former Carnival queens in this group?" And the next thing I know she is talking to Anne Charbonnet. Anne says, "So she is asking me about being queen," and this is on the plane. So we are all right there coming home. So I say, "Wait a minute. No, no, no, no, no, no, no. You want to talk about Mardi Gras? Do a completely separate article. We can set you up with some interviews with some Rex guys if you want to, that's fine. But just don't put it in this article." I mean, come on. We had three former queens of Carnival on the plane. We also had three Loving Cup recipients on the plane. We had the head of the Bureau of Government Research on the plane. Carol Bebelle was on the plane. I mean, Mary Fitzpatrick from the Preservation Resource Cen- ter. I mean, shit, there was a lot of heavy hitters on the plane. I mean forget about Mardi Gras queens. Oh god [inhales]. I mean, we just didn't need that. That was not what we needed.[18]

Extravagant descriptions of elite women's clothing choices are not uncommon in the seasonal coverage of Carnival. But in this post-Katrina context, participants saw attention to clothing and jewelry as casting them in an unfavorable light and distracting from their mission. The comments about designer bags and pearls cut deep because they saw the focus on these details as pulling attention away from their larger goals as a group, regardless of class status or past accomplishments as individuals. Moreover, some group members felt that these accounts reproduced stereotypes of elite women who tend to be portrayed, as Diana Kendall tells us, as being either the idle socialite or the Lady Bountiful:

> Dedicated volunteers have tried for many years to overcome the image of the first of these stereotypes, that of the idle socialite, a term initially used to describe women such as "Mrs. Astor" (Caroline Schermerhorn Astor), who was famous for giving lavish parties for her wealthy inner circle of socially acceptable New Yorkers in the late nineteenth century. They also have attempted to distance themselves from the stereotype of the Lady Bountiful, a "naive, but well intentioned 'do-gooder,' sympathetic to the plight of the lower classes but not truly understanding. She has nothing better to do. The lady bountiful is utterly removed from the hardships of the world around her."[19]

Kendall concludes that these portrayals function to "trivialize" women's philanthropy and volunteerism even as more and more women have entered the "economic, political, and social mainstream."[20]

Depictions like this of WOS felt dismissive. One woman said, "I mean, we all know that we've been stereotyped—I know that I've been stereotyped in a heartbeat, because it happens a lot when I go out and try to get behind a cause. So, I mean, in order to balance my image or whatever I come across as, it's going to be much more effective if I'm with someone who is not from the exact same background that I am." In my interviews it became increasingly clear that many of these women had fielded similar charges before, which may be why the organizers sought to diversify from WOS's inception. Participants and the AP reporter that interviewed them appear to have seen the situation differently. Whereas many participants viewed themselves as showcasing racial and ethnic diversity, the reporter seemed instead to be fixated on members from a certain class.

WOS participants had gone to great lengths to avoid such a limiting focus on their appearance, and they wanted to be judged by their actions and accomplishments. On the whole, participants saw themselves and their work in a more positive light. They felt unified, heterogeneous, inclusive, and diverse. They saw their work as reflecting their moral investment in the broader community and as using their privilege for a greater good. In this sense, they wanted to be recognized for their "community-building activities," which feminist scholar Shulamit Reinharz defines as "those actions engaged in by a group of people on their own intiative in order to increase social cohesiveness of unrelated persons or to enhace the opportunities or redress the injustices of persons with whom the group identifies by beyond their own family."[21] Participants understood criticisms by reporters as overshadowing the moral community they had sought to create and by extension the moral selves they sought to craft.

Another interviewee used the criticism to examine the social functions of elite women in non-crisis times. She recalled a conversation with a relative:

> My daughter-in-law said, "Throughout history, women of means have"—and we're not saying we all have—we're not gazillionaires, but we have certain

means—"have built hospitals, have built museums, have been the people who get behind the arts and the things in the city that other people don't have the ability to do. It's a *good thing* to have people like that in a community. If you don't, you're really in trouble." So we didn't have to answer it [the media coverage]; we just kind of let it go away. Some people on the committee do have designer bags. But a lot of people don't. So it was just unfortunate that they got spun that way.

These social contributions she describes are a contemporary version of noblesse oblige, an ideal that Kathleen D. McCarthy notes has taken a uniquely American form in urban settings through "civic stewardship—the notion that successful citizens owe a dual obligation of time and money to the communities in which they have prospered." McCarthy writes, "In a highly mobile society such as ours, it has continually served to graft people's loyalties to their adopted cities, rekindling their commitments to the community ideal, and encouraging them to assume responsibility for the provision of essential social and cultural institutions."[22]

Because participation was often guided by moral and political commitment, the women also had a sense of self at stake in how the group was represented. That is why they criticized the media coverage. The women had intended to minimize signs of affluence and distinction, and they felt that reporters placed too much emphasis on their class positions, which functioned to overshadow the women's goal to unify behind a single cause. Their diversifying of what could have easily been a homogeneous group representing the most prominent of white New Orleans nonetheless attests to their efforts.

One African American woman, a Links member, commented on the positive social functions of group participation:

I thought it was good, because I know women who are involved in this group, and their husbands are so involved in the recovery process and rebuilding businesses, and they're just sitting at home, getting depressed, feeling lonely. I thought this was great, because it got some of these women out of the house, involved, engaged. I thought it was a good therapy for a lot of women. With some of them, it was just a cool thing to do, a cool thing to be involved with Women of the Storm. If that floats your boat, hey, we were it for a little while. We were the fashion.

CHAPTER 8

Divergent Paths

In which some women focus on other things

As the women waited for lawmakers to visit New Orleans, they sought to recharge the sense of group unity they had felt during the Washington trip. At 11:30 A.M. on Friday, February 17, WOS attended a fund-raiser—the Blue Tarp Fashion Show and Luncheon. The tongue-in-cheek event combined culture and politics, using the peculiar sense of humor that proliferated in New Orleans's post-Katrina culture to raise awareness about the erosion of Louisiana's wetlands.

Staged at Antoine's, a famous and, for many, expensive French Quarter restaurant, the $35–$40 per head fund-raiser featured costumes by local artists and designers who transformed storm-related materials into trendy outfits donned by runway models. The fashion show took place on the restaurant's first floor, where a stage had been erected amid tables covered in white linens. The restaurant's Proteus Room, named after one of the city's oldest Carnival krewes—the mostly male, majority white, overwhelmingly affluent, exclusive old-line social clubs and organizations that in many ways epitomize the social structure of New Orleans—became the backstage, where costume designers prepared their models for their moments in the spotlight.[1] On the walls and in the display cases, one could see krewe memorabilia, including black-and-white photos of white Carnival courts dating back to the 1880s; invitations to Mardi Gras balls; and a sparkling array of crowns, scepters, and jeweled accessories. These Carnival items revealed the restaurant's long tradition of catering to the city's white elites.

In the main room, guests sipped cocktails and champagne as they were treated to a fashion show featuring some unconventional materials, such as blue tarps, protective hats and gloves, and hazard masks, some of which had been made into costumes by members of the satirical and often crude group known as Krewe de Vieux.[2] A week earlier, on Saturday, February 11, the nine-hundred-member krewe, the first to parade after Katrina, marched to the sound of the Rebirth Brass Band through the Faubourg Marigny neighborhood and the French Quarter with the disaster-related theme "C'est Levee," a play on the French phrase, "c'est la vie," meaning "that's life."[3] Whereas some questioned whether the city should hold Carnival when thousands of Katrina evacuees were still displaced, the krewe's guiding principle was simple: "Preserve our culture and heritage first, and the recovery will follow."[4] I attended the parade along Decatur Street, which featured ribald political commentary on the disaster; for example, the Krewe distributed a handbill titled "Le Monde de Merde," which declared: "As they swim, splash, paddle and piddle their way through the Quarter, the evacuators, ejaculators, speculators, snorkelers, scuba divers, dumpster divers, muff divers, divas and deviates of the Krewe will spill out of their breaches, breach all etiquette, have sex in the breach, breach for the stars, and prove that they are truly canal retentive."[5]

Krewe de Vieux toned down its satire for the occasion at Antoine's. In this venue, Southern manners and etiquette reigned, even as participants engaged in parodies of elite culture. One media observer described a model as wearing the "season's hottest look, a five-tiered tutu and matching corset in the fabric du jour: blue tarp."[6] Designer Amanda Anderson created a garment that she titled "Katrina Butterfly," made of trash bags wound around a hoop skirt to symbolize a cocoon, along with wings made of blue tarps for the butterfly that she likened to New Orleans's rebirth.[7] Other notable garments from the twenty-five-piece collection included a "Blue Tarp Geisha" outfit and a Christian Dior–inspired "New Look" gown, complete with a blue tarp sunhat, created by Sand Marmillion, whose Lakeview home had been inundated with seven feet of floodwater, and Wes Davis's "Blue Tarp Debutante," a *Flashdance*-inspired pink T-shirt paired with a pleated miniskirt.[8] As local couturier Tracy Thompson said, "After all, blue tarp blue is the new black."[9]

Sponsored by WOS, AWF, and the Louisiana Department of Culture, Recreation, and Tourism, the luncheon helped disseminate information about Louisiana's eroding coastline. Sidney Coffee, who in September 2004 was appointed by Governor Blanco as executive assistant of coastal activities, gave audience members a "forceful presentation about the importance of Louisiana's coastal wetlands to the United States."[10]

After the runway show and presentation, the costumes were auctioned, with proceeds totaling six thousand dollars benefiting AWF and the Louisiana Cultural Economy Foundation.[11] Fusing fashion and the politics of rebuilding, disaster philanthropy and good old-fashioned hobnobbing, the luncheon showed new forms of "conspicuous consumption for a good cause" arising out of crisis.[12] A few weeks later, WOS began selling its blue-tarp umbrellas, one thousand of which were donated by a group member, at fund-raisers and in local boutiques for twenty-five dollars each, with priority given to women-owned retail stores. At one store they were featured alongside a display of storm-related merchandise, including children's raincoats, waterproof totes, and jelly shoes. A style writer for the local paper wrote in anticipation of April showers, "Don any of these waterproofed accessories or ensembles and you're guaranteed to receive a flood of compliments."[13]

This WOS luncheon resonates well with sociologist Diana Kendall's point that "the power of elite women—both through their wealth and their good deeds—is essential for fundraising activities that raise large sums of money for good causes." She notes that these women have "clout to attract the sponsorship by and participation of other elites; however, in return, the women must make elites feel special and provide them with opportunities to enjoy themselves in the company of others who are similar to themselves."[14] WOS's activities are an illustration of what Kendall describes as the reproduction of the upper class: "elite fundraisers serve to reproduce the upper class by providing a venue in which privileged people only associate with one another and in which the social boundaries between elites and nonelites are pronounced."[15]

While all who traveled to Washington were invited to attend the luncheon, there were several factors that would have made it difficult for some participants to attend. First, the event was held in the middle of a workday; attendance presumed a certain amount of leisure time and flexible work schedules. Second, the event required excess cash to spend on tickets, and those strapped for money were excluded. Compared to many other New Orleans fund-raising events, the tickets were inexpensive, but for some women it might have seemed like a frivolous expense. Although the ostensible goal was to bring participants together again, one unintended consequence of decisions about scheduling, cost, and location was that preexisting social and economic boundaries resurfaced, which in turn changed the group's composition.

This dynamic illustrates a central point of my study: WOS's composition fluctuated greatly over space and time. If one were to describe WOS using observations from a single moment, this would obscure the social processes involved in recruitment, attrition, and retention. As Kathleen Blee has stated, micro-level decisions have a cascading effect, tilting the future of groups in particular ways over time; with respect to a group's composition, the "tendency of activist groups to become more homogeneous over time is due more to attrition and retention than to patterns of joining. Those who are similar to current members—in ideas or other factors—stay; those who differ, leave."[16] On the Washington trip, WOS had come together for a single day, mobilizing behind a single cause, aiming to speak with one voice. Yet it did not take long before group participants would begin to take strikingly different paths on the road to recovery. After the trip, WOS faced the challenge of sustaining its heterogeneity. The varying life experiences that made WOS diverse also made it difficult for some women to continue their participation. Many had more pressing obligations.

Sharon Alexis, an African American woman, was one WOS member who lived worlds apart from some of WOS's elite participants. Her experiences were typical of the working- and middle-class participants, especially those whose pre-Katrina everyday lives involved helping impoverished communities. At the time of Katrina, Alexis worked as director of the Gert Town Family Center, a community space run by Catholic Charities in Gert Town, a predominantly African American neighborhood that is one of New Orleans's poorest areas and was hard hit by Katrina.[17] The low-lying area of Gert Town has a rich cultural history. The famed jazz musician Ellis Marsalis grew up there.[18] Singer-songwriter Allen Toussaint, who spent the first two decades of his life in Gert Town, described the neighborhood as "a poor section of New Orleans that was rich in spirit." It was in a "dingy-blond 'shotgun' house on College Court," as Toussaint would recall, that he learned to the play the piano, and he remembered the sense of community: "Everyone in the neighborhood knew each other. If your mother forgot to leave you the key to the front door, you bothered your neighbors, since everyone's skeleton key worked in all the locks."[19]

As Hurricane Katrina approached New Orleans in late August 2005, Alexis evacuated to a hotel in Houston. When the levees failed, Gert Town was flooded with over six feet of water. The Gert Town Family Center sat underwater, and her two-bedroom home, not far from Tulane University, was flooded as well. In the weeks after the storm, the New Orleans Catholic Charities offices relocated to Baton Rouge, and Alexis sought housing there too, along with many others; the Louisiana capital took in nearly two hundred thousand Katrina evacuees. Alexis was welcomed into the home of Darwyn and Carmen Williams, who had contacted Catholic Charities and offered to host a Katrina evacuee indefinitely. Throughout October 2005, Alexis stayed with the Williams family in their house in Country Club of Louisiana, a gated community in south Baton Rouge that boasts centuries-old trees and a "majestic Louisiana plantation clubhouse with tennis and swimming facilities."[20]

During her time in Baton Rouge, Alexis worked in a mobile trailer stationed at the Catholic Community Services building, tracking down displaced Gert Town residents by phone. At night she spent time with the Williams family talking about life in Gert Town. Alexis told a reporter for *New Orleans CityBusiness*, "It's all about trust. Just as they get a perspective from me, I get a perspective from them. If everyone learns to trust, we can get through this and rebuild a better New Orleans and take down the class and race boundaries. You look at people who make comments about the way African American people live, but they don't do anything about it. You need the knowledge to help them and instead of talking about the negative, people need to open up their hearts and their heads. Out of darkness comes light."[21]

In January 2006, when WOS made its trip to Washington, Gert Town remained in shambles. Although the floodwaters had receded, there were painful reminders of the horrors that neighborhood residents had faced during the storm. Not far from the Gert Town Family Center, a wheelchair sat empty on a front porch. Alexis told a journalist that during Katrina the elderly man who lived there had survived for three days in the wheelchair with floodwaters up to his chin as he waited for help, only to die a few days after being rescued.[22]

In addition to worrying about the extra burdens faced by the poor throughout the city, Alexis was concerned that the floodwaters had been contaminated by materials in an abandoned warehouse on Earhart Boulevard, which had once been home to Thompson Hayward Chemical Company. According to documents from the State of Louisiana Department of Environmental Quality, the property was used for "pesticide formulations operations" from 1940 through 1977 and for the "bagging of soda ash material and the warehousing and distribution of several industrial chemicals that included dry cleaning fluids and commercial pest control products." In the late 1980s it was discovered that dry-cleaning chemicals had been released into the city's drainage system and that banned pesticides and contaminants were present in the surface and subsurface soil of the property, leading to its closure in 1988. Some on-site remediation took place, but not of the areas suspected of "most impacts." Nearly a decade later, in 1997, a risk assessment was conducted to identify "contaminants of concern," followed by a feasibility study that resulted in a recommendation for "excavation and off-site disposal of contaminated media."[23] A concrete slab was poured over the contaminated soil, and barrels and drums remained within the warehouse doors.[24] Years went by without action, and then Katrina hit.

Alexis and other Gert Town community leaders and residents had been worried about this chemical site long before Katrina, and they now believed that floodwaters had carried contaminants from the site to the homes in surrounding neighborhoods. Alexis remained convinced that those who had waded through Katrina's floodwaters had come into direct contact with chemicals and pesticides from this site, and she used the media to bring attention to these issues, thereby extending a long tradition of women's participation in environmental, health, and toxic waste activism.[25] "This is a crime that this is allowed to take place, both pre-Katrina and post-Katrina," Alexis told *New Orleans CityBusiness*.[26]

The implementation of the remediation would not begin for months, which kept many displaced Gert Town residents from deeming it safe to return to their homes. Only in October, over a year after the storm, did the remediation activities begin, and these lasted well into August 2007. During that period 751 tons of hazardous debris were brought to disposal facilities in Oklahoma; 4,800 tons of soil excavated from the site and deemed hazardous would be incinerated in facilities in Texas and Nebraska; and 5,800 tons of construction debris would be brought to landfills in Louisiana. A new chain-link fence was erected around the site, and the backfill was covered with grass.[27]

As a WOS participant, Alexis was able to express her frustrations with lawmakers in Washington and share concerns about contamination threats to her community, not to mention the challenges she faced in rebuilding her flooded home. "It's easy for our officials to stand up and talk about what we're doing around the world to bring peace," Alexis told a writer for the *Chronicle of Philanthropy*, whose article "When the Helpers Need Help" focused on the personal post-Katrina challenges for New Orleans charity workers. "For people who are distraught here in Louisiana, they need some peace," Alexis said. "I feel sometimes I just have to take some time off to deal with what I have to deal with."[28] Her frustration was warranted; her neighborhood had remained without electricity five months after the storm, and, like Cecile Tebo, who lived not too far away, Alexis had engaged in a months-long battle with her insurance company. "I had my FEMA trailer delivered in November. Just had my lights turned on two weeks ago," she said in a February 2006 article.[29] In addition to going to Washington, Alexis found that counseling Katrina survivors became a way of dealing with anger and frustration. She also met with a trauma counselor provided by Catholic Charities to talk through her anxiety.[30]

Environmental injustice was not limited to Gert Town. Several other communities contended with the deleterious effects of storm wreckage and demolition debris hauled into their neighborhoods as other parts of the city were cleaned up. Fifteen miles from Gert Town is Versailles, a small, ethnic enclave in New Orleans East, which has served as the hub of New Orleans's Vietnamese American community since refugees began arriving there in the 1970s.[31] Versailles is home to Mary Queen of Vietnam Church, which according to Father Vien Nguyen, the church's pastor at the time of Katrina, served over six thousand parishioners, many of whom were drawn from the twenty-two thousand Vietnamese residents in the greater New Orleans area.[32] During the storm, Father Nguyen helped parishioners evacuate, and later, after the levees broke, he engaged in search and rescue efforts using a fifteen-passenger van to help bring those in the surrounding neighborhood to the church, which served as an evacuation point. As the floodwaters rose, blocking the headlights of the van, Father Nguyen and others began conducting their searches for survivors by boat.[33]

In January 2006 Father Nguyen received a phone call from Anne Milling, who told him about the newly formed women's group and their planned trip to Washington, D.C. Father Nguyen put Milling in touch with Kim Dung Nguyen, a New Orleans native working at Mary Queen of Vietnam Church, as well as two of the church's nuns, one of whom was Sister Anne Marie Kim-Khuong of the Daughters of Our Lady of the Holy Rosary.[34] These three women were joined by Tina Owen, who immigrated to the United States in 1975 as a refugee and later co-founded the Vietnamese Initiatives in Economic Training (VIET), an organization that helped Vietnamese residents apply for citizenship, obtain work permits, and find resources to overcome language barriers.[35] For the most part, participation by Vietnamese women after the one-day trip to Washington was limited; they, like Sharon Alexis, had more pressing concerns.

On February 14, just days before the Blue Tarp Fashion Show, Mayor Nagin signed an executive order that led to the opening of a massive dumpsite along Chef Menteur Highway at the edge of Versailles. The Chef Menteur Landfill, as it was soon dubbed, was intended to hold about one fourth of Katrina's storm debris. Father Nguyen said that the projected 6.5 million cubic yards of trash would become "one of the tallest structures in New Orleans East."[36] But it wasn't the eyesore that raised concerns among the nearly one thousand families that lived within two miles of the landfill; it was the fear of toxins from the unsorted debris leaking into the community's water supply, potentially contaminating the gardens where elders in the community grew vegetables.[37]

Over the next few months, Kim Nguyen would join other community members in organizing to close the landfill, a fight that would continue well into August 2006, when the executive order was set to expire. During that period, Nguyen took on many tasks related to the rebuilding of the Vietnamese community, including coordinating volunteers, writing grant proposals for the estimated three hundred thousand dollars needed to repair the damaged church and seeking assistance in replacing the computers and furniture destroyed during the storm. But the main focus for Nguyen and others in this community remained the landfill; the primary concern was the immediate and long-term health of neighborhood residents.

Another part of the city faced similar problems. The Agricultural Street Landfill is equidistant from Gert Town and Versailles. It was opened by the city in 1909 and was in operation for nearly fifty years. In 1971 the Housing Authority of New Orleans (HANO) opened the Press Park townhomes, a newly formed, largely black neighborhood sited on the former landfill, one that covered nearly 190 acres.[38] Gordon Plaza, another subdivision of sixty-seven homes built on the former municipal dump, opened in 1980. In 1983 the Orleans Parish School Board purchased land on the site and built Moton Elementary School, which opened in 1989, serving over four hundred students.[39] In 1993, under pressure from residents, the Environmental Protection Agency (EPA) performed soil tests and found that the site was laced with hazardous materials. The following December the Agricultural Street Landfill was declared a Superfund site, an area identified by the Environmental Protection Area as contaminated with hazardous waste and thus eligible for clean-up.[40] In 2003 the Louisiana Department of Health and Hospitals reported that the incidence of breast cancer among Gordon Plaza residents was almost 50 percent higher than in other areas.[41]

On September 29, 2005, Beverly Wright, director of the Deep South Center for Environmental Justice at Dillard University and co-chair of the National Black Environmental Justice Network, testified before a subcommittee of the U.S. House of Representatives. During her testimony, Wright, a sociologist, explained how the Agricultural Street Landfill was just one episode in a larger history of environmental racism in the area, both pre- and post-Katrina. "Dozens of toxic time bombs along Louisiana's Mississippi River petrochemical corridor, the 85-mile stretch from Baton Rouge to New Orleans, make the region a major environmental justice battleground," she said. "Black communities all along the corridor have been fighting against environmental racism and demanding relocation to areas away from polluting facilities."[42]

Wright's experiences of Katrina were personal and political. Her home in New Orleans East, an area she described as "predominantly African American and middle to upper class people," was flooded during Katrina, and she lost all of her belongings.[43] In an interview she gave shortly after the storm, she reported that some of the most difficult losses were the photographs of her mother, who had died the April before Katrina. Wright also reflected on the experience of temporary downward mobility after the disaster, standing in line with others to receive public assistance:

> What people don't recognize—I recognized this when we were standing in the food stamp line—is that Katrina was a big equalizer. You had single mothers who had been living in subsidized housing, physicians, and ministers all in the Red Cross line trying to get food stamps because we had no money. The banks were under water. So if you had money, you couldn't get to it. And if you had money in the bank for that month, your job was gone, so you wouldn't have any the next month. We have such an unsure future. We have thousands and thousands of people, from every occupation, who no longer have a livelihood who now have to take handouts. When I got the food stamp card, I didn't know what EBT [Electronic Benefit Transfer] stood for. There are all kinds of things we are just finding out, and it is a humbling experience. Those of us who have nothing are appreciative, but you recognize that you are in a completely different position than where you have ever been in your whole life.[44]

Wright used her time and energy to draw attention to environmental and health disparities among communities of color. Her work as a prominent researcher, coupled with her decades-long participation as a scholar-activist in the environmental justice movement as well as her membership in the Crescent City Chapter of The Links, likely led to the invitation to participate as a WOS member.[45] But after the trip to Washington, she returned to her community and academic work, publishing numerous books and articles with fellow environmental justice scholar Robert D. Bullard, including *The Wrong Complexion for Protection: How the Government Response to Disaster Endangers African American Communities* and the anthology *Race, Place, and Environmental Justice after Hurricane Katrina: Struggles to Reclaim, Rebuild, and Revitalize New Orleans and Gulf Coast*, which includes a contribution by Sheila J. Webb, another WOS participant. Webb's chapter, "Investing in Human Capital and Healthy Rebuilding in the Aftermath of Hurricane Katrina," examines the health disparities among African American communities and argues for redesigning the health care system in post-Katrina New Orleans. Webb was born in New Orleans and after seventeen years working at the New Orleans Health Department would go on to serve as director of the Center for Empowered Decision Making.[46] In the aftermath of the storm, she helped coordinate mobile health clinics with EXCELth Incorporated to serve evacuees at Renaissance Village, a FEMA trailer park in Baton Rouge.[47] When Webb was honored in July 2006 as one of *New Orleans Magazine*'s "Top Female Achievers," she was pictured wearing a WOS button.[48]

Immediately after the Washington trip, WOS reached another turning point in which group members took divergent paths that mapped out, to some great degree, along racial lines. As peripheral members of WOS, Alexis, Nguyen, Wright, and Webb returned to their communities still reeling not only from the storm but also from old and new forms of environmental racism, while those in the core membership hurriedly prepared for the first congressional visits.

CHAPTER 9

Invitations Accepted

*Relating the decisive first visits to
the scenes of destruction*

WOS imagined that planeloads of lawmakers would seize the opportunity to visit post-Katrina New Orleans. But to the women's disappointment, the vast majority of their invitations were turned down. In the first weeks of February 2006, WOS members called congressional offices and sent follow-up e-mails, pressing lawmakers to visit—"persistence," they reasoned. Some lawmakers asked if aides could attend on their behalf. The women struggled with this request, because they wanted representatives themselves to visit. But it was a compromise that they would ultimately accept, albeit begrudgingly; a visit by an aide would be better than no visit at all. Many congressional offices had even stopped responding. In a correspondence shared with me, one pair of women e-mailed back and forth for days, updating each other about their follow-up work. One of the two left numerous voice messages with lawmakers and felt that they had chosen not to take her calls; she was planning to send a final e-mail and then "wave the white flag." Her WOS partner had similar news. After initially hearing back from a congressional staffer who said that the lawmaker might consider a trip that August, this participant said a visit was needed much sooner. Then came silence: "I NEVER got a return e-mail or call! SHAME!"[1] To WOS's dismay, the first three of the four time slots offered to lawmakers went by without a single visitor.

But the tide would soon turn. The first lawmakers to accept the invitation planned to visit New Orleans in mid-February 2006, on the last of WOS's four proposed dates. On Sunday, February 19, Rep. Lynn Westmoreland (R-GA), and Rep. Scott Garrett (R-NJ) visited New Orleans, along with Chandler Morse, aide to Rep. Jeff Flake (R-AZ).[2] Michelle Presson, Garrett's chief of staff, reflected on WOS's Washington trip by saying, "They did a pretty persuasive pitch up here."[3] A *Times-Picayune* reporter noted that Westmoreland arrived in New Orleans wearing not only a tan suit and brown leather cowboy boots but also a "cloak of skepticism," believing the "faces of Katrina were the looters, the crooked politicians, and the derelict police officers."[4]

This first visit was crucial because WOS would execute the itinerary that it had spent weeks refining. As with hosting guests at any formal event, there was much planning to be done. Decisions had to be made about what the lawmakers would see, with whom they would speak, where these meetings would take place, and what would be said. The disaster tour for lawmakers was intended to be nothing less than comprehensive—showing that locals had a plan, demonstrating the range of affected populations in the city, and putting another face on Katrina. It included a two-hour aerial tour aboard a Blackhawk helicopter, conducted by Gen. Hunt Downer of the Louisiana National Guard, that was intended to reveal the erosion of Louisiana's wetlands, which were washing away at a rate of "tens of square miles per year (approximately 100 acres per day)."[5] WOS also recruited speakers to provide expert testimony about the wetlands' role in reducing hurricane storm surge.[6] There was a stop at Jackson Barracks, the Louisiana National Guard headquarters; a three-hour land tour of damaged neighborhoods, including the Lower Ninth Ward, Gentilly, Lakeview, and New Orleans East; and visits to the major levee breaches at the London Avenue Canal, Industrial Canal, and 17th Street Canal. After seeing the destruction in a range of areas (poor black neighborhoods, affluent white enclaves, middle-class black communities,), the representatives met with local civic and business leaders, including R. King Milling; Jay Lapeyre, president of the New Orleans Business Council; Rod West of Entergy and the LRA; and Mel Lagarde, chairman of Mayor Nagin's BNOB Commission.[7]

Several core members joined lawmakers on the tour, and the group organized meals for the lawmakers at the end of the day. After discussing the possibility of having a private dinner in a FEMA trailer, WOS chose instead to host the dinner at a beautiful Uptown home unscathed by floodwaters.

The following day, Monday, February 20, the women "put everyone on the plane after a powerful breakfast meeting" with representatives from the LRA, the BNOB Commission, and the New Orleans Business Council.[8] The core organizers then met at Milling's residence to discuss the first visit. The group agreed that if pressed for time, seeing neighborhoods—and the storm's concrete effects on residents' lives—would be more important than seeing the erosion of coastal wetlands.

The first congressional visit marked a major turning point for WOS and also for federal support for the Gulf Coast recovery. Representatives Westmoreland and Garrett were among eleven lawmakers who had voted against the September 2005 bill to provide $52 billion in aid to the region, claiming it was an "invitation to fraud."[9] After his tour, however, Westmoreland said, "This visit definitely helps. I'm so glad to see some different faces of people who are trying to make a difference. All we had seen in Washington and on TV were people that did not give a real good

representation of what was going on down here."[10] His "we" statements suggested
that many lawmakers were not moved by the plight of impoverished black residents
whose suffering was broadcast nationwide during the catastrophe.[11] "You have to
see the massive scale of the devastation and get a greater perspective on the enormity of it," he said. "I'm glad I got to see it first-hand."[12] Garrett called WOS "very
persuasive."[13]

After the trip the *Times-Picayune* published an editorial praising WOS's abilities
to get the lawmakers to visit.[14] The paper printed the running count of congressional
visits, based in part on WOS's statistics: 57 of 435 representatives and 30 senators
had visited post-Katrina.[15] These representatives became advocates of WOS's cause,
and they vowed to return to Washington to encourage their peers to accept WOS's
invitation. Westmoreland said, "I'm definitely going to talk as many as I can into
coming down and taking a look for themselves. I definitely have more confidence
that the people in this community are trying to do this the right way."[16] The women
were satisfied with the outcomes. Peggy Laborde, for example, told reporters, "We
are extremely pleased with how the visit went. It was important to show them that
we are behind changing the way we do business in New Orleans and let them know
that we are going to demand accountability at all levels of government."[17]

What was the rationale behind the tour? One white woman told me about how
they tried to project a particular image of the devastation by showing lawmakers
the destruction in both rich and poor neighborhoods:

> To me the most important thing to see is, if you're only going to take people
> two places, they need to see the Lower Ninth Ward and they need to see either
> Lakeview or Northline, someplace where there are big, expensive homes. Because
> I personally—and I know a lot of people I know—feel the media has not done
> us justice. It's all about the poor blacks in the Lower Ninth Ward. As you know,
> some very expensive homes got hit. And some of those people do have a whole
> lot of money, but a lot of them in Lakeview don't. Once again, the media is con-
> centrating on that, but what goes along with that concentration is the fact that it
> brings back the pictures of people at the convention center and the Superdome,
> which then brings in, "It's nothing but the poor blacks," and a lot of them did live
> down there. But once again, it's very much a slanted story.

In these ways, some WOS participants attempted to "expand the circle of the we"
by expanding the circle of loss.[18]

Another white participant gave the following account of her own touring practices when she showed visitors the devastation across the city:

> I also like to start out with million-dollar houses and then I personalize things. I
> say I went to my friend's mom's house. She had lived here for fifty years, probably

more, actually. Probably sixty years. Raised four kids. She's in her eighties. Everything in her house is purple, because she loved purple. And she had absolutely every new appliance in her kitchen, because she loved toys. I mean, you know, like the latest in blenders, the latest in choppers, the latest in coffeemakers. Seven feet of water. You know. Then my personal tour goes down to the Lower Nine.

Reflecting on the tours for lawmakers, a white participant said, "There are fifteen-million-dollar homes that had ten, fifteen feet of water in them. It's not just a poor problem, it's not just a black problem. And even when you don't have a home that flooded or washed away and you didn't lose everything, your life is hugely impacted."

While many in WOS acknowledged that poor people of color were disproportionately affected by Katrina, some members also sought to expand the circle of loss to include whites and the affluent. It is useful to think about how some contemporary social theorists might approach these activities, especially because WOS and its participants were involved in the process of constructing a particular Katrina story during this lawmaker's visit. The women, the speakers, and the local media all served as "carrier groups" in articulating a claim to some "fundamental injury" at the level of the collectivity; the lawmakers served as the audience to whom these claims were directed, and the tours functioned as the situation in which these claims were communicated.[19] Group members, together with the civic and business leaders, were involved in constructing a "framework of cultural classification" and crafting a "new master narrative" of Katrina. For these lawmakers, the "face of Katrina" involved subjects who embodied racialized poverty and who constituted a singular group that bore the brunt of the pain and suffering. But these tours organized by WOS aimed to expand what Jeffrey Alexander calls the "nature of the pain" as well as the "nature of the victim." By communicating the social, economic, and political effects (the nature of the pain) on new historical subjects (the nature of the victim), the tours encouraged lawmakers to reconsider the "relation of the trauma victim to the wider audience."[20]

Whereas the women were the principal participants on the trip to Washington, their role during the congressional visits to New Orleans was noticably different. They often receded into the background. One woman explained how she saw their role: "Because none of this tap dance we are doing. All we are are facilitators. We in no way represent ourselves as experts on any of this. We try to get the best and the brightest to make these presentations so that what they're hearing is one hundred percent credible."

While many of the women were arguably among the best and the brightest, having an encyclopedic knowledge of Congress, their city, and the catastrophe, prevailing notions of credibility and masculine authority pressured the women to remain facilitators and defer to those with political or business credentials. Several interviewees commented on the absence of women's voices in these meetings with elected officials. This is what one white woman had to say about it:

> But whenever they bring dignitaries in, they don't have women speak to them. They have about four or five men that speak to them and tell them what the business of New Orleans is and the business of the wetlands and how to conduct it. That seems a little one-sided. It seems strange to me that the Women of the Storm have men speak for them. But in our society I don't know whether it's that way everywhere, but down here, men are in much more important positions business-wise than women are, and they've been appointed to these boards. There's one woman who's very knowledgeable. She's on the Bureau of Governmental Research. She's a smart lady. They don't have her speak to these people. But I think she could, easily. If we bring people down, I think women should be more involved. . . . I'm talking about knowledgeable women to say knowledgeable, important things to these men as they come through.

Indeed, many WOS members were civic and business leaders as well—attorneys, small-business owners, community activists, and university professors and presidents. Some group members were key public figures with the ability to communicate knowledge of the catastrophe and the recovery efforts to the broader public.

Participants were aware of gender hierarchies in politics and gave consideration to the challenges that accompany organizing as a group of women. As another white woman said about the Washington trip, "I am not going to say that maybe some of the congressional leaders wouldn't have rather seen men. And talked business. Because they are certainly more comfortable talking to men about business than they are to women. However, most of our women can talk to them on just about every subject that they would have wanted to. But we were told by a couple of senators, 'Why don't you get the men of the business community to give us a call? We might take them more seriously.'" Remembering how these gender dynamics played out during conversations with Sen. Lamar Alexander (R-TN) and White House economic adviser Allan B. Hubbard, WOS participant and matriarch of Louisiana's "first family of football," Olivia Manning, told one journalist, "They all want to talk football, even if just a little bit."[21]

A white woman critiqued these gender hierarchies and suggested that gender relations could have been reconfigured differently in the wake of the catastrophe. In the reconstruction of community and everyday life, she saw a unique opportunity to guide women into positions where they could demonstrate their knowledge about the recovery. She said, "I think the Women of the Storm was wonderful. No men stood up and said, 'Let's do this.' The women did this. But in order to have the senators pay attention, they have to have men talk to them. I would like to see a couple of women thrown in there." She proceeded to name a number of prominent women who ran community organizations and who could have spoken to elected officials. But this vision of transforming gender was fleeting. Finally, as though defeated by the pressure on women to fade into the background in male-dominated political arenas, she expressed her discontent and then conceded: "I'm just amazed that we don't have more women making presentations. But men listen to men. You know that." In this sense, the women took the position of facilitators rather than presenters, of hostesses rather than experts, reproducing conventional gender inequalities.[22]

Engaged in both highly visible work and behind-the-scenes labor, WOS members were participating in civic action that helped shape the broader Katrina recovery movement. But were they also performing a new form of movement "housewifery"?[23] In many ways their roles during congressional visits supported the existing gender order. However, there were subtle ways in which the group did challenge gender relations. It was clear that they had orchestrated the visits and that the male speakers were participating in tours organized and administered by the women. And though the women did not self-identify as feminist, at least in their interviews with me, the critiques by some members resonated with strains of feminist discourse that have sought to increase women's standing within existing social and political structures. Some told me that prior to the storm they had advocated for women's equality through educational opportunities, occupational placement, or dress-to-impress initiatives, to name a few examples. And many engaged in community work in order to improve the lives of others. Some saw the meetings with officials as missed opportunities for women's leadership in the post-Katrina recovery. Only a few women said this, but their critical remarks show that not everyone in WOS believed their role should be in the background.

The dominant discourse among WOS was that women did this work out of selflessness, deflecting credit rather than trying to receive personal gain. After describing herself as a full-time, stay-at-home mom, one white woman I interviewed said, "You know, somebody said to me, 'The women in this state will be the saving grace.' And my husband said, 'I've got this speech prepared, what I need to say to Congress, and I should be going on this trip.' And I said, 'Well, you know, you're not a woman, now, are you?' And we agreed that there could be no Men of the Storm. There are too many agendas. Their egos are too big. There are too many chiefs and not enough Indians, and the women are happy to be the Indians." Many women seemed more than willing to do their work without recognition, and they framed women's civic participation as nonpolitical. This echoes sociological research on how women often refuse to characterize their community work in political terms.[24]

On Tuesday, February 21, Westmoreland and WOS member Beverly Church appeared on CNN to discuss the lawmaker's tour of New Orleans.[25] Reflecting on his visit, Westmoreland said, "Well, I—it—it was kind of a—a shock to see the—the total devastation, especially where those breaches were at in—in the levees, just an unbelievable thing to see people's clothes hanging out of trees, and, you know, cars turned upside-down."[26] When Westmoreland was asked why he went to New

Orleans, he responded in ways that foreground WOS's effectiveness: "Well, number one, I was invited. I think that makes a difference when somebody goes, being invited, than they do trying to get a good photo-op for their local newspaper."[27] These words are among the first public commentaries on the invitation's efficacy. He continued: "But the Women of the Storm made a big difference for me, because it really put some real-life faces with the situation, and not just politicians."

On February 23 the Bush administration released a report on the federal response to Katrina. First ordered by President Bush during his address to the nation from Jackson Square on September 15, 2005, this comprehensive review included specific recommendations for preparing for the 2006 Atlantic hurricane season, and it was less severe in its assessment of the failure of government response than a report released just nine days earlier by House Republicans, which offered a scathing analysis of the inadequte response at all levels of government. That morning, a CNN broadcast from New Orleans featured three prominent WOS members—Cecile Tebo, Anne Milling, and Madeline West—who remarked on the report and the current conditions of the city. As they spoke, a ticker ran across the bottom of the television screen, reading, "Women of the Storm seek to keep NOLA from being forgotten." Reflecting on the upcoming Hastert-Pelosi bipartisan visits and the White House report, West told the CNN interviewer, "I think the report coming out, . . . it's only looking at the initial phase of it. Now we're in the recovery phase, which is still in a crisis and it's very important."

CHAPTER 10

New Orleans at Six Months

Amid Carnival, a city takes stock of the recovery,
some plans unravel, and yet the women persist

In February 2006, six months after Hurricane Katrina, New Orleans began count-ing down to its first Mardi Gras after the storm. The convergence of the six-month mark and Carnival meant that residents, the media, and city leaders were taking stock of the recovery. The Gulf Coast Reconstruction Watch, a joint project between the Institute for Southern Studies and the institute's journal, *Southern Exposure*, released a special report titled "The Mardi Gras Index." Analyzing over 135 indicators, the report provided a "statistical snapshot" of the disaster recovery and concluded that "beneath the uplifting veneer, it's clear that New Orleans is being left behind again."[1] A few key points from the report are worth noting. Estimates of the city's repopulation varied greatly and were changing rapidly, but the report estimated that by Mardi Gras only 156,000 residents had returned. It highlighted the lack of housing for displaced and returning residents, noting that homeowners were in "limbo" and that renters remained without help. Around 21,000 residents in New Orleans had filed requests for FEMA trailer homes, but as of early February 2006, only 3,000 had been installed; because of the agency's rules about the placement of trailers in flood plains, nearly 11,000 sat empty in Hope, Arkansas.[2] The report noted that only 17 percent of public schools in New Orleans had reopened, which made it difficult for families with school-age children to return to the city.[3] The start of the 2006 hurricane season was just three months away, but neither Congress nor the president had authorized funding for levee fortification projects or wetlands restoration projects.[4]

Given this situation, questions arose about whether to hold the 2006 Mardi Gras celebrations at all.[5] But there were many people who felt that it was emotionally and psychologically important for Carnival to be held. On Thursday, February 23, the

After arriving on the evening of Thursday March 2, the House co-delegation, which included Rep. John Boehner (R-OH), Rep. Jim Clyburn (D-SC), Rep. Deborah Pryce (R-OH), Rep. John Larson, and Rep. Tom Davis (R-VA), attended a press conference at the Royal Sonesta Hotel in the French Quarter. The next morning, the group toured the destruction in the coastal communities of Mississippi; on the itinerary were Gulfport, Bay St. Louis, and Waveland, a town flattened by Katrina's storm surge. In the afternoon they returned to New Orleans to visit Lakeview and the Lower Ninth Ward, where they were briefed about the levee breach at the Industrial Canal by Daniel Hitchings, director of the Army Corps of Engineers' Task Force Hope.[13] When the delegation arrived in the Lower Ninth Ward, residents had been cordoned off a block away from the briefing. A *Times-Picayune* photographer documented the interactions that took place when a few Congress members approached the residents: Rep. Lois Capps (D-CA) hugging Yvonne Wise, a Lower Ninth Ward resident, and Pelosi embracing another resident, Mattie Mack.[14] On one evening during the three-day trip, Louisiana representative Charlie Melançon (D) organized a nighttime bus tour through Chalmette to emphasize the sense of desertion; according to Melançon, fourteen Democrats but no Republicans went on the excursion. Brendan Daly, Pelosi's spokesperson, said of the twilight tour, "There's no people. There's no dogs, cats; no kids."[15]

On Saturday, lawmakers were scheduled to meet with WOS members and civic and business leaders. However, as the day unfolded, the itinerary the women had worked so hard to arrange was seized from their control. One participant told me that the trip was being run by Hastert's office and FEMA, which refused to alter its program at the recommendation of local groups. In the words of one WOS member, who left a phone message for me at the time, "The Congressional delegation coming today have pretty much kept us out of the loop. They want to run things their way with no interference from us. It's pretty frustrating, but we will persevere."

WOS was given a brief window to meet with lawmakers. On Saturday morning at the Royal Sonesta Hotel, some WOS core committee members—Anne Milling, Beverly Church, Becky Currence, Peggy Laborde, Madeline West, Dolly Simpson, and Liz Sloss—held a breakfast with Hastert and other members of the delegation.[16] But the meeting was cut short because Hastert arrived late, and at least one lawmaker, Rep. Jeb Hensarling, who had been skeptical of the Baker Bill, left the meeting even before hearing presentations about the city and state recovery plans, consequently inciting outrage from the *Times-Picayune*. During the trip, Hensarling said that state and local officials wanted a federal handout, and he questioned what able-bodied people were doing to help themselves, a dismissal that the newspaper, in an editorial titled "Clueless on the Hill," would go on to call a "nasty assessment of the people who live here." In response to those lawmakers who seemed reluctant to back the rebuilding efforts, the newspaper said, "The job of recovery is hard enough without leaders in Washington working against it."[17]

Lawmakers who attended the breakfast meeting seemed impressed by the presentation on the local recovery plan. As one reporter observed, "Although a spokeswoman for the delegation said the members of Congress had not come at the bidding of any one group, the pins the politicians wore belied the importance of this little-known sisterhood, which was moved to action after failing to see sufficient progress in the cleanup of their storm-battered city."[18] Lawmakers praised WOS as an integral part of the recovery. "When these women visited Washington, they literally took the town by storm. They were the unlikely messengers of this disaster," said Pelosi.[19] Another lawmaker, Rep. Sheila Jackson-Lee (D-TX), reacted similarly: "When I look at these women, I'm reminded of John Adams and what his wife told him as he was drafting the Constitution: Abigail Adams said 'Don't forget the ladies.' If you want to get something done, put the women in charge. The Women of the Storm have galvanized this community. They're uncowering and undeterred. They cannot be stopped."[20]

"Stunned by the scale of the tragedy," Pelosi said that she would support a recommendation by President Bush to allocate another $4.2 billion in housing recovery aid as well as an additional $1.5 billion for storm protection measures. Hastert was less committal, although he seemed deeply moved by the scenes of destruction,

FIGURE 5. House Minority Leader Nancy Pelosi is greeted by Women of the Storm members Peggy Laborde, Madeline West, and Nancy Marsiglia (*from left*) at a breakfast before a tour of New Orleans, Saturday, March 4, 2006. AP photo/Cheryl Gerber.

saying, "I saw some amazing things here, things that I never thought I would see in my lifetime, the scope of this."[21] Pam Bryan remembered, "His demeanor seemed to warm significantly while he was here. He seemed to change."[22] Just like Representatives Westmoreland and Garrett, many from the bipartisan House visit pledged to encourage other lawmakers to accept WOS's invitation.

WOS was not alone in supporting revenue sharing from offshore energy production. Several figures with national political clout argued that such a plan was needed to finance the state's coastal restoration projects. On Monday, March 6, Newt Gingrich, former Speaker of the House, and John M. Barry, author of *Rising Tide: The Great Mississippi Flood of 1927 and How It Changed America*, published an article in *Time* titled "Why New Orleans Needs Saving." Gingrich and Barry described how engineers, working to control the Mississippi River in order to service the shipping and oil and gas industries, ended up "greatly accelerating the washing away of coastal Louisiana" by stopping sediment from replenishing the Mississippi deltas over time. The numbers they cited were grim: more than nineteen hundred square miles had already been lost, and another seven hundred square miles would vanish, "putting at risk port facilities and all the energy-producing infrastructure in the Gulf."[23]

After giving an estimated cost of $40 billion, an amount they considered reasonable when compared not only to the cost of rebuilding the port elsewhere but to the amount spent on wetlands restoration in Iraq, Gingrich and Barry wrote: "Washington also has a moral burden. It was the Federal Government's responsibility to build levees that worked, and its failure to do so ultimately led to New Orleans being flooded. The White House recognized that responsibility when it proposed an additional $4.2 billion for housing in New Orleans, but the first priority remains flood control. Without it, individuals will hesitate to rebuild, and lenders will decline to invest." The two proposed a solution congruent with WOS requests:

> How should flood control be paid for? States get 50% of the tax revenues paid to the Federal Government from oil and gas produced on federally owned land. States justify that by arguing that the energy production puts strains on the infrastructure and environment. Louisiana gets no share of the tax revenue from the oil and gas production on the outer continental shelf. Yet that production puts an infinitely greater burden on it than energy production from other federal territory puts on any other state. If we treat Louisiana the same as other states and give it the same share of tax revenue that other states receive, it will need no other help from the government to protect itself. Every day's delay makes it harder to rebuild the city. It is time to act. It is well past time.[24]

On the same day that Gingrich and Barry's article appeared in *Time*, search teams with cadaver dogs set out to once more comb through damaged homes in the Lower Ninth Ward before demolition crews began hauling away debris from the areas where lawmakers had convened just two days earlier. Search teams had already gone through the 120 homes slated for demolition, but with more than 400 people still missing, Army Corps of Engineers officials decided to check one last time.[25] On Sunday, March 5, on the same weekend of the bipartisan visit, a Lower Ninth Ward resident with no relatives, a fifty-five-year-old man by the name of Joseph Naylor, was found dead in his attic.[26] On the other side of the city, in the mostly white, affluent Lakeview area, where similar efforts were under way, search dogs helped discover a body in the attic of a rental home. According to an account by Louisiana's medical examiner, the man had entered the attic in an attempt to escape the rapidly rising floodwaters and tried to crawl through an air conditioning vent.[27] These stories continued to emerge, extending the pain of Katrina well into the spring months of 2006. In March 2006 alone, nine bodies of storm victims were discovered throughout New Orleans, including that of a girl about six years old, who was found in the Lower Ninth Ward with her blue backpack.[28] In a *New York Times* article about those who remained missing, forty-year-old New Orleans resident Wanda Jackson, whose nephew was swept away by Katrina's floodwaters as his mother watched, said, "We never reached out to anyone to tell our story, because there's no ending to our story. Because we haven't found our deceased. Being honest with you, in my opinion, they forgot about us. They did not build nothing on 9/11 until they were sure that the damn dust was not human dust, so how you go on and build things in our city?"[29]

Like Cecile Tebo in her December 2005 letter, "We Are Not OK!," Jackson expressed concern about the place of the city in the national imagination. Their lives and their suffering were vastly different, but both Jackson and Tebo, like many others living the post-Katrina life, believed that the city had been long forgotten. In what seemed like an ongoing disaster, an open wound rather than a scar, WOS continued its activities to help keep the city on the national agenda. On Tuesday, March 7, WOS members spoke at a panel discussion about the Washington trip at the Newcomb College Center for Research on Women (NCCRW), which was moderated by member Diana Pinckley and organized by the Tulane Women's Association. WOS panelists also included executive committee member Pam Bryan, Pamela Pipes, Norma Jean Sabiston, and Tania Tetlow, a Tulane University law professor. Sister Anne-Marie Nguyen of the Vietnamese community was scheduled to speak, but she was unable to attend. As part of the careful staging of the room for the dozen or so audience members, a blue-tarp umbrella was stationed on a small side table, along with copies of the book *Why New Orleans Matters*, wrapped in blue ribbon to show how the book had been presented to lawmakers.

Also at the table was Jeanette Bell, known among the women for her work in historic preservation as well as for the roses she grew in her garden that was once an overgrown lot; four bouquets of her roses were evenly spaced out on the seminar table that day.[30] Bell's account was particularly interesting, not least because she talked about how she felt pressured to participate in the group, not by the women sitting at the table, but by her daughter. For nearly thirty years before joining WOS, Jeanette Bell had worked in historic preservation, first in Detroit, where she moved in the early 1970s from her home in Mississippi, and later in New Orleans's Central City neighborhood, where in 1990 she bought and restored a dilapidated nineteenth-century home in a poor area suffering from crime and disinvestment. In 2000, census data show that 87.1 percent of Central City residents were African American while 9.9 percent were white. Nearly 84 percent of the occupied housing units were renter occupied.[31] The average household income for residents in 2000 was $31,984 (in 2015 dollars), and nearly 42 percent of households reported total incomes of less than $10,000.[32] This was worlds away from the "sliver by the river."

It was in Central City that Bell continued her decades-long efforts to combat urban blight through preservation and beautification projects. She began with modest projects to enhance her surroundings in the community. For example, she tried to bring cheer to the neighborhood with Christmas decorations meticulously hung up on her home. She recalled a memorable compliment from a ten-year-old boy who deemed her holiday decorations better than any other home on the block; she remembered the boy saying to his friends as they walked by her home, "Now you see, her shit's on the map."[33] In the years that followed, she began to take on larger projects in the neighborhood, trying to save historic homes from demolition. These preservation efforts began to be recognized by influential people in the city. In 1995 Mayor Marc Morial appointed Bell to a four-year term on the Historic District Landmarks Commission, which has legal enforcement powers over the city's historic districts.[34]

In 2003 Bell bought a blighted lot from the city, cleared the yard of its weeds, and planted more than five hundred rose bushes. When Diana Pinckley introduced Bell at the NCCRW event, she highlighted Bell's garden as a sign of resilience in Katrina's wake. "All those rose bushes made it through the hurricane, though a few of them turned over," Pinckley said to the small crowd. "But she turned them back over. With Jeanette, those rose bushes figured they had no choice but to live. So they did." Bell's good fortune and pluck highlight another casualty of Katrina: many of New Orleans's parks and leisure spaces. The fierce winds had not only destroyed roofs and shattered windows but also upturned trees, including over a thousand trees in City Park.[35] Almost 90 percent of City Park was flooded, with water depths ranging from one foot to ten feet; for several weeks more than 40 percent of the park remained underwater.[36] At the New Orleans Botanical Garden, one thousand rose bushes died after sitting in floodwaters for weeks. On the other side of town near the New Orleans Country Club and the Metairie Cemetery, Longue Vue House and Gardens was flooded with murky waters from the breached 17th Street Canal.[37]

Two weeks after Hurricane Katrina, when Mayor Nagin began allowing a staggered reentry by zip code into the storm-ravaged city, Bell returned to New Orleans to check on her home and her garden. She would soon discover that she was the only person on her block, or in the whole neighborhood, for that matter. Luckily her home was spared any major damage. The flood that inundated 80 percent of the city had stopped just a few blocks away. But almost as soon as she found that her home had escaped the flood, she and the small regiment of residents who had trickled back to the city were forced to evacuate again when Hurricane Rita was reported to be heading their way. When Rita made landfall near the Texas border, parts of New Orleans reflooded, forcing an already on-edge population into yet another stage of uncertainty.

When Bell returned to New Orleans four days after Rita, she was relieved once again that her garden had been saved. As an attempt to respond to the pain around her throughout the city, she began cutting roses from her garden and passing them out to anyone and everyone who walked by: "We needed as much positive energy, given that much of our landscape had been decimated by the storm." She gave roses to Red Cross workers passing by in mobile food trucks distributing meals to those who stayed through the storm, to early returnees she encountered on the street, and to members of the Army Corps of Engineers.

Bell's work in Central City both before Katrina and in the days and weeks after the storm made her a desirable candidate for WOS participation, and at the panel discussion at Newcomb, she recalled Anne Milling's January phone call inviting her to be part of WOS. But unlike many of the women I spoke with, Bell initially hesitated. She felt stretched thin, having already committed to other projects in the city. She remembered telling Milling, "I'm sorry, I'd love to, but I don't think I can do it." Milling, not one to give up, asked her to think about it and get back to her, Bell said.

Shortly after the call, Bell told her two daughters that she was on the fence about the trip. One daughter said, "What's this vacillating about? You're the person who was out there, always on the pavement, always on the soapbox, and you're vacillating? I'm going in your place."

Bell recounted feeling floored by her daughter's insistence. "Oh, I am not at an age where I need my daughters to go and represent me! So I said, 'Well, I think I'll do it.'"

"You can call her right now," said her daughter.

"OK, I'll call her," Bell said.

"I'll wait here by the phone," said her daughter in this cross-generational showdown.

"I mean, that is what you do to your children!" Bell exclaimed to the Newcomb audience.

With help from her daughters, she began to see the connections between her nearly thirty years of work in historic preservation and the more immediate efforts to help New Orleans recover. "Because I've always been involved in neighborhoods. I think that strong cities are cities that have healthy neighborhoods," she recalled. "I've been involved in historic preservation for over thirty years. I've been involved in helping send people to Washington, send the bright people to Washington for almost forty years. I hosted a fund-raiser for a senator who was trying to unseat another senator, because I feel like having the right people in Washington makes all the difference in your hometown." She commented on the importance of law-makers visiting the city and then returned to the role her daughter played in her decision: "We have people who are coming here from all over the world and this is something that needs to be saved, and I need them to make an informed decision about the appropriations that come to New Orleans. That is why I realized that . . . well, I knew that, I just needed my daughter to come and tell me." At this point in the conversation, with her eye on the bouquets from her garden, she said, "So I just spent the last five months spreading positive energy in any way that I can."

CHAPTER 11

The Breach

Involving a visit by two important persons,
a chance encounter, and a revelation

The congressional visits by Westmoreland and Garrett, and then by dozens of House members, were major turning points for WOS. Another milestone came when senators John McCain (R-AZ) and Lindsey Graham (R-SC) visited New Orleans in March 2006. Unlike the previous visits, the McCain and Graham tour featured a WOS press conference at the 17th Street Canal levee breach in the Lakeview neighborhood. Intensifying their efforts, WOS sought to turn the visit into a media event.

WOS members and their supporters began arriving around 10 A.M. on Friday, March 10, for the press conference at 6814 Bellaire Drive, directly adjacent to the breach. The setting provided a startling backdrop. Several homes had been lifted off their foundations and dropped in the middle of the street. Blue tarps covered the roofs of homes overlooking the press conference. Behind the podium stood what would later be described as the "most photographed house in Lakeview."[1] The front porch steps led to what used to be an entrance to the home; now they led to an architectural shell, through which one could see to the home behind it. The home's interior had been exposed after floodwaters tore away the salmon pink stucco façade, revealing a chandelier that swayed ever so slightly in the wind. A red, white, and blue patriotic ribbon, like those left on roadside memorials, had been placed on what remained of the drywall. An orangeish flood line, resembling a dirty bathtub ring, stretched across its exterior walls and the plywood covering the first-floor windows. Search-and-rescue marks spray painted on plywood indicated that this home had been visited on September 22. Surrounding streets were still covered with debris, long after the floodwaters had receded.

As the crowd awaited the lawmakers' arrival, there was an unexpected turn of events. Just minutes before the senators arrived, two bright yellow school buses rounded the street corner—a vivid contrast to the devastation site, where the colors had been muted by mud and dust—and parked about two blocks down Bellaire Drive. Nearly three dozen girls, mostly white, from Academy of the Sacred Heart, dressed in school uniforms, exited the buses and gathered in front of the breached canal as part of a field trip that serendipitously coincided with the congressional visit.

This wasn't the girls' first encounter with the politics of the Katrina recovery. Two months earlier, on January 12, hundreds of Sacred Heart girls converged on Jackson Square to demand levee protection for New Orleans and coastal restoration for the Gulf Coast Region. That rally, which I observed from Decatur Street, was planned for one of President Bush's visits to the city.[2] The girls marched in circles wearing life jackets and flotation devices, shouting impromptu chants such as "For our nation, coastal restoration," "N-O-L-A, Make our levees safe today," and "Category 5 to survive." A pair held a sign reading, "We Can't All Live in a Yellow Submarine." Another sign read, "Dutch do it better." One student had affixed a construction paper fish to the bottom of her blue, green, and white plaid skirt, resembling a 1950s poodle dress. Several wore goggles; some carried paddles.

At the March 10 press conference, the girls were not accessorized with any storm-related gear, just their school uniforms. Peggy Laborde immediately approached the young women and invited them to join the press conference—to "witness the government process in action," I overheard her saying. Dressed in pink, she then led them down the once-flooded street to the press conference site at Bellaire Drive and Spencer Avenue. They stopped in the middle of the street between two destroyed homes. It was an unforeseen, cross-generational, gendered convergence on the site of loss. One WOS member I spoke with at the press conference attributed the encounter to "divine intervention." A second woman from the core leadership agreed with the explanation, saying, "I don't think there is anything else you can attribute it to." A third concurred: "It was perfect."

With the levee breach in the background, exposed pilings of the temporary floodwall rising along the horizon, trees uprooted from the violent rush of water, and Caterpillar construction equipment in the neighboring lots, Laborde welcomed the Sacred Heart girls and told them about the importance of women in community organizing. She mentioned that the girls would be the next generation to take on the task of rebuilding New Orleans and that this was their city. Then she pronounced them "Girls of the Storm." At this point, sirens signaling the approaching motorcade could be heard in the distance, and there was a great deal of movement in the crowd. One woman yelled over the sirens, "Does anybody need an umbrella that doesn't have one?" Organizers searched for extra umbrellas, which were then distributed to the women in the crowd. A few schoolgirls were given blue-tarp umbrellas and voiced their thanks; the others expressed desire for the prized possession. This scene marked a particularly gendered event; none of the men at the press conference held an umbrella, not the male civic or business leaders and not the local politicians who arrived to publicly align themselves with WOS, including New Orleans city councilman Jay Batt.[3]

The crowd included veteran members as well as newcomers and supporters who had read about WOS's actions in the local paper.[4] Members of the reform group Citizens for One Greater New Orleans and Katrina Krewe were also in attendance, demonstrating some overlapping membership. Many women wore fleur-de-lis pins or "Rebuild NOLA" shirts. In a performative reference to the storm's destruction, one participant appeared on the scene dressed in a T-shirt and bright yellow rubber boots, a sharp contrast to her normal business attire. Most of those with existing ties to the group wore WOS pins on their lapels.

As the motorcade approached from Robert E. Lee Boulevard and drove toward the breach, the schoolgirls shouted at one another to make room for the vehicles: "Back up! Back up!" When McCain and Graham arrived, having spent the day with their tour guides, Louisiana senator David Vitter and his wife, Wendy Vitter, they shook hands with people in the crowd while making their way to the podium.[5] As the press conference began, the women unfurled their umbrellas. "We have to get started, we have to get started," said some of the organizers, trying to stick to the schedule. They did not want to lose a single moment with the lawmakers. Anne Milling interjected, "We're taking them to the breach." The senators were surrounded by the schoolgirls, shaking hands and posing for photos, before being led by Milling and members from the National Guard to be briefed about the levee breaches by representatives from the Army Corps of Engineers.[6] The crowd followed the senators through a security fence surrounding the worksite, ascended the canal's embankment, and eventually stood on the rocky ground that filled the levee breach. As the senators listened to the engineers, the women, in an improvised action, ascended the levee and encircled the elected officials. The senators stood between the exposed pilings of the once-breached levee and a crescent formed by women with open blue-tarp umbrellas.

FIGURE 6. Women of the Storm's press conference at the 17th Street Canal levee breach, March 10, 2006. Photograph by the author.

After the briefing, the senators and the crowd descended the levee and gathered near the podium. Wendy Vitter opened the press conference by thanking the lawmakers "for coming to see what is our national disaster." McCain approached the podium and thanked the politicians, the schoolgirls, and WOS. Then he said, "You cannot appreciate the enormity of it until you see it. I know that has been said a thousand times already by previous visitors, but it still remains true and needs to be repeated." McCain continued: "The president was very clear when he visited here just a short time ago about his support for additional funding. I support the president."[7]

"Yeah, I support the president, too!" shouted one WOS participant. "Yay, George Bush, I love the president!" This participant, whom another interviewee described as "very flamboyant," was immediately reprimanded by nearby group members. "We're supposed to be nonpartisan, nonpolitical. We're not supposed to do that!" said another woman, who remembered the collective response to this audience member's political outburst. In moments like these, when unstated rules were broken, group members were swift to police each other.

Anne Milling concluded by issuing a request to McCain and Graham: "We have a favor to ask of you. We ask both of you to return to our nation's capital, to encourage your peers to accept the invitation of the Women of the Storm to come and do exactly what you have done today. Secondly, we urge you to be ever mindful that a national disaster has occurred and, in our opinion, we deserve a national response."[8] Immediately after the press conference, as the women discussed the senators' remarks, one in the core leadership commented, "It couldn't have gone better. They said all the right things." And another participant told me, "The one thing, and you were there, that needs to be said, and John McCain said it, is, 'You can't believe it until you see it.' And he didn't see half of it. The vastness of it is the thing, the wide expanse is what people don't get." Another reflected on McCain's visits: "I think he will do wonders for us. I think he will go back up to Washington, explaining to people, to congressmen, that they have to come down. I think that was one of the best people to have gotten down here."

In their interviews with me, many referred to this event as particularly meaningful. It recharged group sentiments, clarified a sense of political and civic commitment, and confirmed that their actions in Washington were making a difference. One of the older women in the audience, a white woman in her seventies who had been assigned to visit McCain during the Washington trip, was thrilled that he had visited New Orleans: "I was at a meeting at Anne's house, a garden club meeting, and she said, 'John McCain's coming,' and I said, 'Yippee! That's my man!'" She continued by clarifying a little: "Not really my man, but my man because I went to see his aide. I played a teeny little part in it." Others were moved by the chance encounter with the girls. A white woman in her sixties told me, "When I saw those Sacred Heart girls, I said, 'Now I understand why we're here.' It was just a revelation. I kept thinking, we're gonna be working so hard and we're gonna try to do this. I'll

FIGURE 7. After Women of the Storm's press conference, March 10, 2006. Photograph by the author.

be a hundred and ten when I see this. But then I saw the kids, and it reminded me about my daughter and her child and everybody else who has kids. It's for them."

In addition to the visual evidence, the stories of loss were a crucial part of McCain and Graham's visit. As one reporter commented, "Debby Landry, a Lakeview resident and member of Women of the Storm, told McCain her three-bedroom home a few blocks away was completely flooded, and that she has lived in a FEMA trailer for the past few months. The homes of her parents and children also were damaged by the flood. 'We lost everything,' Landry said through tears as she hugged McCain. 'We have no family home. We have no family home.'"[9]

McCain and Graham appeared to be sympathetic to WOS's cause and the plight of New Orleans. But not all lawmakers were entirely moved by the group's tours. After completing a disaster tour in New Orleans, Representative Hensarling told reporters, "The camera lens doesn't do it justice." But he maintained the skeptical attitude, saying he wasn't entirely convinced that there was a unified plan across levels of government, despite the women's attempts to have recovery leaders confirm that various levels of government and civic and business leaders were on the same page. "I saw public officials who took very little responsibility [for failures in responding to the hurricane] and are looking for large checks from the federal government," he said. "Where's the plan? Where's the accountability? What is the city doing? What is the state doing? Those able-bodied individuals under 65, what are they doing to help themselves?"[10]

Hensarling was not alone in expressing skepticism. During a Senate Appropriations Committee hearing in early March, Sen. Bob Bennett (R-UT), for example, questioned allocating funds to rebuild New Orleans, which he described as "a place that the laws of physics say doesn't make sense for people to live in." Bennett, who had yet to visit New Orleans, went on to say, "Building a city 10 feet below sea level does not strike me as inherently, basically a good idea. If someone makes a really stupid decision in the name of nostalgia that we want to rebuild this neighborhood just like it was, maybe Katrina said to us, you don't want a neighborhood there."[11] When asked by a journalist about Bennett's remarks, Mary Landrieu responded, "It is not nostalgia that motivates us to rebuild. It is common sense and in our nation's best interest to revitalize this great city. Its seaport, trade gateway, and hub for the energy resources necessary to keep Americans from freezing this winter are all essential to our nation. Senator Bennett owes the people of New Orleans a visit and an apology."[12]

On March 23 Milling reminded participants to continue contacting Washington: "Ladies . . . once again we ask you to 'nag' your representatives. . . . Since storming the capital on Jan. 30 . . . about 45 representatives have come."[13] The tragedy of Katrina was an ongoing challenge for residents of New Orleans, and the strain and emotional toil seemed to be unending. The day after Milling reminded the women to have ongoing contact with lawmakers, two more bodies were found in the Lower Ninth Ward.[14]

Besides Newcomb, many other educational institutions were also calling on WOS members to share their stories. For example, a WOS member, along with representatives of Katrina Krewe and Citizens for One Greater New Orleans, spoke about their participation in the recovery at the elite Louise S. McGehee School on the occasion of its annual Founder's Day event.

I had the opportunity to attend this event, and I must have stood out like a sore thumb. Upon my arrival, an assistant to McGehee School headmistress Eileen Powers said to me, "You're not alumna," before darting away to photograph arriving guests. A WOS participant had invited me to attend the event before our scheduled interview later that day. I made my way into the assembly room of the school's main building, a massive Italianate villa built in 1872 for Bradish Johnson, one of Louisiana's richest and most powerful men both before and after the Civil War.[15] I sat down near the back of the assembly room, behind rows and rows of mostly white school girls (and due to Katrina, a few boys who were attending the school temporarily). McGehee alumna, both middle-age and older women, many of them parents and grandparents of the girls, began arriving. Some chatted outside on the elevated porch that overlooked Prytania Street.

Gatherings like these were increasingly common in post-Katrina New Orleans, an effort to return to normal. But life was still raw. The events still seemed very close, and residents seemed to require an acknowledgment of their collective loss and the struggles to move forward.

After an introduction from the McGehee student body president, the girls sang a piano-led rendition of "America the Beautiful," followed by the collective reciting of the Pledge of Allegiance. The headmistress approached the podium and held up a wooden plaque embossed with the word "Believe," which she said she had purchased for fifteen dollars at a Steinmart in Houston during her evacuation. She said it had served as a source of inspiration and reminded her of the need to reopen the school as soon as possible. She addressed the girls and alumna:

> As we commemorate our ninety-fourth year . . . we want to recognize these women in the McGehee community, all of the women who have taken a leadership role in the rebuilding of New Orleans. For close to a century, Louise S. McGehee School has graduated young women who know what it means to be leaders and who are ready to take charge of their futures. Now more than ever before, it is critical that our girls understand that they can do anything because at McGehee, girls fill every role—math whiz, sports star and community activist! [16]

The assembly continued with words by Ruthie Jones Frierson, class of 1958, who had formed Citizens for One Greater New Orleans in Katrina's wake and traveled to Washington, D.C., with WOS, demonstrating that the group drew upon women from similar social circles. She told the story of the emergence of her group, known colloquially as the "Ladies in Red," many of whom sat in red blazers in the audience. Frierson was followed by Becky Zaheri, founder of Katrina Krewe, and then by Jill Nalty, a WOS participant and mother of two girls at McGehee, who spoke about the trip to Washington.

By March 2006 WOS's educational outreach was taking place mostly in areas such as the Garden District and Uptown and in places like McGehee, Loyola, and Tulane. Very little, if any, work was being done in educational institutions that served racial and ethnic minorities. In one of G. William Domhoff's many analyses of the ruling class, he notes that "private schools" serve as an "important avenue through which the upper class infuses new blood into its ranks."[17] This can be seen not only in the strictly educational aspects of such schools (McGehee's website boasts about French instruction beginning in pre-kindergarten classes and the Latin requirement for middle schoolers), or the friendship networks that develop among students, but also in events like the assembly at McGehee, which give students a model for engaging in philanthropy and civic activism in ways that are proper for their class. The "new blood" here includes the children of New Orleans's elite attending the school along with the aspirational students on financial aid who, with the school's training and extracurricular activities, may one day enter the elite.

CHAPTER 12

Going National

*In which several women's organizations lend
support for the resurrection of New Orleans*

On Sunday, March 26, Milling e-mailed WOS participants to announce a newly
formed partnership with four national women's organizations: Association of Junior
Leagues International, the National Council of Jewish Women, The Links, and the
Women's Initiative of the United Way. Milling wrote, "We are going from a humble
force of the initial 130 women who flew to D.C. on Jan. 30 to over 275,000 women!!!
Indeed this will make a huge difference . . . and hopefully no longer will anyone
in the United States Congress ignore our invitation. . . . Now we have soul mates
throughout America who believe as we do . . . the leadership of the United States
must see the devastation."[1] These partnerships signal an important shift in WOS's
organizational structure. No longer an emergent group, WOS began to resemble
what disaster sociologists have characterized as an "expanding organization."[2] The
tasks or group goals remained the same (most importantly, inviting members of
Congress to visit the destruction), and the structure and membership grew, at least
in theory. Whether or not many of these hundreds of thousands of women made
calls on WOS's behalf is not the point, although members of the group's steering
committee had every hope that this would happen. This partnership enabled the
women who did take action to say they were speaking for a larger constituency that
was spread across the country. They believed lawmakers would have a harder time
saying no to their own constituents. These new allies also contributed to WOS's
mobilization of images of diversity to bolster claims about values the group considered important.

For the steering committee, this shift in numbers seemed like a good occasion
for another public event. On Wednesday, March 29, several core members held a
press conference in Washington to announce the endorsement by the four women's

organizations. A *Times-Picayune* editorial observed that WOS was "getting some reinforcements. Lots of reinforcements."[3] The editorial praised the partnerships, saying, "If the women elsewhere are even remotely as energetic and organized as the Women of the Storm, this community will be in much better shape in no time."[4]

Pledging support for WOS's cause, leaders from each of the four organizations released statements that called on lawmakers to accept the group's invitation. For example, Stacy Kass, executive director of the National Council of Jewish Women, urged representatives in Washington "to walk the walk—to make the trip to Louisiana."[5] Emphasizing women's solidarity, Gladys Gary Vaughn, national president of The Links, made the following statement: "The Links, Incorporated understands the importance of working together and the necessity of collaborating with like-minded organizations to strongly urge Members of Congress to tour metropolitan New Orleans, pass legislation to rebuild the Gulf Coast Region, and protect our most vulnerable citizens. . . . Congress must make this journey in order to experience the needs of the people." Statements by Anne Stallard, chair of the National Women's Leadership Council, United Way, and Pam Newby, president of the Association of Junior Leagues, expressed similar sentiments.[6] Each pledge commented on the importance of accepting the invitation, and there were great hopes that these national partnerships would increase the number of congressional visits. According to WOS's count of visits at the time of the partnerships, only thirteen senators and forty-two representatives had accepted their invitation.[7]

Some New Orleanians were taking note of WOS's progress. In the *Times-Picayune*, Nathan Jones described WOS's activities as a "refreshing" alternative to local government, which he saw as only focused on "restoring its lost slice of the pie." Jones continued: "These brilliant women have swooped in to do what others could not: Bring federal lawmakers to Louisiana." Then, after commenting on the new partnerships with national organizations, Jones said, "The new sets of issues they're tackling makes me want to ask 'Is there a MEN of the Storm I can join?'"[8]

There were other big changes taking place on the heels of WOS's announcement about going national. The group was also going online. Whereas other emergent groups, such as Citizens for One Greater New Orleans, were able to launch websites within days of forming, it took WOS nearly two months to create a virtual presence. On March 29 WOS's website went live, thanks to the work of Diana Pinckley, a former director of public relations at Tulane University, who would become central to WOS's newly formed media subcommittee.[9] It might be surprising to learn that it took so long for WOS to develop a website. But these details reveal much about how WOS operated in its early existence.

In its early days WOS relied heavily on direct contact and communications—face-to-face meetings, phone calls, and even e-mail, faxes, and handwritten notes—and there wasn't an immediate concern for establishing a web presence to increase their sphere of influence. That all changed when WOS members realized they had missed a great opportunity to mobilize the national media during the 2006 Carnival season. Several members believed their message was so clear and their cause so compelling that the media would simply jump at the opportunity to give them coverage during Mardi Gras. After listing a number of news outlets—CNN, Fox, *Good Morning America*, the *Today* show—that were in town for Carnival, one woman said, "We had a captive audience. The entire world was watching on Mardi Gras day, and we didn't get on [the major networks]. And if we could have gotten on and said, for three minutes, 'Women of the Storm. All we're doing is trying to get the legislature to come down here. You tell everybody in your city and state to accept the invitation of the Women of the Storm.' Stupid that we weren't on." While group members did appear on CNN, they felt their voices were noticeably absent in other venues. At that point it was decided—"We need a media committee," as one woman recalled with frustration, and a website was part of this initiative. This moment of organizational self-reflection reveals that participants evaluated their work in relation to their larger goals, reflecting on past actions and missed opportunities, and sought to make changes to work more effectively.

The exponential increase in members allowed WOS to make strategic claims, both in person and on their newly formed website, about widespread support from across the nation, bolstering the claim that their cause was not just local but indeed national. Yet the everyday workload fell largely on the shoulders of the core leadership, a tiny group by any measure. Their calendars were completely full, and there was little time for leisure. By April 2006, WOS had adopted a polished routine, although the ongoing work of planning and coordinating so many moving parts meant much time was spent attending to details, including a visit on April 7 by Sen. George Allen (R-VA), a potential 2008 presidential candidate and longtime supporter of plans to expand offshore drilling. The morning of the planned visit, Allen announced that he would have to reschedule his trip to New Orleans due to a pressing immigration vote, adding, "I remain deeply interested in touring the city of New Orleans to observe the recovery process that's all underway and where they can improve as we make continuing recovery decisions."[10]

While some lawmakers would cancel their trips, others made their visits as planned. During the week of April 17 alone, WOS hosted three separate though nearly overlapping visits by lawmakers: Sen. Harry Reid on Monday, April 17; Sen. Blanche Lincoln (D-AR) and Sen. Maria Cantwell (D-WA) on April 20; and Donald Powell on Friday, April 21.[11] The core met regularly, and the newly formed media committee, led by Pinckley, had begun to deal with a number of press requests and to work on the website, documenting its past actions and posting testimonials from lawmakers. Members also accepted invitations to speak at local schools and to give presentations to various organizations visiting the city to volunteer. They fielded a wide range of requests and proposals—for example, a woman called to propose the idea of "Students of the Storm," to pressure elected officials with student letter-writing campaigns modeled on the women's efforts.

At the time, New Orleans was facing a contentious mayoral race. On April 1 thousands of residents marched across the Crescent City Connection Bridge towering over the Mississippi River, demanding that local elections be postponed. Critics such as Jesse Jackson and Al Sharpton rallied protesters in an effort to protect the voting rights of residents displaced by Katrina, arguing that satellite polling places be set up in cities outside of New Orleans.[12] While the political climate was intensely focused on issues of race and class, gender was central to voter turnout. Early reports of voting in the first mayoral race after Katrina showed women making up nearly two-thirds of the early voters, which Beth Willinger, a research professor at Tulane, attributed to the fact that so many women still hadn't returned to the city.[13] In this context WOS steered clear of local politics, although many members were active in political campaigns. The emphasis on being "nonpartisan and nonpolitical" meant refusing to endorse specific mayoral candidates. Instead, WOS maintained its focus on bringing members of Congress to New Orleans. In late April, Milling updated the membership on the number of visits: "We're delighted to announce that to date 47 senators have visited and 87 members of the House of Representatives. . . . To keep you informed about your assignments, attached is the latest list of those who have been here."[14]

On May 6, Marie Corinne Morrison Claiborne, better known as Lindy Boggs, U.S. Representative (D-LA) from 1973 to 1991 and the first woman to serve as U.S. ambassador to the Vatican, a post she held from 1997 to 2001, was awarded the Congressional Distinguished Service Award, an honor given to former members of Congress for their public service and commitment to democracy and freedom. After being introduced by Sen. Barbara Mikulski (D-MD) at the awards ceremony in Washington, Boggs used her acceptance speech to reissue WOS's invitation:

> I would like to extend a personal invitation, on behalf of the Women of the Storm, to those of you who have not yet come to New Orleans and the region to see firsthand the devastation, which exists still eight months after Hurricanes Katrina and Rita. . . . We need your continued help and support in rebuilding our levees, our economy, and our community and in healing our families. I deeply appreciate this honor and sincerely hope that you will honor my invitation. It is a very special city and there are many wonderful people there who are proud to call it home. Please come down to New Orleans and of course come to see me in my funny old home when you do.[15]

Boggs's request was another instance of using politeness in political ways, extending a seemingly benign invitation that was in fact a powerful demand.

CHAPTER 13

Storm Warnings

Containing a brief account of a media event

In late May, WOS met to consider how the June 1 start of the Atlantic hurricane season could be used to refocus national attention on its mission. Just the idea of another hurricane season evoked visceral reactions of fear and anxiety for many residents who had survived the destruction of the previous storm season. It reminded them that New Orleans remained vulnerable. During one brainstorming session about a possible event, many proposals were put forward, including a march through the streets of New Orleans, but this potential action was shot down immediately. Referring to the summer heat, and suggesting that street actions were out of the question, one woman exclaimed, "I am not going to march!" Another idea was much more grandiose: WOS could organize a flotilla along the Louisiana coast. According to this plan, a fleet of boats, positioned at nightfall at a particular distance from the shore to represent the amount of wetlands lost to coastal erosion, would shine bright, industrial-grade lights into the sky. The action would be photographed by satellite and the images circulated worldwide to garner attention to coastal issues. There was a positive response to this idea until one member cautioned that the whole production might look "elitist," too spectacular and too wasteful; the plan was abandoned. More ideas were generated until WOS finally settled on the action that they would go on to name "Storm Warnings II."

It was yet another highly orchestrated media event, which the women held in the Tad Gormley Stadium in New Orleans's City Park.[1] WOS, along with AWF, mapped congressional visits and absences on a football field–size map of the United States. States that had at least one elected official visit were covered with blue tarps, and silver tarps covered states that had no members visit since the storm. The football field represented the rapid loss of coastal Louisiana, which was washing away at the

FIGURE 8. Storm Warnings II, June 1, 2006. Photograph by the author.

rate of one hundred yards—the size of a football field—every thirty to thirty-eight minutes, making the area more vulnerable to floods and storm surge impacts.[2]

The event included music by the Soul Rebels Brass Band, as well as singer Jep Epstein, who performed "Our Home, Louisiana," a song he had composed after Hurricane Katrina. When the program began, the stadium was nearly empty. About seventy-five audience members sat between two huge banners with the words "Levees 5," which referred to levee protection able to withstand a Category 5 hurricane. Garland Robinette, a host on local radio station WWL, gave a welcome address, in which he called not just for enhanced flood protection but also for action against the loss of wetlands. A moment of silence was held for those who had lost their lives, homes, and businesses during Katrina. Robinette said, "Today we gather here in a football stadium to bring to light the fact that Louisiana loses [pause]. Now, this I don't think people really believe. But take a good look at this football field. Every 30 minutes, every 30 minutes. If this were in Boston, Manhattan, San Francisco, if you lost one football field in a day, it would make worldwide news. We lose one of these every 30 minutes. We are losing a football field every 30 minutes. That has got to stop."[3]

Then Milling spoke: "We are a group of approximately 300 women from metropolitan New Orleans. Our mission is a simple one, from the get-go. Fill in the blanks." The map of the United States became a stage on which the women would dramatize the number of members of Congress who had visited post-Katrina New Orleans. Anne Milling stated, "While we thank the Members of Congress who have visited and gained an understanding of our plight, we remain shocked that 400 U.S. Senators and Representatives have not found the time to visit the site of the worst natural disaster ever to strike our nation." At the time of the event, 135 members of Congress had visited, but "seven states [had] yet to send a single member of their Congressional delegations to the devastated region, while 21 states [had] not sent a senator and 19 states [had] not sent a member of the House of Representatives."[4]

Milling read a list of the fifty states in alphabetical order over a loudspeaker and reported for each state the number of senators and representatives who had visited and the number yet to come. Like ritual chanting, Milling's reading relied on rhythmic, stylized speech.[5] When a state was called out, several women walked to its place on the map, opened their blue-tarp umbrellas, and stood silently before the small crowd and cameras. At one point during a planned helicopter flyover, the women dispersed to cover each state, thus symbolically tying themselves, and Louisiana, to the nation. As the band played and the helicopter swooped overhead, the women collectively raised the blue-tarp umbrellas to the sky. Unlike the solemn performative unfurling on Capitol Hill, the women popped and twirled their umbrellas in second-line style.

WOS also drew upon symbols that had cut deeply into the city's body politic. On each state, the tarp was marked with the search-and-rescue marks that covered homes across the region and served as vivid reminders of the storm. It is important to note the weight of these symbols at the time of the June 1 event; decaying bodies were still being found in the wreckage, and even two months after this event, remains of what was believed to be yet another Katrina victim were discovered under piles of debris.[6] The X-shaped markings reflected an organized effort to account for human life during Katrina and contained information on the date of the search (top quadrant), the search-and-rescue team (left quadrant), the number of living people found upon entry (right quadrant), and the number of dead, if any, at that location (bottom quadrant). In their presentation, WOS transformed the search-and-rescue marks, as well as the blue tarps, as part of their goal of communicating visually the number of congressional visits to the city. The top quadrant of the X indicated the state's abbreviation; the number on the left communicated the number of members of the Senate that had visited; on the right were the number of House members; and on the bottom quadrant, the total number from each state yet to visit.

Local media covered the action and interviewed several participants. During the event, WOS criticized members of Congress from six states that had yet to send lawmakers to visit, including Senator Bennett from Utah. Peggy Laborde said, "Our mission is not completed. We will not give up. We are relentless. I got news for them—they've just met their match."[7]

The following day, June 2, the U.S. Army Corps of Engineers accepted some responsibility for the condition of the levees before Katrina and, at the same time, made a public statement that the city remained at risk of flooding from future hurricanes. Kathleen Blanco, who spoke at the event, discussed the historic adoption of a comprehensive master plan for coastal restoration and hurricane protection, and she used the opportunity to pressure the federal government to support oil and gas revenue sharing for Louisiana. Blanco, like Mary Landrieu, WOS, and many others, argued for a 50 percent share of royalties to be distributed among oil-producing states with coasts along the Gulf of Mexico.[8] She threatened to block a massive August 16 sale of oil and gas leases in the western Gulf of Mexico, which in August 2005 had brought in $283 million for the federal government's general fund, none of which went to Louisiana. "I definitely mean business," Blanco said. "Some may view this as an idle threat. They shouldn't. I will stand firm. I will not back down."[9]

Although WOS's events at the beginning of June focused attention on as-yet-unachieved goals, the next few weeks were marked by some significant successes. On June 8, for example, the Senate reached agreement on a $94.5 billion emergency supplemental spending bill that included $4.2 billion for housing recovery programs and $3.7 billion for levee upgrades.[10] On June 13 Milling invited participants to her house to write thank-you notes to lawmakers. Although these letters acknowledged lawmakers' support of some of WOS's primary goals, the women had no intention of disbanding, especially with the issue of revenue sharing still on the table. There was still work to be done.

Throughout the summer, trips to visit the devastation were becoming almost mandatory for politicians considering a 2008 White House bid. Brian Brox, a political science professor at Tulane University, said, "If you are going to be a serious, credible politician, you are going to have to be able to talk intelligently about what Katrina did to this region, and the first step in that is going to be to come and visit now."[11] In late June, just a few weeks after Storm Warnings II, two potential 2008 presidential candidates, Sen. Evan Bayh (D-IN) and Sen. George Allen, who had canceled his April trip, toured the city with Landrieu and Vitter and met with business leaders to talk about wetlands restoration. After touring the Lower Ninth Ward and St. Bernard Parish, Allen, wearing what one journalist described as his "signature cowboy boots," was reported to have said, "It's just so heartbreaking. If this were a carpet-bombing in a war, you couldn't have more devastation."[12] The trip culminated in a press conference just one hundred feet from one of the levee breaches.[13]

The one-year anniversary of Katrina was approaching, so in late summer WOS began to consider another potential action. In the meantime, as more residents came back to the city, group members began involving themselves in normal activities tied to their pre-storm lives. For example, on July 13 WOS core member Nancy Marsiglia, along with Barbara Turner, spent time packing hundreds of children's books for distribution to eighteen child-care centers as part of a project of the Women's Leadership Initiative of the United Way.[14] Two days later, reporters observed that WOS had reason to "take Utah off its hate list."[15] Sen. Bob Bennett, the outspoken Utah lawmaker who, like Hastert, had questioned rebuilding New Orleans, and Senate Majority Whip Mitch McConnell (R-KY), made a weekend visit to the disaster zone at WOS's invitation. During the trip, they received a briefing by civic and business leaders in the McIlhenny Company's Tabasco boardroom on the eighteenth floor of One Shell Square on Poydras Street in New Orleans's Central Business District.[16] After touring New Orleans, Bennett told reporters at the *Deseret News*, a Salt Lake City newspaper, "I always understood how devastating it was, but there is nothing quite like seeing it firsthand."[17] WOS had once again succeeded in convincing a reluctant lawmaker to accept its invitation.

WOS members were pleased. Donna Fraiche, a member of WOS and the LRA, told the *Salt Lake Tribune*, "It's one thing to see it on CNN and talk about it on the Hill. It's another thing to walk the walk."[18] Speaking about touring uninhabited neighborhoods and echoing WOS's language, Bennett said, "I should have realized it's as big as it is, but when you're driving through the streets, street after street after street, you realize the scope. . . . It's eerie to see the same flood line on every house in the neighborhood. Floodwaters actually were higher than the rooftops, but the floods settled to a point 3 or 3½ feet high and stayed there for months—and that is the mark you see."[19] Then he offered remarks about razing the damaged housing: "My instinct is to bulldoze it and start over again."[20] In a significant departure from earlier words about not rebuilding the city, Bennett remarked, "By no means do I support letting it wash away and forget it." He qualified his position by adding, "There may be places that should not be rebuilt. Don't just automatically assume that everything that was has to be rebuilt the same way."[21] Bennett, a Senate Appropriations Committee member, noted that the federal government had thus far spent or approved $50 billion for the Katrina recovery. He added, "They certainly have enough money for now, and didn't ask for any more money—for now—although they reserved the right to do so in the future."[22]

Counting the trip by senators Bennett and McConnell, WOS had brought to New Orleans at least one lawmaker from every state except New Hampshire, North Dakota, West Virginia, and Wisconsin.[23] WOS's organizational structure was in place, and the recent successes had given them political legitimacy. Another high-profile visit came in late July, when Sen. Barack Obama (D-IL), another presidential hopeful, made his first trip to post-Katrina New Orleans, becoming the fifty-fifth U.S. senator to tour the disaster zone. It was also his first trip to the city; he stated that he had never had the occasion to be there and didn't want to visit too soon after the storm for fear of appearing too political. At Louis Armstrong International Airport, on Friday, July 21, Obama, who made the trip with Sen. John Kerry (D-MA), was greeted by Landrieu and several WOS members. Later that day, like other politicians before him, Obama rolled up his sleeves and picked up a brush and blue paint to engage in relief work; Kerry gave a speech in the Upper Ninth Ward; and Hastert led an eleven-member delegation to survey the recovery in Lake Charles, an area hit hard by Hurricane Rita. Obama then took a two-hour city tour in a white van with Capt. Michael Benoit, of the Louisiana National Guard, prompting Obama to say, "I've never seen something that stretches so far in every direction. You are awestruck. To see mile after mile of abandoned homes and businesses is remarkable."[24]

WOS's goal to have every member of Congress visit New Orleans remained unfulfilled, and thus the women's efforts continued. And as the one-year anniversary of Katrina neared, WOS's confidence grew, as reflected by even more ambitious initiatives, including a second trip to Washington.

CHAPTER 14

Women of the Storm Return

*Involving another trip to Washington
and some concrete achievements*

At the one-year anniversary of Hurricane Katrina, roughly 181,000 people were living in New Orleans. The repopulation was racialized: the city's black population had decreased by 57 percent, while the white population dropped by only 36 percent.[1] The post-Katrina population was also older, more educated, and more affluent than pre-Katrina, and its households were more likely to be childless.[2] Households with children under eighteen years old returned at lower rates than any other type of household, although households headed by women with or without children under eighteen also had low rates of return.[3] The storm had additional differential impacts that varied by gender, especially with respect to earnings. After Katrina, while men's earnings rose—around 20 percent—earnings and employment opportunities for women worsened. Sociologists Beth Willinger and Janna Knight found that in the year after the storm, "the significant increase in men's median annual earnings was largely attributed to the earnings of white men (up 46 percent), while the decrease in women's wages fell largely on black/African American women (down 14.4 percent). It took nearly three years before this would stabilize."[4]

On the eve of the first Katrina anniversary, WOS claimed that only one-third of the 535 members of Congress had accepted their invitation to visit—55 senators and 123 of 435 representatives.[5] In its first year of existence, WOS's efforts had limited success. But the sense of abandonment was still quite profound, and members continued to pressure lawmakers to visit. Over the summer, the group had been soliciting donations through personal requests and phone calls, seeking to raise funds for another trip to Washington to spotlight the Katrina recovery and focus attention on coastal issues. By September 8 the fund-raising for the trip was already complete. "Finished with that," Milling told one reporter.[6] She went on to say, "We've been doing our homework for the last six to eight months. We feel that we're stronger and wiser and more knowledgeable. When we went initially we were 130 novices. Now we've learned a great deal, and we're all totally confident knocking on any door of any member of Congress."[7] With this newfound confidence and sizable donations in hand, WOS decided that it was time to return to Washington. At this point WOS was becoming more like an established organization and less like an emergent group; their beliefs and organizational structures had become more and more fixed.

As WOS prepared for its second trip to Washington, every state except New Hampshire had sent at least one member of its delegation to see the destruction. Among the lawmakers who had not made the visit were two with immense political clout: California Republican representative Jerry Lewis and Wisconsin Democratic representative David Obey, both members of the House Appropriations Committee. And despite the claim that the legislators in the region were all supportive of a unified rebuilding plan, several senators from Gulf Coast states had not accepted WOS's invitation, including Alabama Republican Jeff Sessions, Florida Republican Mel Martinez, and Florida Democrat Bill Nelson.[8]

The WOS core leadership called upon many of the participants who had gone on the January 2006 trip and invited them to participate in the group's second visit to Washington. The vast majority obliged, but others were unable or perhaps unwilling to attend. New individuals were then invited to participate in their place. On September 14, about a week before the trip, a list of three talking points was sent to the group to use in their conversations with lawmakers. First, the group was encouraged to thank Congress for providing billions of dollars for the Gulf Coast recovery, including funds for levee repair and upgrades, infrastructure improvements, and the housing recovery plan known as the Road Home Program. Second, the group was instructed to target lawmakers who had yet to visit by reissuing the invitation to see the progress that had been made as well as the disaster-related challenges that remained. Finally, the group was to stress what was now considered its most critical issue: the sharing of royalties from oil and gas exploration in the Gulf Coast's Outer Continental Shelf (OCS) and the use of those funds for coastal restoration. The talking points provided statistics about Louisiana's oil and gas production, its seafood industries, and its coastal erosion. The group was to propose a solution, which included a request for $15 billion over the next twenty years for massive restoration projects of the barrier islands and the wetlands, which included a proposal to redirect parts of the Mississippi River. The talking points also listed two pending bills in Congress, both related to revenue sharing, one of which proposed opening up over eight million acres in the Gulf of Mexico to new drilling. The document concluded by saying that the group endorsed neither bill; however, they framed themselves as "proponents of coastal restoration and the receipt of a percentage of the oil and gas royalties." This third point, the group's primary objective for the second trip, was accompanied by a parenthetical note:

"Ladies ... This is the most significant message as you meet with members of the U.S. Congress!"[9]

On September 20, a month after the Katrina anniversary and just before the first anniversary of Hurricane Rita, WOS made its second trip to Washington, and I traveled with the group to and from New Orleans on the chartered plane. Everyone met at Louis Armstrong International Airport at 5:45 A.M. and departed for Washington soon thereafter. More than 130 women were on the plane, whose seventy-thousand-dollar rental cost was funded in part by contributions from sources who remained unidentified at the time.[10] In the months leading up to the second trip, the group's general ledger, now found in the Newcomb archives, registered contributions into the WOS Fund, administered by the GNOF, from numerous banks, corporations, and foundations, including Shaw Construction ($5,000), Whitney National Bank ($10,000), the Almar Foundation ($10,000), Capital One/Hibernia ($10,000), Tidewater ($25,000), J. P. Morgan/Chase ($10,000), Regions Bank ($5,000), Superior Energy ($5,000), and Entergy ($50,000).[11]

One journalist noted that roughly two-thirds of participants had been on the first WOS trip in January.[12] Indeed, according to internal WOS documents, at least eighty of the women had participated in both trips, with about fifty others participating for the first time. Many of the women discussed in this book, including Jeanette Bell, Barbara Blackwell, Pam Bryan, Marvalene Hughes, Cecile Tebo, and Beverly Wright, were on the second trip. Others, such as Sharon Alexis, Olivia Manning, Sister Anne Marie Kim-Khuong, and Sister An Nguyen, were not.[13]

As the plane descended on Washington, the core committee moved to the front of the plane near WOS's most prominent passengers assigned to seats in first class—Rose Campagna, Alva Chase, Leah Chase, Bonnie Conway, Joan Coulter, Sybil Favrot, Marvalene Hughes, Gloria Kabacoff, Verna Landrieu, Betty McDermott, Catherine Packer, Joyce Pulitzer, Sandra Rhodes Duncan, Alexis Robinson, Valerie Sholes, and Nicole Spangenberg—where they began a last-minute recap of WOS's agenda over the plane's intercom system.[14] Pam Bryan told the women, "Don't hesitate to be dramatic. What we're asking for is $15 billion. When you think about it, that's not a lot of money. Don't be afraid to ask for that. Please pass on the sense of urgency ... that we need this money now!"[15]

Just as in January 2006, drama and public performances were an important part of the visit. WOS held another press conference, with speeches by Landrieu and Vitter, where members again unfurled their trademark blue-tarp umbrellas. Once again they split into twos and threes, often as interracial groups, and spent the day extending, and at times reissuing, invitations to the 45 senators and 329 representatives who had yet to visit New Orleans a year after the devastating storm. They also invited members to a screening that evening of a documentary about coastal erosion, giving them a small admittance ticket that made the showing seem like a special event.[16]

But on this trip something was different. Many lawmakers immediately recognized the group of women, and more time was spent discussing issues rather than

FIGURE 9. Gloria Kabacoff, Betty McDermott, U.S. Senator Mary Landrieu, and Landrieu's mother, Verna Landrieu (*left to right*), greet one another before a press conference on September 20, 2006, in Washington, D.C. Getty Images/Chip Somodevilla.

explaining who they were. The trip's late-September timing was important because WOS aimed to convey their message before Congress took action on the issue of OCS revenue sharing and coastal restoration before the October 6 recess.

Even more than the first trip, this was a statewide effort. Representing southwest Louisiana, the area hit by Hurricane Rita, which often remained in Katrina's shadow, were women like Sharon Bergeron of Houma and Myrna Connor of lower Cameron Parish, whose home was destroyed by Rita and who was reluctant to rebuild without increased storm protection and coastal restoration. Demonstrating her personal investment in the trip, Connor said, "If we don't do anything about coastal restoration, the shoreline will be at my new home." Echoing Connor's concerns, Bergeron said, "Our issue is we have no hurricane protection, none. We've been waiting and waiting and waiting."[17]

Anne Milling and her partner Rita Benson LeBlanc met with Sen. Hillary Clinton. The twenty-nine-year-old LeBlanc was executive vice president and co-owner of the New Orleans Saints (with her billionaire grandfather, Tom Benson), only one of five women owners in the NFL. LeBlanc was a spirited advocate of the city's football team, saying that "the health of the [city's] economy is directly tied to our [the Saints] health."[18] One of WOS's youngest participants, LeBlanc would use her football connections to help support WOS's causes.[19] Working with Milling and other WOS members left a lasting impression on LeBlanc, who in 2014 told a *Times-Picayune* reporter that the women had used their Southern charm to open doors in Washington. Reflecting on the trip, she said, "When we went lobbying in D.C., I pretty much describe it as being with a bunch of southern Obi-Wan Kenobis. . . . Because there were all these charming women that would say, 'You don't mind if we bring our documentary photographers in?'"[20] Reporter Mark Schleifstein, who quoted LeBlanc as saying, "They would just magically do things that normal people just can't," went on to write that she "imitate[d] the Jedi mind-trick speech pattern in the Star Wars movies."[21]

At 6 P.M. the women convened in Caucus Room 325 of the Russell Senate Office Building for a reception. It was there that Pelosi addressed some members of Congress, their aides, and WOS participants: "We are all so honored that you are back in Washington. Because of you, 57 senators and over 100 members of the House have visited Louisiana, and we have seen for ourselves. It has been a transforming experience for all of us who have gone there, and for that we are grateful to you." She continued: "To the Women of the Storm, know your power."[22]

Former Louisiana senator John Breaux addressed the crowd: "There is nothing like an agitated, dedicated woman." The women laughed, as did the men. Breaux continued by saying hurricanes Katrina and Rita were perhaps "almost a blessing in disguise." His reason: "because it allowed us to tell the rest of the country the story of Louisiana and the tragic consequences of us not paying attention to our environment, to our wetlands." Breaux ended with praise: "You did what we couldn't do in 32 years that I was in Congress, and that was to educate the rest of the country, to educate members of Congress, Republicans and Democrats alike from all over this country, that yes, this was a national issue."[23]

Then R. King Milling took the stage to roaring applause. He summarized the women's accomplishments, saying, "I need not remind you that you came just eight months ago, and you won over senators and members of the House, on both sides of the aisle, with both perseverance and Southern charm." After declaring WOS one of the most successful groups in Louisiana's history, King Milling continued with praise—"They are persistent, tenacious, and utterly charming"—and then quoted Val Marmillion, head of the public relations firm that had helped brand the group, as calling Anne Milling a "force of nature."[24]

The reception was followed by the screening of *Washing Away: Losing Louisiana*, a Louisiana Public Broadcasting documentary narrated by Susan Sarandon. The film profiled six Louisianans whose lives had been affected by the vanishing coastline and by hurricanes Katrina and Rita. One subject was chef Leah Chase, a WOS member who had participated in both trips to Washington and who sat in the audience that evening.

Leah Chase, creole chef and owner of the legendary Dooky Chase's restaurant, is arguably one of the best known African American members of WOS and was an active participant in the group over the years. Born in New Orleans on January

6, 1923, she grew up in Madisonville, Louisiana, and returned to New Orleans in 1942 at age eighteen.[25] In the early 1940s, Chase married into the family that owned Dooky Chase's, at the corner of Orleans Avenue and North Miro Street in the Tremé neighborhood; her mother-in-law lived next door. "But you have to understand, now, in '41, African Americans did not eat out. Well, they had no place to eat out to begin with. They had no restaurants, as we know restaurants today. Everybody. Duke Ellington, as great as he was, there was no place for him to eat, he had to eat here. King Cole had to eat here. Everybody had to eat here," she explained in an interview for PBS's *American Experience*.[26] Throughout the turbulent 1960s, civil rights leaders would come to Chase's restaurant not only for food and a table but also because she provided a gathering place and "safe haven" for strategy sessions in the upstairs meeting room.[27] Whether it was black artists or civil rights activists passing through New Orleans, Chase would cook for many of them, preparing gumbo in twenty- to thirty-gallon batches. She went on to say, "Well, I cooked for a lot of people. I cooked for Thurgood Marshall on this stove. I cooked for Big Daddy King on this stove. I cooked for everybody on this stove."[28] Elsewhere, she recalls cooking for Reverend Martin Luther King Jr., Ray Charles, and James Baldwin.[29]

After Katrina five feet of water sat in her restaurant for weeks on end. Nearly a year after the storm, Chase, then eighty-three years old, was still living in a FEMA trailer across the street from her restaurant, which was still being rebuilt.[30] Across Orleans Avenue, the Lafitte public housing projects, which had contained 896 rental units when Katrina made landfall, remained unoccupied, the doors shuttered with impenetrable steel plates.[31] In August 2006, a few weeks before the first Katrina anniversary and a month before WOS's second trip to Washington, Chase told the Associated Press that she thought that socioeconomic class had played a larger role during the storm than race or racism: "People get mad at me because I don't talk about race or racism. To me, poverty is the thing. If you don't have money, you're going to have a hard time at everything, no matter what your skin color is."[32]

Chase's restaurant would reopen only in 2007. A year later, when she served a bowl of gumbo to President-elect Barack Obama during his visit to her restaurant, she reprimanded him for pouring hot sauce on her cuisine before trying it. Reflecting on the infamous "hot sauce incident," Chase told *Ebony* magazine, "No one pours hot sauce on my gumbo. Of course, I had to stop him."[33] And in 2016, the year that the "Queen of Creole Cuisine" turned ninety-three, Chase would make a brief appearance in Beyonce's "Lemonade" video.[34] But this was all still in the future. On the night of WOS's film screening in Washington, the story of Chase's rebuilding was still being written, and the film painted a painful picture of how Katrina had changed the lives of the entire Chase family. Chase narrated how her daughter, son, and sister had lost everything in the storm. The film crew documented groups of volunteers helping her gut her restaurant, tearing out drywall and flooded appliances. Her profile ended with a producers' note telling viewers that eleven months after Katrina, Chase finally received "mold remediation" clearance, official paperwork

FIGURE 10. Leah Chase wearing Women of the Storm pin in 2010.
Photograph by Cheryl Gerber.

following an inspection that would allow her to begin renovations.[35] The Washington trip ended with an intense feeling that for many residents along the Gulf Coast, Leah Chase included, there were many hard days of work ahead.

On the plane ride back to New Orleans, many of the WOS participants enjoyed a few glasses of wine. But this was not the celebratory atmosphere that they experienced on the first trip, when the women believed the seats on the donated planes would quickly fill to capacity with interested elected officials. This time they were more sanguine about the possibilities of bringing about rapid social change. Nonetheless, the second plane ride home to New Orleans represented another sign of progress, and the women still shared a strong sense of purpose. Leah Chase took the opportunity to make an impromptu address to the women over the plane's intercom system. She said, "I just couldn't go home without saying how much I appreciated being here today, how proud I was of everyone. You really made a difference." She went on to say, "This was unbelievable. And I call you ladies, but truly, you are women. And that is a great gift."

The following Tuesday, September 26, WOS members made another appearance in New Orleans, along a bridge crossing the once-breached 17th Street Canal, to advocate for the passage of several amendments to the Louisiana constitution that were on the ballot that Saturday, September 30. Joined by members of Citizens for One Greater New Orleans, the Coast Guardians, and AWF, WOS encouraged citizens to vote for these amendments, two of which were directly tied to coastal restoration and protection. After Kathleen Blanco stressed the point that Louisiana had lost over two hundred square miles of wetlands during hurricanes Katrina and Rita, Anne Milling said, "Louisiana feeds and fuels the nation, but we're washing away," and "Coastal restoration gives us the front-line hurricane protection."[36]

Twenty percent of eligible voters turned out at the polls, 80 percent of them supporting the two amendments related to coastal restoration. R. King Milling said, "The degree of the victory . . . should give a message to Washington . . . that when this state suggests it is serious about retargeting dollars to this effort, it is absolutely serious."[37] Amendment 1, the Coastal Protection and Restoration Fund, dedicated potential federal revenues shared with Louisiana from OCS oil and gas activities to coastal restoration and protection. Amendment 2, Consolidation of Coastal Funds, was similar in its aims, directing a percentage of proceeds from the sale of its remaining shares of a 1998 national tobacco lawsuit settlement to the Coastal Protection and Restoration Fund. These amendments, which were fiercely opposed by some local environmental groups that wanted to delink conservation and oil and gas drilling, were central to convincing lawmakers in Washington that federal monies would be spent wisely in Louisiana, a state often viewed with suspicion due to its long history of corruption; they also aimed to protect residents and to create a system that was self-sustaining.

Back in Washington, Congress went on recess in early October, failing to vote on oil and gas revenue sharing legislation. This was a major blow to WOS's recent efforts, because chances were low that lawmakers would address the issue before the new session in January. "We were disappointed that they recessed without passing some legislation," WOS member Rebecca Currence told reporters. "We've got two scenarios facing us. There's the six-week lame-duck session, but traditionally not a lot of stuff happens in a lame-duck session. Then the other scenario is that we start over in January."[38] If Congress waited to tackle these issues when they reconvened in January, members of WOS reasoned, new members of the legislature would not be as supportive, since they would not have heard the group's pitch in Washington, and they likely would not have seen the destruction in New Orleans, something the women thought was central to convincing lawmakers to support their cause.

November 2006 brought with it the next round of midterm elections, and the women anticipated some legislative turnover. Immediately after the election, WOS sent informational packets to new lawmakers in Washington to catch them up on hurricane recovery issues, coastal restoration, and oil and gas revenue sharing.[39] Not long afterward, a small WOS delegation was back in Washington lobbying for the passage of oil and gas revenue sharing legislation, which was part of the Gulf of Mexico Energy Security Act, co-sponsored by Landrieu and Sen. Pete Domenici, a Republican from New Mexico, who at the time was chair of the Senate Energy

Committee. The bill was designed to give oil-producing states in the Gulf of Mexico—Alabama, Louisiana, Mississippi, and Texas—a share of royalties generated from offshore oil and gas production; it would also open up 8.3 million acres of oil and gas drilling in the gulf. At the time of the women's lobbying trip, the bill, which was supported by President Bush and had already passed the Senate, needed to pass in the House.[40]

In early December the House approved the measure, and on December 20 President Bush signed this legislation that gave Louisiana a share of offshore oil and gas royalties, which, as Amendment 1 stipulated, would be channeled into a "trust fund" for enhanced flood control, hurricane protection, and coastal wetlands protection.[41] Landrieu told the Associated Press, "It was the best gift that the President could give to the people of Louisiana. It'll be the gift that'll keep on giving for decades."[42] By the end of the year, Bill Walsh of the *Times-Picayune* wrote, "The story of how Louisiana managed to turn history around is one of maddening legislative near-misses, political perseverance and good timing. High energy prices, an unexpected political shift in Congress and the ravages of Hurricane Katrina helped focus a nation's attention on finally allowing a state to share in the energy bounty off its shores."[43] There was no mention of WOS, despite the group's well-documented efforts.

CHAPTER 15

The Presidential Debate

On the crafting of another grand proposal,
resulting in a bid, a rejection, and a rejoinder

In March 2007, in anticipation of the 2008 presidential elections, WOS took on another big project with the hope of keeping national attention on the Katrina recovery: a bid to host one of the presidential debates in New Orleans. By embarking on this new undertaking, WOS once again adapted to changing sociopolitical conditions and began to resemble what disaster sociologists call an "extending organization," which is an organized response to disaster in which a group whose organizational structure remains in place ends up taking on new activities.[1] Following the actions of WOS over time, one can see that the group occupied numerous places in the typology of organizational responses to disaster; they evolved from an emergent group (when the group first formed), to an expanding organization (with their efforts to increase membership by partnering with national women's groups), to an extending organization (hosting a presidential debate).

Around this time there was also a second wave of participation in the core; the executive committee increased to fourteen members. The core members of 2006—Anne Milling, Pam Bryan, Beverly Church, Rebecca Currence, Peggy Laborde, Nancy Marsiglia, Diana Pinckley, Dolly Simpson, Liz Sloss, and Madeline West—were joined in 2007 by a new cohort: Naydja Domingue Bynum, Carmen Duncan, Alexis B. Robinson, and Sally Suthon. Holding a doctorate from Louisiana State University, Naydja Bynum served as president of the Historic Faubourg Tremé Association among numerous other volunteer activities tied to the architecture and culture of the historic neighborhood. Carmen Duncan, originally from Havana, Cuba, was a New Orleans real estate agent who was active in many groups ranging from the Junior League to the Trinity Episcopal Church. Alexis Robinson, a member of The Links and National Girl Friends, was a retired administrative assistant at ExxonMobil; her husband, Virgil Robinson Jr., served on the board of the LRA. The last newcomer was New Orleans native Sally Suthon, a past president of the Junior League of New Orleans and the incoming president of the Garden Study Club.[2] Together these newcomers brought a needed burst of energy and division of labor to the latest initiatives.

Partnering with four universities—Dillard, Loyola, Tulane, and Xavier—WOS filed an application with the Commission on Presidential Debates to hold one of the three debates in New Orleans that October. Among the application materials was the seventy-five-hundred-dollar fee and a letter addressed to Janet Brown, director of the commission, by Anne Milling, who highlighted numerous educational, medical, and governmental post-Katrina recovery initiatives. WOS saw the debates as critical to the ongoing recovery because it would attract thousands of journalists to the city and generate intensive media coverage. Milling summarized the importance: "Timing is everything—and, in our opinion, the timing for New Orleans to serve as a presidential debate site is now."[3] Importantly, WOS redeployed the strategy of invitation. "We invite you to experience our 'new' New Orleans by allowing us the privilege of hosting a presidential debate in the fall of 2008," Milling wrote in her letter, which emphasized the collaborative aspect of the invitation. Although traditionally a single institution hosts a debate, this proposed event would be organized by multiple universities and held at the Ernest M. Morial Convention Center. Milling argued that the convention center would serve as "an ideal venue for this occasion," because each participating university had suffered millions of dollars in damages to their facilities. The proposal emphasized that the convention center "surpassed" the requirements of the commission, calling it a "state-of-the-art facility." It also highlighted the facility's proximity to nearly twenty-five thousand hotel rooms and "America's finest restaurants." After describing the city's resources and facilities, WOS attempted to establish its credibility by recapping its accomplishments:

> Though your organizational host is not a household name, the non-political, non-partisan Women of the Storm, composed of ethnically, socially, and economically diverse women of New Orleans and the region, has a proven track record. Individually these women have expertise comparable to those in the best corporate board room; collectively their success in bringing national leaders and members of the United States Congress to see firsthand the devastation and challenges facing New Orleans is unquestioned. We have the organizational ability, tenacity and passion necessary to host a debate![4]

Indeed, WOS members were convinced that they could come up with the $1.35 million required of the host group to cover debate costs. And in addition to stressing the accomplishments of WOS, this description marks one of the first occasions that the expertise of its members was mentioned.

On Thursday, March 22, 2007, Mary Landrieu sent a letter to the commission supporting WOS's proposal, endorsed with signatures by six senators who were, at the time, also presidential candidates: Joseph Biden (D-DE), Sam Brownback (R-KS), Hillary Clinton, Chris Dodd (D-CT), John McCain, and Barack Obama. The letter echoed WOS, insisting on the national significance of the recovery efforts: "There is no doubt that the next President of the United States will bear a significant responsibility to address the ongoing and momentous challenges of this recovery. This duty is highlighted by the region's vital role in our nation's economy and national security and the statement our efforts make about how America protects and cares for its own people in times of crisis." To address concerns that New Orleans might not be able to handle the influx of journalists and politicians to the area, the letter emphasized that "the city's transportation and hospitality services are more than capable of supporting the event," noting that hotels had returned to 90 percent of their pre-Katrina capacity, and that more than thirty thousand people had recently attended a major conference in the city. Landrieu's letter tied post-Katrina struggles to broader themes on the national agenda, making it an appropriate venue for candidates to discuss their platforms: "With new school and health care systems being rebuilt virtually from scratch, small businesses struggling to reopen, a devastated law enforcement community facing a growing crime epidemic, and families forced into tough choices on housing and other life-or-death questions, New Orleans also provides a unique forum for a discussion of broader issues in the campaign." The selection of the city, Landrieu argued, would also help rebuild the area: "The Commission can itself contribute to the recovery and renewal of this vibrant region."[5]

Local media, including the *Baton Rouge Advocate* and the *Times-Picayune*, offered support, calling the city a "fitting debate site" and adding, "The eyes of the nation and the world were on this city during the Hurricane Katrina crisis. Holding a debate here would ensure that a similarly large and influential audience would see us in the midst of recovery."[6] LRA chairman Norman Francis and vice chairman Walter Isaacson also offered their endorsement, saying, "Presidential debates are historic in their own right, a chance for the voting public to see the candidates for president square off in spirited discussion of the critical issues facing this nation. Couple this with the historic recovery—the largest rebuilding this country has seen since the Reconstruction—and there clearly is no better place than New Orleans for those vying to be the next president to lay out their plans for improving this country from coast to coast."[7]

Support went far beyond local and state interests. The nation's most prominent newspapers argued that New Orleans would be the perfect backdrop for presidential candidates to address domestic issues. The *New York Times* editorial board supported WOS's efforts and wrote, "If there's any sense of justice, relevance, even poetic stagemanship at work, New Orleans should emerge hands down as the site for the debate that will be dedicated to the nation's domestic problems."[8] The editorial reminded the public that two years after Katrina, there were still more than thirty thousand families displaced and more than thirteen thousand other families still living in trailer parks. Another endorsement came from the *Washington Post*, which said "hosting one of the debates would be an enormous psychological boost for New Orleans."[9] *USA Today* argued, "The city's main strength as a debate location is in the many challenges it still faces. Name any major domestic policy issue and in New Orleans it's a major problem, a promising solution or a grand experiment."[10] Similarly, the *Boston Globe* gave its backing "because many American metropolitan areas are vulnerable to earthquakes, storms, fires, floods, and terrorist attacks. A question for each presidential candidate is: What would you do if another catastrophe strikes U.S. soil?"[11] A column by editor Richard Stenge in *Time* magazine also supported bringing the presidential debate to New Orleans.[12]

Did New Orleans have a chance? WOS's university partnership was in competition with nineteen institutions. The commission's announcement was not scheduled until October 2007 and then was postponed to November 2007. While WOS waited for the commission's decision, there were numerous recognitions that cemented their place among Louisiana's most influential women. For example, on April 29, Anne Milling and Ruthie Frierson were named Newcomb College's Alumnae of the Year.[13] And on May 12, at Loyola University's commencement ceremonies, WOS was awarded an honorary doctor of human letters degree for its service to New Orleans and the region. For Milling, the honorary doctorate was "nothing that one would dream of in your wildest dreams and imagination. We were just taken aback and terribly flattered."[14]

One week later, on May 19, presidential candidate Hillary Clinton received an honorary doctorate during the commencement ceremonies at Dillard University, the historically black university where WOS member Marvalene Hughes remained university president. During the outdoor ceremony at the university's campus in Gentilly, Clinton called the conditions in post-Katrina New Orleans "a natural disaster that has become a national embarrassment and an international disgrace." Using the occasion to make comparisons between 9/11 and Katrina, Clinton said, "If New York had been flooded and the president had treated it the same way as he has Louisiana, we would have dogged him everywhere, holding signs and talking to the press." A day earlier Clinton once again toured devastated neighborhoods, including the Ninth Ward, Broadmoor, and Central City. She made an appearance at a fund-raiser, with tickets ranging from one thousand to twenty-three hundred dollars per person, and she had a private dinner with WOS members at Milling's home.[15] After the trip Clinton sent a letter to Milling extending thanks for making her visit to New Orleans a success. Clinton ended the letter by writing, "Working together, I know we can make great strides in rebuilding New Orleans and the entire Gulf Coast."[16]

In the meantime, as summer rolled on, New Orleans entered its second hurricane season after Katrina. Thursday, June 1, marked the beginning of the 2007 hurricane season. As in 2006, WOS used the occasion to shine the national spotlight on the city. In the third annual Storm Warnings event, which they called "The Up River Tour," WOS tried to draw attention to coastal wetlands issues by arguing that the

FIGURE 11. Anne Milling followed by Rita Benson LeBlanc and other members of the Women of the Storm stepping off a boat at the Port of New Orleans to announce their river tour in New Orleans, Thursday, May 31, 2007. AP photo/Alex Brandon.

city was tied economically to the rest of the country via its port at the mouth of the mighty Mississippi River. Joined by environmentalists and civic, business, and industry leaders, WOS arrived at the Port of New Orleans aboard the Coast Guard vessel *General Kelly*, some wearing white linen with blue-tarp umbrellas in hand.

WOS launched Storm Warning III with presentations by Anne Milling and R. King Milling, as well as Gary LaGrange, director of the Port of New Orleans; Conrad Appel, chair of the board of directors for the Port of New Orleans; Sidney Coffee, chair of the Coastal Protection and Restoration Authority; and Mike Dunne, author of *America's Wetland: Louisiana's Vanishing Coast*. Each spoke about the economic links between Louisiana and places in America's heartland. Together, this entourage spoke about the coastal industries in Louisiana and the threat that disappearing wetlands would pose to the security and economic stability not only for the region but also for the entire nation. For example, LaGrange spoke about how the Port of New Orleans is tied directly to thirty-three states and three provinces in

Canada, all of which rely on the 14,500 mile inland waterway system. Others spoke about goods that pass through the port or that are produced in Louisiana's waters, from coffee to cargo, oil, and gas, to rubber, fish, and seafood. Hoping to communicate that Louisiana "fuels and feeds the nation," WOS emphasized that one-third of all oil and gas production comes from Louisiana's coast, that 30 percent of U.S. seafood comes from Louisiana's waters, and that New Orleans serves as the largest port, measured by tonnage, in the United States. After the launch in New Orleans, WOS members traveled to Memphis, Dubuque, and Chicago to raise awareness about regional and national connections to Louisiana. In many ways this shows that WOS's ideas of New Orleans were like the relational constructions of place examined by geographer Doreen Massey, who stresses the importance of "a sense of place, an understanding of 'its character,' which can only be constructed by linking that place to places beyond."[17]

In mid-July a WOS delegation drove to Mud Island outside of Memphis to describe the effects of vanishing wetlands on communities upriver. In September WOS members were in Iowa at the National Mississippi River Museum & Aquarium, where Dubuque mayor Roy Buol commented on how wetlands loss in Louisiana affects the Midwest: "Anything that threatens the Mississippi River means we are impacted in Iowa. Keeping the mouth of this great river secure means that goods and products from our state make it to market. And, when the Gulf Coast is threatened by hurricanes, the citizens of Dubuque feel the impact at the gas pump. This area is vital to our economic and energy security and we should not let it deteriorate."[18]

But hosting a presidential debate remained WOS's primary goal. In June representatives of the Commission on Presidential Debates (CPD) began visiting potential host sites to determine if they had the resources required to pull off the event successfully. WOS's chances increased slightly when Ohio State University dropped out of the competition, citing concerns about raising the $1.35 million required of each of the three winning bidders. On Tuesday, June 19, the committee visited New Orleans. Local media erupted with stories about the importance of the debate for the economic recovery of the city and region. That day, Tammy Johnston, a representative from the commission, toured the convention center to evaluate its capacity for the national broadcast. And during an hour-long presentation, she heard expert briefings by top officials, politicians, and civic leaders, including Lt. Gov. Mitch Landrieu, Norman Francis, Anne Milling, and NOPD chief of operations Anthony Canatella.[19]

On August 10 a nonprofit group based in Colorado known as Friends of New Orleans (FONO), which formed in the year after Hurricane Katrina, held a panel discussion in Aspen titled "New Orleans: The Role of Higher Education, Local Business, and Cutting-Edge Nonprofits in the City's Rebirth." The event, moderated by Walter Isaacson, featured numerous panelists involved in higher education, business, and nonprofit organizations, including Rev. Kevin Wildes, president of Loyola University New Orleans; Norman Francis; and R. King Milling. The panelists spoke about wetlands restoration, green home construction, and the charter schools movement in New Orleans. Also in attendance were Anne Milling and Phyllis Taylor, then chair and CEO of Taylor Energy, one of the largest oil and gas companies operating in federal waters in the Gulf of Mexico. It was at this event, according to Isaacson, that Anne Milling gained a verbal pledge of support from candidate John Edwards for the bid to hold a presidential debate in New Orleans.[20]

In August 2007, as the second anniversary of Katrina approached, Nancy Pelosi, who was now Speaker of the House, brought a fifteen-member bipartisan delegation to observe the recovery efforts in New Orleans and in Mississippi. The group met with local and state officials at the Hotel Monteleone on Royal Street and also with residents still living in FEMA trailers. House majority whip James Clyburn said, "We took our work from that trip (last year) and applied it immediately, and in six short months of a new majority we delivered on our promises. Next week we must assess the progress in the Gulf Coast region, and establish a partnership for the future."[21] House Democrats took credit for passing thirteen bills related to the hurricane recovery, including a waiver of a rule that required Louisiana to match 10 percent of the federal dollars allocated for rebuilding, a proposal that was supported by numerous parties ranging from Hillary Clinton to the National Council for Jewish Women.[22]

And on the eve of the two-year anniversary of Katrina, nearly fifty members of WOS members appeared on the *CBS Evening News* to discuss with Katie Couric the struggles of a city that had lost nearly two-thirds of its population.[23] As they walked the deserted streets of the once flooded Lakeview neighborhood, Couric reported that $60 billion of the $116 billion earmarked for the Gulf Coast recovery was to go to Louisiana. After describing how much of it went to disaster relief and flood insurance, Couric reported that the remaining $25.5 billion was to be spent on rebuilding. But Couric noted that only $6.78 billion had been spent on rebuilding New Orleans.[24] The levees were still being rebuilt, and throughout the city, only half of the public schools had reopened. When Couric asked the group whether rebuilding New Orleans was another disaster waiting to happen, Marvalene Hughes said, "It doesn't need to be. It can be a city that welcomes people and redevelops itself if the right investment is made in the city. . . . It was not Katrina that caused the problem, it was the lack of attention to the levees."[25] Milling added, "We don't want people to forget us. . . . This was a man-made disaster. America was built on the foundation of people helping one another. And we feel like Congress and the federal government should do the same for us."[26]

But WOS's recovery work wasn't all politics and economics. It also found a place in the sports arena. The link to the New Orleans Saints vis-à-vis the team's owner and executive vice president, Rita Benson LeBlanc, put WOS front and center during a Saints game at the Louisiana Superdome. On September 24, WOS lined up, umbrellas in hand, on the fifty-yard line during the halftime show for a salute that spotlighted the recovery work of local groups.

Nearly two years after it emerged, WOS continued to make steady progress with its initiatives, its momentum matched by increased confidence and recognition. For participants, even small advances were significant. But WOS's so-called winning streak was about to come to a controversial end. In November 2007, WOS had to face its first major defeat. Despite receiving endorsements from seven presidential candidates (five Democrats and two Republicans), as well as support from major newspapers across the country, the eleven-member Commission on Presidential Debates rejected the New Orleans bid on Monday, November 19. Many explanations emerged as disappointed supporters tried to ascertain the reasons for rejection. Anne Milling said that Paul Kirk, co-chair of the commission, told her the city was not ready to host a major event. He later denied making the statement, telling the Associated Press, "I don't think that is exactly what I said. That may have been her interpretation." He added that hosting the debates would be an "expensive proposition" and that "all things considered, New Orleans did not measure up."[27] Other explanations ranged from claims that the commission was concerned that New Orleans couldn't afford the police overtime, to questions about who would take responsibility for legal requirements, to doubts about technology at the convention center. But documents about the panel's deliberations remained sealed and were never released.

Michael D. McCurry, a member of the commission, told the *New York Times* that despite the fact that multiple groups participated in the proposal, there was only one signature, that of Anne Milling; yet Milling claimed that Janet Brown told her there could be only one signature. Ultimately, the commission was concerned that WOS could not guarantee that it could pull off the event. McCurry said, "It was the amorphous collection of people promising to put on the debate with no sense at the end of the day of who would be accountable. You had one person representing all these diverse interests, from the universities, to political leaders, to local law enforcement. We said we need full confidence that people will be accountable for what's promised, and we didn't get that." He added that "the only person at the table was Anne."[28] In response to the decision, Anne Milling said, "I was shocked to say the least. This is exactly the sort of thing we do so well. I can't understand the reasoning."[29]

In a unanimous decision by the committee, the three debate sites chosen were University of Mississippi in Oxford, Mississippi; Belmont University in Nashville, Tennessee; and Hofstra University in Hempstead, New York. Despite being given a second site visit during the selection process, New Orleans wasn't even considered as one of the alternates, slots that went to Danville, Kentucky, and Winston-Salem, North Carolina.[30] The vice-presidential debate went to Washington University in St. Louis.

New Orleans supporters were not satisfied with the panel's explanations. When the panel claimed that New Orleans could not meet logistical requirements, such as having 3,000 hotel rooms for journalists, critics responded to the panel's selection of

Oxford, Mississippi, whose Convention and Visitor's Bureau claimed that it offered only 650 hotel rooms, compared to the 24,000 available in New Orleans.[31] Those across New Orleans felt outraged by the rejection. Norman Francis said of the commission's decision, "They missed an opportunity to help America."[32] In a written statement about the rejection, Milling said, "Politics trumped the moral decision." Many saw the political debates as an opportunity to showcase pressing issues on both the local and national agenda. One local columnist observed the impossibility of holding "empty debates" in a place like New Orleans, adding that the "nation has been spared the inconvenience of seeing its failure at one of the precise times when national shortcomings are most visibly discussed."[33] The *Times-Picayune* called the commission's explanation "a slap in our face" and went on to say that because no historically black university had ever hosted a presidential debate, the panel "also bypassed the opportunity to make history."[34] And at the end of an editorial rebuffing the panel, the *Times-Picayune* published commission members' telephone numbers, which led to some committee members receiving angry calls by bid supporters. Frank Fahrenkopf, the commission's co-chair, reflected on the irate responses, saying, "Maybe Women of the Storm is an apt description."[35]

Locals weren't the only ones upset. Three Democratic presidential candidates reproached the commission for its decision. Clinton said the commission "missed a golden opportunity to show New Orleans that the entire country is committed to its recovery." Mentioning a collective responsibility to rebuild, Edwards said, "Holding national events in this city, like a presidential debate, will help New Orleans move forward." Obama asserted that the event would have reminded the nation "about the unmet promise to rebuild and restore the Gulf Coast."[36]

Another *Times-Picayune* columnist compared the debate site rejection to the unspoken rules of a dating breakup: "The Commission on Presidential Debates is now discovering that New Orleans is not the woman who cries quietly into her napkin at the news of her rejection. To the contrary, she is the woman who demands to know what the hell's wrong with the person walking away."[37]

One week after the commission's announcement, Anne Milling released a twelve-hundred-word statement rebutting the decision. She challenged the panel's reasoning that there was only one signature on the proposal, stating that Janet Brown had told bidders that the proposal could have only one signature, one entity that would assume responsibility for legal and financial liabilities. Milling added that obtaining additional signatures would not have been a problem. She reemphasized the partnerships with local universities and provided quotes by Nagin, Blanco, and Warren Reuther, chair of the convention center board, each pledging their full support to meet the commission's requirements. Then Milling questioned, "If multiple signatures were necessary, then why was that not asked of us?"[38]

Anne Milling's pointed response addressed each of the commission's explanations with a carefully crafted counterargument. She stated that the CPD continued to misrepresent the state of the New Orleans recovery. In response to co-chair Paul

Kirk's statement to her by phone that "New Orleans is not ready," Milling gave a slew of recent examples of major events hosted by the city, including mega-conventions and national sporting events. New Orleans would soon host other major events in the city, including the Sugar Bowl in January 2008, the National Basketball Association All-Star game in February 2008, and numerous major conventions. She added, "What an incorrect, unsupported and damning statement this was to a city on the mend." She concluded by claiming that New Orleans was the "right moral choice" for a debate site. There were historical-comparative references as well, further bolstering her claims. Drawing on recent history, she referenced the decision to hold the GOP party convention in New York after the 2001 terrorist attacks: "After 9/11, when New York suffered tremendously with its tourist economy lagging and the perception of safety in question, the Republican National Committee made a conscious decision to select New York as its venue for its next national convention. New York truly was never seen as a 'favorite among Republicans,' but it was the correct and moral choice to make. Other contenders for the 2004 Republican convention, including New Orleans, supported that choice. Why did the CPD not support the correct moral choice this time?"[39] Throughout the debate controversy, many in New Orleans and beyond saw this decision as imbued with moral significance.

In December 2007, WOS was still reeling from being rejected as a host for the presidential debates. But there was some support from afar that helped replenish the group's financial accounts. An end-of-the-year twenty-five-thousand-dollar donation came in from Michael Bloomberg, the Republican-turned-Independent mayor of New York City and one of the richest people in the world, who must have been persuaded by WOS's efforts and interested in supporting its cause.[40]

WOS decided that if New Orleans couldn't hold the debate on location, then it would try to do so virtually. In the first half of 2008, WOS teamed up with Google and YouTube to host a presidential forum in New Orleans on September 18 at the convention center right before the first of the scheduled presidential debates.[41] Once again the city was abuzz with the possibility of showcasing recovery efforts. A *Times-Picayune* editorial described the potential online forum as "sweet justice for New Orleans."[42] By this point in the nomination process, McCain had solidified his spot on the Republican ticket, with Clinton and Obama still vying for the Democratic Party nomination, but none of the candidates immediately confirmed participation at the virtual forum. Despite all the fervor about the forum, the proposal began to fizzle. By early August the idea came to a screeching halt, with lawmakers citing late party conventions; the GOP convention was scheduled for early September, just two weeks before the proposed virtual forum. The *Times-Picayune* made one last push by stating, "No doubt both candidates have a full schedule between now and Election Day. But New Orleans ought to figure into those plans. There are lessons for the entire nation in what happened here during and after Hurricane Katina. Another debate—especially one held here—would be time well-spent for the candidates and the American people."[43] The virtual forum never materialized, and New Orleans remained left out of the public debates. Despite this second rejection, the bid had unified many New Orleanians. Anne Milling said the effort had "rallied every facet of our diverse community" and that the New Orleans community "proved to be a united and resilient voice."[44]

Two years after the group's emergence, Milling summarized WOS's accomplishments during expert testimony given to the DNC Platform Committee on August 1, 2008: "After two charter flights to Washington in 2006—each carrying 130 women from the metropolitan area and south Louisiana to invite and educate our nation's leaders in person—and continued persistence in 2007 and 2008, we can report that, of the current 110th Congress, 57 senators and 142 members of the House have visited."[45] After this summary, WOS members in attendance tried to persuade Democrats to support a comprehensive national disaster plan. Suggesting that lessons learned from New Orleans were more than just local issues, Milling emphasized vulnerabilities across the nation: "No place can claim immunity. Every American community and city is vulnerable, as recent floods in the Midwest and fires and earthquakes in California have reminded us."[46]

In the midst of the 2008 presidential race, as well as the third anniversary of Hurricane Katrina, WOS aimed to keep the Katrina recovery on the U.S. political agenda. If political heavyweights wouldn't come to New Orleans, then WOS would go to them. On August 24 eight group members traveled on the discount carrier Southwest Airlines from New Orleans to Denver for the Democratic National Convention. Upon their arrival in Colorado, group members rented two minivans, checked in at the Embassy Suites hotel in suburban Aurora, and then met up with Beverly Church's son, Ford Church, who lived in Denver and volunteered to help transport ten boxes of foam footballs for distribution during the convention and at an event later that evening.[47] At 3 P.M. the convention kicked off New Orleans–style in a Colorado Convention Center ballroom, where delegates saw performances by the Wild Tchoupitoulas, a group of Mardi Gras Indians, who appeared in full regalia of lavish handmade costumes of beadwork and feathers. Also, performing R&B hits and contemporary jazz were the "Soul Queen of New Orleans," Irma Thomas, and Terence Blanchard, a Grammy-winning trumpeter. WOS tossed hundreds of custom-made yellow-and-turquoise foam footballs bearing the group's logo to emphasize that the coast was eroding at the rate of one football field every fifty minutes.[48] This was followed by a FONO-organized panel titled "Louisiana Three Years after Katrina: How Far Have We Come? What Are the Next Steps?" The briefing included Lt. Gov. Mitch Landrieu, Sen. Mary Landrieu, Donna Brazile, James Carville, Walter Isaacson, and Harry Shearer.[49] Outside the hall, WOS members and Citizens for One Greater New Orleans set up tables and passed out information about Katrina.[50] Collective efforts were highlighted by Milling, who told reporters, "We will deliver our message that America must learn from New Orleans—about emergency planning and disaster response, infrastructure reliability, and restoration of coastal wetlands and other threatened habitats. All citizens and elected leaders need to understand that the crisis du jour could occur in any community, today or tomorrow."[51] At 6 P.M. that evening, WOS and their supporters attended a five-hundred-dollar-per-person benefit at the Fillmore Auditorium organized by FONO titled "New Orleans All-Star Jam-Balaya," where FONO gave the "Heroes of the Storm" award to WOS. Other recipients included the Tipitinas Foundation, the New Orleans Jazz and Heritage Foundation, the Broadmoor Improvement Association, the Holy Cross Neighborhood Association, Beacon of Hope, Citizens for One Greater New Orleans, the St. Bernard Project, New Schools New Orleans, Idea Village, and Reconcile New Orleans. A week later, on September 1, and on the cusp of Hurricane Gustav's landfall along the Gulf Coast, a similar event was organized at the Republican National Convention in Minneapolis. The RNC event was hosted by actor and FONA board member John Larroquette and former Louisiana House representative William "Billy" Tauzen along with Hon. Tommy Thompson, former Health and Human Services secretary in the George W. Bush administration and FONO board member, and Mary Matalin, a Republican political strategist—although some from the WOS delegation could not attend because Gustav interrupted their travel arrangements.[52]

The presence at both national party conventions ensured that WOS adhered to its nonpartisan identity, and the events gave WOS yet another opportunity to showcase New Orleans's food, music, and culture, which they deemed important for the city's cultural recovery. Along with an all-star cast of New Orleans musicians that rivaled the talent gathered at annual events like Jazz Fest and the French Quarter Festival, audience members broke out in second lines while po'boys, red beans and rice, and muffulettas were served, with sponsorship from the Louisiana Seafood Promotion Board and the National Restaurant Association.

WOS's social ties to FONO reveal some financial and economic connections to corporate sponsors. On a flyer for the event, FONO thanked its sponsors and supporters, which included oil, energy, and biotechnology interests such as PhRMA, Shell Oil, American Chemistry Council, Comptel Coalition, Edison Electric Institute, Entergy, Nuclear Energy Institute, Lockheed-Martin, American Petroleum Institute, and the International Petroleum Association of America. These connections to energy industry interests weren't called out publicly for another two years (until the BP oil spill), but they demonstrate the concrete ways that oil and gas were woven into the very fabric of Louisiana business and politics. Additional insight can be gleaned from some of the group's financial records in the Women of the Storm records at Newcomb College. For example, in the WOS treasurer's report submitted that October, the group's assets were $110,113, comprised of line items from August to October such as a $250 donation given to the organization after a speech by Milling at the Junior League of Mobile; a $5,000 donation from Cindy H. McCain; and a $30,000 grant from GNOF.[53]

During the 2008 presidential debates in September and October, the post-Katrina recovery was mentioned only once during the three presidential debates and one vice-presidential debate. In response to this, Anne Milling told reporters that this lack of attention was "rather sad considering the magnitude of our problems and federal dollars allocated."[54] Once again the recovery was overshadowed by other pressing issues facing the nation. In November 2008 Barack Obama was elected president, and it seemed that change was in store for the nation, and perhaps for the Gulf Coast. But national attention was squarely on the economic recession. Katrina was fading from public discourse, but the women continued to pressure Congress to visit New Orleans and to support long-term wetlands restoration projects.

At the beginning of 2009 one could see the effects of WOS's work and historical influence in New Orleans and beyond. On the evening of President Obama's inauguration in January 2009, watching television and toasting with mimosas, a small group of nine African American women, all under forty, and calling themselves "Women of the Storm of Color," met at Lacrecia James's Gentilly home, which had been flooded with five feet of water during Katrina.[55] Printed in *USA Today*, the article mentioning "Women of Storm of Color" didn't reference WOS, but in the name that James and her group members crafted, there seems to be a nod to WOS's existence and, perhaps, a critique of the original group's whiteness. I could not find evidence that Women of the Storm of Color existed beyond the night of the inauguration.

In a period of abeyance, WOS members planned a next wave of actions. It was just a matter of time before they would reappear, again in relation to dates on the summer calendar. On June 1, at the beginning of the 2009 Atlantic hurricane season, WOS held its annual event, this time titled "Storm Warning IV: Last Stand for America's Wetland," which included a concert held at Woldenberg Riverfront Park along the Mississippi River. The group gained additional star power by inducting soul musician Irma Thomas into WOS, just before her performance at a Saturday concert. Thomas, who had performed at WOS's events at the 2008 national party conventions, and whose home in New Orleans East as well as her nightclub, the Lion's Den, were flooded during Katrina, became an avid supporter of coastal restoration, telling the *Times-Picayune*, "We must rebuild the marshes. Without marshes to protect us, we're going to be in a lot of trouble here in New Orleans."[56] WOS members joined performers on the stage, toting their blue-tarp umbrellas, raising them in sync with Thomas's beats, and tossing their small yellow-and-turquoise footballs into the audience.

By the end of August 2009, four years after Katrina, President Obama, who had made five trips to New Orleans after the storm, spent the anniversary on Martha's Vineyard rather than in New Orleans, a cause for widespread public criticism from residents hurt by his absence. In October 2009, however, he returned to the city, visiting the Dr. Martin Luther King Jr. Charter School in the Lower Ninth Ward. As the school prepared for the visit, WOS arrived to bolster support among the pupils, passing out over 200 yellow-and-turquoise footballs to students. At day's end the group promised to return with more footballs so that each of the 736 students would receive one.[57]

As with the umbrellas, using footballs to illustrate their message turned out to be a smart move, especially during the 2009 NFL season, when the Saints became the league's Cinderella team. On January 15, 2010, Vice President Joe Biden visited New Orleans and met with WOS members Becky Currence, Pamela Pipes, and Naydja Bynum during an event at the St. Bernard Recreation Center in the Seventh Ward, near the devastated areas of Gentilly. The next day, January 16, the Saints had a divisional playoff victory against the Arizona Cardinals, and on January 24 the team defeated the Minnesota Vikings, a playoff win that secured their place in the Super Bowl, set for February 7 in Miami. On Wednesday, February 3, four days before the Super Bowl championship, several WOS members descended on Washington and gave out another seven hundred miniature footballs, affixed with small maps of Louisiana's disappearing coast, to members of Congress, the Obama administration, and journalists. The card attached to the football with yellow ribbon emphasized the rate of coastal erosion and included the text "Be a Saint, save our Coast—invest in America's future." Rita Benson LeBlanc said, "We hope that our winning ways will add to the attention to save one of the most essential natural resources in the world." LeBlanc hoped that the Saints' popularity and the Super Bowl coverage would help bring attention to coastal restoration.[58]

In New Orleans, fans rallied behind the Saints as the team reversed a losing streak and marched into the Super Bowl against the heavily favored Indiana Colts, whose quarterback was the beloved New Orleans native Peyton Manning. Across the city there were divided loyalties, perhaps no more so than for Manning's parents— retired Saints quarterback Archie Manning and Olivia Manning, a WOS member who was widely admired for her charity work. New Orleans was mesmerized by the Super Bowl and overjoyed when the Saints upset the Colts. It's common for fans and revelers to take to the streets after their hometown team wins a sports championship, but in New Orleans the sense of rebirth made the celebrations more meaningful and marked an important turning point in the Katrina recovery. Thousands upon thousands of fans (one WWL-TV reporter estimated crowds of eight hundred thousand) attended the victory parade, which fell a week before Mardi Gras. Milling drew a connection between the Super Bowl and the recovery: "In my humble opinion, New Orleans is poised to soar in the second decade of the 21st century, and the country better keep its eyes on us Who Dats."[59] The 2010 Super Bowl had a healing effect on the city, and it came to be seen by many as the antithesis of the city's defeat, suffering, and shame. For many in New Orleans, the Saints' unlikely Super Bowl championship represented the "anti-Katrina," a sign and article of faith that the city was entering a new chapter in the recovery.[60]

CHAPTER 16

The BP Oil Spill and Beyond

*How Women of the Storm become Women of the
Spill; how a project is almost derailed; and how a
third visit to Washington creates new alliances*

The elation of the Saints' 2010 Super Bowl win was soon countered by a devastating blow to the city's morale. On April 20, 2010, the BP-leased *Deepwater Horizon* oil rig exploded off the Louisiana coast, killing eleven men. Almost five million barrels of crude oil poured into the Gulf of Mexico in the worst oil spill disaster in U.S. history. Over several months the oil slick spread, washing up on the beaches of five states, killing wildlife, damaging the fragile wetlands along the Mississippi River delta, and endangering the livelihoods of all those who relied on the water. Many observers anticipated that the cleanup would take months, if not years. Without a doubt, the BP catastrophe brought back painful memories of Katrina and Rita, as Gulf Coast residents were still dealing with long-term effects of the two hurricanes. Conflict, cleanup, and recovery seemed destined to remain a part of their everyday life.

In the BP oil calamity, environmental concerns were at the forefront of political debates. Statistics on the importance of the coastal wetlands were flying fast and furiously, and questions arose about Louisiana's long-standing dependency on the energy sector. WOS members, who helped popularize the wetland-recovery connection over many years, were now well versed in these data. Academics, scientists, community groups, and environmental activists pointed out that for decades coastal wetlands had been razed for oil pipelines and navigation canals, including the infamous Mississippi River Gulf Outlet, almost always referred to by local residents as "Mr. Go." The energy industry also played an important role in these post-Katrina discussions, framing itself not as a threat to the environment but as a key player in wetlands revitalization. Many proponents of the Katrina recovery, like WOS, had successfully pushed for the expansion of the oil and gas industries. After Katrina over eight million acres of federal waters in the eastern Gulf of Mexico were opened up to new offshore oil and gas leases, and royalties became a primary funding source for coastal wetlands restoration in Louisiana. It was in federal waters that the *Deepwater Horizon* drilling rig exploded.

For several months the WOS remained surprisingly quiet. In 2010 even the June 1 start of hurricane season, which WOS had drawn attention to annually since 2006 with its Storm Warning events, went unmarked. Two weeks later, in mid-June 2010, there were signs that WOS had been busy organizing a plan to address the spill. On June 16, 2010, Anne Milling contacted WOS supporters by e-mail to announce a campaign: "Many of you may have wondered about Women of the Storm's activity in the face of the oil spill and urgent coastal restoration needs. Believe me, we've got a major project under way—with major star power involved!"[1] She went on to describe their "Restore the Gulf" campaign, an online petition in which WOS would seek one million signatures that group members would then present to Congress, requesting that lawmakers support "sustainable long-term funding to restore and protect the Gulf Coast and our valuable wetlands." In a significant departure from their previous activism, WOS planned to pair their signature campaign with a public service announcement (PSA) in the form of an internet video in which New Orleans luminaries and Hollywood celebrities demonstrated their support for coastal restoration. WOS worked quickly, and in the first weeks of July 2010 the group had begun recording the video. WOS planned to make a third trip to Washington later that year, signatures in hand, to demand that Congress and President Obama's administration give the Gulf Coast funding from oil and gas royalties immediately rather than in 2017, as stipulated in the Gulf of Mexico Energy Security Act, which WOS had worked to pass in 2007. WOS again focused attention on visits by members of Congress and sought to cast the oil spill as a national issue. By July 12 the *Times-Picayune* reported that only nine chairpersons from the nineteen committees and subcommittees investigating the oil spill had visited the scene of the destruction—"Second-hand accounts, no matter how vivid, can't substitute for seeing things for yourself"—and described these congressional trips as "an eye opening experience."[2] These familiar slogans, which, as the editorial mentioned, can be attributed to WOS's work in the years after Katrina and before the spill, took on new meaning as the Gulf Coast confronted yet another catastrophe. The newspaper called the congressional visits "crucial" and praised the more than thirty lawmakers who had made a trip since the spill began. The editors quoted Rep. Edolphus Towns from New York, a Democrat and chair of the House Committee on Oversight and Government Reform: "You know things are bad, but when you go there you know that things are a lot worse."[3]

Despite the fact that Gulf Coast states were bearing the brunt of the oil spill's consequences, Milling told the *Times-Picayune* that the spill remained a national issue. Directing her remarks to federal officials, she stated, "We want them to know that it's not just a local issue. It's a national issue. We will have support from Seattle to Maine to the plains of Indiana and Missouri and Iowa."[4]

On July 20, ninety-two days after the spill began and just five days after the oil well was finally capped, WOS held a news conference at P & J Oyster Company, a famous seafood restaurant in the French Quarter, to launch its "Be the One" campaign, recharge local support, and update group members on plans to descend on Washington. The day before the news conference, supporters were e-mailed the link to the campaign website, giving them a "sneak preview" of a YouTube video to be unveiled the following day.

At the press conference, Milling described the use of digital technology in WOS's campaign. To the crowd's amusement, she said, "The Women of the Storm is going viral. And I want you to know a month ago I thought it was a disease. But now they tell me this is the goal, and it's good. I'm getting e-mails saying, 'It's good, Anne, go viral.'" Many of the women were beginning to adopt the language of the Web 2.0 era. This awkward relation to new media should not be surprising, considering that in 2006 it took several months for WOS to develop a website. But the group now understood much better the power of digital media. Milling went on, saying, "We are launching a twenty-first-century high-tech campaign. We are going to Tweet and Twitter. We're going to YouTube, blog, e-mail, Facebook. We're going to do it all. We're going to harness this social media that we've learned so much about to our benefit. We are going to use the social media to harness and garner hundreds of thousands, maybe a million, signatures to support our petition, a very simple petition, which demands funding—'funding' is the key word—for coastal restoration and its many projects."[5] The final cut of the YouTube video was released later that day, and many hoped it would draw much needed attention to the plight of the Gulf Coast. It featured a lineup of celebrities, each holding up an index finger while saying, "Be the One." The two-minute-long video opened with actress Sandra Bullock, who owns a home in New Orleans. She was followed by many stars and household names, including musicians Lenny Kravitz, Dr. John, and Dave Matthews; actors Bryan Batt, John Goodman, Harry Shearer, and Wendell Pierce (the star of the HBO series *Treme*); New Orleans chefs Emeril Lagasse and Leah Chase; and the dynamic political power couple who lived near the Millings, GOP strategist Mary Matalin and the "Ragin' Cajun" Democrat, James Carville, who is also Milling's cousin. The PSA also featured football stars Peyton Manning and Eli Manning, who taped their part just before their annual football camp in Thibodaux, Louisiana.[6]

WOS's petition asked for signatures supporting the following statement: "I demand that a plan to restore America's Gulf be fully funded and implemented for me and future generations." By the day after the news conference, July 21, WOS had obtained sixty-one thousand signatures, and Milling sent another e-mail encouraging members to help the video "go viral." A week later the petition had more than one hundred thousand signatures, receiving national press with a July 28 *Washington Post* article in which journalist Kathleen Parker wrote, "In a crisis-saturated world sodden with cynicism and conspiratorial ennui, these women inspire."[7] But this moment was short lived, and WOS soon found itself at the center of a media firestorm.

The day after the *Washington Post* article appeared, Bullock suddenly requested to be removed from WOS's Restore the Gulf campaign. Her abrupt withdrawal was motivated by an article in the *Huffington Post*, which claimed that WOS's campaign was sponsored by America's WETLAND Foundation and that AWF was a "front group" for big oil and industry interests.[8] AWF declares on its website that it receives money from the oil and gas industry; for the bloggers, this showed that the organization was "funded chiefly by the same oil companies who have ruined the Gulf and endangered the planet with their global warming emissions."[9] Bullock's spokesperson wrote, "At no time was [Bullock] made aware that any organization, oil company or otherwise had influence over Women of the Storm or its message. We have immediately asked for her participation in the P.S.A. be removed until the facts can be determined."[10]

Two days later, Darwin BondGraham, an investigative journalist, posted an article on his blog titled "Women of the Spill—And the Oil Men Who Love Them." The article echoed the claims made on *Huffington Post* and then asked, "How is it that Women of the Storm came to be such a pro-oil interest group?" BondGraham continued: "Truth is Women of the Storm was never a grassroots 'women's organization.' It began as an elitist post-Katrina lobby that emphasized broad social and economic issues related to reconstruction of the city and the region." He said WOS was founded by "mavens of New Orleans' Uptown elite" and labeled them a "women's auxiliary group" that supported "corporate and political campaigns run by their husbands to restore the region's dominant extractive and environmentally destructive industries as soon as possible." BondGraham characterized WOS as "pro-oil and gas lobby by virtue of its leadership" and concluded, "As philanthropists, all of their initiatives aligned with big oil and other dominant economic forces."[11]

Many members of the New Orleans establishment came to WOS's defense, engaging in what sociologist Diana Kendall, in her study of news stories about the upper class, calls "consensus framing" (casting "wealthy people as like people in other classes") and "admiration framing" (depicting the wealthy as "generous and caring people").[12] For example, Senator Landrieu said, "Those of us from the Gulf Coast know the Women of the Storm doesn't represent oil companies. These women represent thousands of families from the region who have suffered a string of disasters. I'm not turning my back on them, and I hope no one else does either."[13] A *Times-Picayune* editorial, "Defenders of the Coast," offered additional support, describing WOS as "tireless champions of New Orleans' recovery since Hurricane Katrina," and praising the group's focus on restoring coastal wetlands as "another critical battle that it has willingly waged."[14] Stating that "it's frustrating to see this civic-minded group unfairly castigated as an oil-industry tool," the newspaper challenged claims that WOS and AWF were simply fronts for the oil industry and that the group's video was a way of shifting the bill from oil companies to U.S. taxpayers. The *Times-Picayune* emphasized that BP should remain responsible for the spill's environmental damage and continued by pressing the point that coastal erosion was a crisis that "predates the spill." Echoing many of WOS's claims, the editorial continued:

> Our coast has been washing away for decades, the victim of natural forces and human activity, including but not limited to oil and gas exploration. Louisiana's coastal wetlands are a national resource, and the causes of their destruction also are national. Their preservation and restoration should be a national priority, and that's the message the Women of the Storm were sending in their video. Seizing the national spotlight that the BP disaster put on our coast to push the broader cause of coastal restoration was appropriate and timely. It's a shame that it's being portrayed as something else.[15]

The newspaper gave space to local residents who chimed in on the issue as well. Gary Beauchamp of LaPlace, Louisiana, described what he saw as "knee jerk reactions to BP and the oil industry." He criticized Bullock's request to be removed from the campaign: "Unless there is evidence that these organizations are puppets for the oil industry, her actions show an irrational disdain and bias toward oil companies." Furthermore, he attempted to disrupt the opposition of oil and the environment by asking, "Is it not logical that the oil companies, who bear part of the responsibility for the erosion of our wetlands, donate money to help restore them? If they didn't surely there would be criticism of their indifference to the problem." Beauchamp called Bullock's position "irrational and ill considered" and ended his letter with a strong analogy: "Ms. Bullock acts like receiving oil money is like being funded by organized crime."[16] Executive committee member Peggy Laborde, who is married to the CEO of an oil and gas company, also expressed her views, telling reporters, "The oil business is part of our culture; it's a way of life in Louisiana. That's often difficult for people to understand."[17]

WOS soon posted a rebuttal on its website, claiming that the group had not received any money for the Restore the Gulf campaign from AWF or oil companies. WOS's damage control seemed to have worked. By August 11, Bullock reversed her decision and continued her official involvement in WOS's "Be the One" campaign. Her participation was conditional, though, as she agreed to remain in WOS's PSA only if it was accompanied by a statement noting that her "participation in the Restore the Gulf campaign does not imply support for, or endorsement of, any organization or of any other message than as expressed in the Restore the Gulf public service announcement. . . . She will NOT support anyone who is using these terrible circumstances to advance the self-servicing cause that does not benefit the Gulf Coast or that burdens taxpayers with obligations that should rightfully be the responsibility of others."[18]

By the time Bullock rejoined the campaign, WOS had collected more than 127,000 signatures, far short of the million they had hoped for. Nevertheless, Milling said, "[Bullock] and other celebrities have been instrumental in rallying national support for restoration of our beaches, wetlands and the Gulf Coast environment."[19] Because the video didn't go viral as expected, WOS turned to more traditional mediums to spread its message. It had already invested time, energy, and financial resources in the production of the video, so in the early months of 2011, WOS's PSA was screened before feature-length films at more than sixty-four hundred movie theaters across the country, thus boosting the number of signatures by the thousands.

Timing was important, not only for the women's PSA but also for the regional campaign to save the wetlands and to recover from the oil spill. Harry Shearer, a *Huffington Post* columnist who also appeared in WOS's video, said in a statement, "Coastal Louisiana is on the front page for a limited amount of time, and that time is coming to an end. This is our window to impel political action, without which we lose our wetlands."[20] And in the days before the fifth anniversary of Katrina, the *Times-Picayune* editors wrote:

> When Louisianans talk about coastal restoration, through efforts like the Women of the Storm's Restore the Gulf campaign, we're calling on the federal government to do what only a national government can: Reverse the ravaging of our coast by erosion and make it a national priority—as it deserves to be. Louisiana's coast was in crisis long before the oil spill, and it will remain a crisis long after BP's cleanup is completed if nothing is done to reverse coastal erosion.
>
> This is not just a Louisiana problem. Our working coast provides energy and food for the nation. Indeed, the federal government has reaped tens of billions of dollars in revenues from oil and gas extracted though our region. The canals that were dredged for the oil and gas industry are a prime cause of coastal erosion. Yet Louisiana won't begin receiving a significant share of those mineral revenues, which will be dedicated to coastal restoration, until 2017. That revenue sharing should start now.[21]

That September, in a statement clearly aligned with sentiments in the newspaper, Nancy Marsiglia, of WOS's steering committee, described the group's latest endeavors in the wake of the spill. They wanted Congress to "speed up the oil revenue sharing" with the passage of the Restoring Ecosystem Sustainability and Protection on the Delta Act, or the RESPOND Act, a bill introduced by Mary Landrieu that would require an earlier distribution of offshore oil and gas revenues generated off the coast. The group was aware that the Gulf of Mexico Energy Security Act of 2006 would begin this revenue sharing in 2017, but the RESPOND Act would release funds immediately. In their view, seven years was a long time to wait. WOS also wanted to make sure that any BP fines would be paid to the Gulf Coast states.[22] This all required additional action, and WOS would soon embark on its third major trip to Washington, D.C., bringing stories not only about the hurricanes but about the oil spill as well. And in addition to contacting previous WOS participants from Louisiana, they began extending invitations to women from Alabama, Florida, Mississippi, and Texas to participate as a Gulf Coast coalition.

On March 29, 2011, WOS returned to Capitol Hill for the third time in five years.[23] In the wake of the BP spill, the group had a primary goal: urge Congress to support the RESPOND Act and to dedicate portions of fines collected from BP to the Gulf Coast states for coastal restoration. Under existing legislation, they said, any fines collected would be put into an Oil Spill Liability Trust Fund, which, to the women's dismay, would be dedicated to cleanup efforts but only for future spills. WOS sought to increase support for pending legislation in the House that would dedicate 80 percent of fines to long-term recovery along the Gulf Coast: the Gulf Coast Restoration Act and the Gulf of Mexico Economic and Environmental Restoration Act of 2011. This was a potentially sizable amount of money, considering that BP faced penalties amounting to as much as $1,000 for every barrel of oil spilled, with conservative estimates suggesting that almost five million barrels of oil had been released. At that rate the company faced penalties up to $21 billion if found grossly negligent. Under the existing laws these civil fines would be put into the Oil Spill Liability Trust Fund for future use. Because the fund was capped at $2.7 billion, any additional fines collected from BP, the women argued, would go into the general fund rather than to the Gulf Coast region. Dumbfounded by this logic, they argued that those funds should go to the affected areas and that this would happen only if Congress created a specific Gulf Coast recovery fund.

Like WOS's earlier effort to go national by partnering with women's organizations across the country, the group tried to establish connections to women in places beyond Louisiana. So in contrast to the two previous WOS trips, which had included only Louisiana participants, this third trip brought together 140 women from the five affected states along the Gulf Coast: Alabama, Florida, Louisiana, Mississippi, and Texas. At the press conference, Milling said, "The Women of the Storm went horizontal. Standing with me, behind me, and alongside of me, is a coalition of talented and committed women from diverse economic and political backgrounds. We're bound by a common passion to restore a healthy Gulf Coast that benefits the entire nation with energy security, food sustainability, and natural ecosystems."[24] The women had 131,000 signatures supporting their petition in conjunction with the Be the One video. The support was widespread and national. In a handout intended for members of Congress and their legislative assistants, the women claimed that 55 percent of the petition signers came from the five Gulf Coast states, while the remaining 45 percent came from elsewhere in the United States, including signatures from citizens in every state as well as the District of Columbia.[25] According to WOS, over 44,000 signatures were collected from Louisiana alone.

FIGURE 12. Women of the Storm's third trip to Washington, March 27, 2011. Photograph by the author.

Holding blue-tarp umbrellas and standing behind a banner that read "Women of the Storm: A Coalition to Restore the Gulf Coast," WOS held yet another press conference on Capitol Hill in which speakers from each of the Gulf Coast states made their pitch to urge Congress to support their efforts to dedicate BP fines to the region. They emphasized that their position was in sync with the bipartisan oil spill commission, especially recommendations put forth in a spill-related investigatory document known as the Mabus Report. This report, produced by an Obama-appointed commission led by Secretary of the Navy Ray Mabus, "recommended that the President urge Congress to pass legislation that would dedicate a significant amount of any civil penalties recovered under the Clean Water Act from parties responsible for the Deepwater Horizon oil spill to those directly impacted by that spill," and that a "portion of any Clean Water Act civil penalties be directed to the Gulf states (Alabama, Florida, Louisiana, Mississippi, and Texas) to enable them to jumpstart their own recovery efforts."[26] A similar suggestion was made by the National Commission on the BP Deepwater Horizon Oil Spill and Offshore Drilling: "The Commission recommends Congress—recognizing that dedicated, sustained funding is necessary to accomplish long-term Gulf of Mexico ecosystem restoration—should direct 80 percent of Clean Water Act penalties to support implementation of a region-wide restoration strategy."[27] Congruent with these recommendations, WOS set out to make an ambitious request of Congress, one that would potentially change the course of the Gulf Coast recovery for many decades to come.

For WOS in 2011 many things had changed, but many things had remained the same. As one editorial at a regional newspaper put it, "Women of the Storm Become Women of the Spill."[28] Just as some group members brought pictures of their flooded homes after Katrina on the first trip to Washington, some women on the March 2011 trip, including Mid-City New Orleans resident Karen Kersting, carried oil-covered seashells that they had collected from beaches along the coast. As in their post-Katrina work, the women's investments in place continued to matter.[29]

Each state along the Gulf Coast was well represented that day in Washington. More than a dozen women from Mississippi joined WOS, including Harrison County supervisor Connie Rockco and Ocean Springs mayor Connie Moran.[30] Rockco made appeals to a moral order by saying, "In the past, the affected areas haven't gotten the money they should. We need the money to come to the counties that were directly impacted by the spill. It's a matter of principle, and it's the right thing to do."[31] Concerned about the fines going into the general treasury, Nonnie Debardeleben of Pass Christian, who served as the organizer for the delegation from Mississippi, said, "Potentially, none of it could come back to the Gulf Coast."[32] Debardeleben also said, "It's not about who gets what amount of money at this point. The point is, the money needs to be allocated, so it won't be spent out of the area."[33] Also speaking at the press conference that March morning was Casi Callaway of the Mobile Baykeepers, which, according to its website, is a "pro-development" group whose "efforts go toward research and education on any issues that may adversely affect the health of individuals and the health of the environment within the watershed."[34] At the speaker's podium, Callaway said, "This oil disaster has been a major component of our work this past 10 months. We firmly believe that the money from the fine must come back to the coast for restoration." She added, "Our Gulf Coast representatives and, frankly, every representative in the country needs to know the money shouldn't go into a big kitty for general fund operations."[35]

Lucy Buffett of Gulf Shores, Alabama, also spoke at the press conference: "I am literally a fish out of water here. I am not very political, but I'm very passionate about where I live." Buffett, a popular Gulf Coast personality with restaurants in Gulf Shores and Destin, Florida, comes from a family that has worked on the waters of the gulf for generations; her brother is singer-songwriter Jimmy Buffett. "You want to learn how to cook a gumbo, I'm your go-to-girl," she said. "You want to know the health of Mobile Bay, Casi is your go-to-girl. So, I'm not really political. So this is a no brainer for me. This is manners 101. You mess up something. You go clean it up."[36]

The Louisiana delegation was by far the largest. One participant from Louisiana, Jennifer Armand, was executive director of the Bayou Industrial Group, an organization of businesses, individuals, and nonprofits from Lafourche, Terrebonne, Assumption, and St. Mary parishes, including the metropolitan area of Houma and Thibodaux, Louisiana. "It's a tremendous event," said Armand, "because of the power of having all of these women gathered together meeting in Washington on one day on one serious issue. It says a lot about the value of our coast and our coastal resources."[37] There were several women from Terrebonne and Lafourche, including Simone Theriot Maloz, director of Restore or Retreat; Carol LeBlanc, member of the Bayou Industrial Group; Arlanda William, member of the Terrebonne Parish Council; Jane Arnette, director of the South Central Industrial Association; and Lori Davis, president of Rig-Chem Inc.[38] "It is a very natural mission for us to undertake," Maloz added in an interview with HoumaToday.com, "especially since we're unfortunately very used to having to fight for things."[39]

The core members emphasized unity across the Gulf Coast states. In the days before the third trip, Nancy Marsiglia spoke on television about the next chapter in WOS's history: "This trip is so crucial to have all five states together, because this is [a] Gulf states coalition to show the Congress and the country how important this part of the country is to the entire nation." A well-informed political strategist, she emphasized unification: "If we all band together, then the smaller states, Louisiana, Mississippi, and Alabama, are with their bigger neighbors, and perhaps they [Congress] will listen a little bit better to the cause."[40] In the group's press release, Milling is quoted as saying, "These women are going to Washington in a spirit of bipartisanship because they know that it is both fair and reasonable for BP to pick up the tab for Gulf Coast restoration, rather than forward the bill to tax-payers in the future."[41] She went on to say, "If Congress doesn't pass legislation to dedicate the fines into a Gulf Coast recovery fund, billions of dollars from the pockets of BP will be washed away into the general fund. At this time, there is no requirement for the BP dollars to be used to restore this region's ability to provide the nation with sustainable food supplies, energy production and other natural resources."[42]

Politicians from the Louisiana delegation were on board with WOS's goals, including Louisiana congressman Steve Scalise, a Republican representing Baton Rouge. In a written statement circulated among reporters, Scalise said, "It is only proper that the Gulf Coast states receive the lion's share of the fines BP will have to pay as a result of this disaster, and it is imperative that we work together without delay to move this legislation forward."[43] Drawing comparisons between the teamwork of the New Orleans Saints and that of WOS, Scalise said, "We are here today to turn what has been a tragedy into something positive for our long-term restoration of the entire Gulf Coast. And I'm sure as Rita Benson LeBlanc would tell you, you don't accomplish great things by yourself, you've got to build a strong team if you want to get those three things done. And what you are looking at here behind us is a great team that has been assembled."[44] Again, the group politics, the teamwork, mattered tremendously. Mary Landrieu joined WOS that morning confident that they would achieve their goals. She chimed in, saying, "I have absolutely no doubt, ladies, that we will be successful with our determination and your stormy personalities."[45] Other famed political leaders championed the group's cause. Speaking on the *Huffington Post* radio talk show, for example, Mary Matalin made a pitch for WOS: "If anyone deserves the disaster relief fund expenses, it is the very location that has suffered the disaster. Look for us on the Hill . . . Women of the Storm, of all stripes."[46]

After the press conference the women split up and fanned out for another round of prearranged Hill visits. And yet again a small group of influential women worked to shape the trajectory of a region in collective distress.

In March 2012 the Senate voted to direct 80 percent of Clean Water Act fines from the BP oil spill to Gulf Coast states as part of the RESTORE Act. This echoed WOS's requests to direct the majority of fine money to the five Gulf Coast states where the damage occurred. Giving some credit to WOS, Landrieu told reporters, "You do not get a Senate vote like we did without major help."[47] In June the House passed the act, and on July 6, 2012, President Obama signed the RESTORE Act into law.[48]

Conclusion

On moral selves and moral communities

On October 5, 2014, the *New York Times Magazine* turned its spotlight on Louisiana's wetlands with its cover story, "Waterworld: The Most Ambitious Environmental Lawsuit Ever." On the magazine's cover was a sweeping, edge-to-edge color photo of the Barataria-Terrebonne estuary in south Louisiana. The focal point of the image was not the green vegetation but rather the water-filled spaces of a shipping canal that cut through the wetlands in a perfectly straight line. It was overlaid with a stark headline in bright yellow: "Every hour, an acre of Louisiana sinks into the sea. Who is to blame?"[1]

When I turned to the article's main text, I was struck by how familiar it all seemed, how closely the words resembled claims that WOS members had been making for nearly ten years:

> Each day, the state loses nearly the accumulated acreage of every football stadium in the N.F.L. Were this rate of land loss applied to New York, Central Park would disappear in a month. Manhattan would vanish within a year and a half. The last of Brooklyn would dissolve four years later. New Yorkers would notice this kind of land loss. The world would notice this kind of land loss. But the hemorrhaging of Louisiana's coastal wetlands has gone largely unremarked upon beyond state borders. This is surprising, because the wetlands, apart from their unique ecological significance and astounding beauty, buffer the impact of hurricanes that threaten not just New Orleans but also the port of South Louisiana, the nation's largest; just under 10 percent of the country's oil reserves; a quarter of its natural-gas supply; a fifth of its oil-refining capacity; and the gateway to its internal waterway system. The attenuation of Louisiana, like any environmental disaster carried beyond a certain point, is a national-security threat.[2]

The rest of the article focused on efforts to explain the causes and consequences of land loss; the heated conflicts over blame, in which the oil and gas industry are often singled out; and questions about who should shoulder the cost of restoring the coast. The story discussed struggles that long preceded Hurricane Katrina and continue to unfold many years after the BP oil spill, but curiously, there's no mention of WOS.

"Waterworld" is revealing of how Louisiana's struggles have made their way into the national discourse. Surely many political actors and public intellectuals have done their share to bring this information to the broader public. But as this book has shown, WOS members helped popularize these discourses and attempted to keep them on a national agenda. Having spent nearly a decade following the group's work, I was both surprised and not surprised that WOS was not mentioned. I was surprised, given that the points made in "Waterworld" were nearly identical to the information shared incessantly by WOS over the years, from small gatherings in New Orleans, to national television broadcasts and social media outlets, to the halls of Congress. Recall for a moment the group's actions at the Tad Gormley Stadium, at the Superdome during a Saints game, or in the Lower Ninth Ward school during Obama's campaign visit, where they used the football field to help visualize Louisiana's land loss. Or consider the group's event at the Port of New Orleans, which was used to show the city's connections to regional and national economic interests through oil and gas production, the seafood industry, and the shipping industry. Indeed, the claims were so familiar that it was as though the reporter had used the group's talking points as the skeleton for the article.

Yet I wasn't surprised that WOS was absent from the text, because I've learned that the work these women do is often part of what Arlene Kaplan Daniels calls "invisible careers." Their lives are part of a very particular social fabric, where wealth, work, capital, and status are tightly interwoven with gender in complex and often contradictory ways. Their contributions to society are routinely overlooked by those who often notice only male leaders whose masculinity seems to be a necessary prerequisite for being "charismatic." Moreover, the women themselves often don't take credit for their own work, especially when working in groups with other women.[3] One interviewee offered this observation: "And people say, 'Well, why women?' Who knows? We don't need the credit. That is a Lindy Boggs thing. If you just give away the credit, you can accomplish anything." Among these women there exists a deeply rooted tradition, revealed in the nod to Louisiana congresswoman Lindy Boggs, of deflecting acclaim, of receding to the background, of doing this work without any apparent direct economic or political gain.[4]

But in a way there is a system that keeps tabs on all of this invisible labor, adding entries to a register that records who is doing what, with whom, and for which particular cause. In many ways, yes, they were not compensated financially, and this is praiseworthy, but there is often another kind of payoff. That is, this individual and collective work—from civic participation to philanthropy to charitable giving to post-disaster activism—has the potential to accrue a particular form of value over time. While many participants said there were few benefits to doing this "community work," interviews coupled with the long list of write-ups in the society pages—once known as the "women's page"—demonstrates that there were indeed benefits. As sociologist Randall Collins has argued, "There is a realm of charitable ritual that may be regarded as financial investments repaid in a different coin: the coin of status."[5] Awards and accolades, mention in prominent media venues, or being named Mardi Gras royalty are among the biggest social rewards in New Orleans. In this context of status and social recognition, one could see why being part of "the List" of WOS participants mattered so much.

All of this reveals the larger social context in which WOS participants lived their lives, which would be a mistake to dismiss as inconsequential, frivolous, or unimportant. One need only peruse New Orleans's publications to see how the ruling class, as G. William Domhoff writes, is constituted by "relatively mundane people doing lots of relatively little things that add up to something very big."[6] Every year *New Orleans* magazine publishes a list of "Top Female Achievers," the *St. Charles Avenue* magazine publishes a list of "Activists of the Year," and *New Orleans CityBusiness* publishes a list of "Women of the Year." Many selected to participate in WOS were previously recognized in these venues or went on to be recognized in them; they often added WOS to their list of affiliations.

Group membership and level of participation varied widely. As this book has shown, some women were ongoing participants who made WOS one of their primary causes for years on end. Other members' participation was more episodic, usually centered on major WOS events rather than day-to-day operations. Others still were onetime participants or nominal supporters who dedicated precious time and energy to other causes deemed more urgent to their communities of origin. Yet the decision to participate, whether for years or even for one day, should not be minimized or taken lightly. In a post-disaster context, a moment when resources were strained beyond belief, the decision to participate in groups like WOS was one social, political, and moral choice, among many other difficult choices, about how to use one's time, energy, and other resources.

There is much to be gained from looking at these social networks and connections in the context of Katrina. It reveals how thoroughly embedded these women were in the social and institutional fabric of the city, both pre- and post-Katrina, and in helping shape dominant discourses of the recovery. Through the membership of key individuals, WOS is linked to almost every major group, organization, and institution in the city. An admittedly incomplete list includes, for example, women's civic organizations such as the Junior League, The Links, and Jack and Jill; cultural institutions such as the New Orleans Museum of Art and the Ashé Cultural Arts Center; religious institutions like Catholic Charities; major universities in New Orleans, including Dillard, Loyola, Tulane, and Xavier (and in Baton Rouge, Louisiana State University); the Preservation Resource Center, the New Orleans Saints, and the *Times-Picayune*, not to mention direct connections to political families and economic dynasties such as the Landrieus and the Kabacoffs. Many of these entities, organizations, and institutions contributed to the amplification and trumpeting of the group's cause. Reflecting on the history of the group, it is clear that one of WOS's major achievements was its alignment of so many vectors of power and influence, from the local and national media to the private and nonprofit sectors, from educational institutions to sports teams and civic groups. The biographies of WOS members are a crucial element of this part of the group's story. Participants drew upon a set of skills and networks that they had spent lifetimes developing and refining, and they used the particular forms of femininity, politeness, and class-specific skills honed over decades to make bold requests. By naming these connections, reflecting on the group's invisible labor, and mapping out the processes by which powerful groups rule and exert their influence, this book contributes to the understanding of the lives of those in the upper echelons of society.

The women expressed a powerful investment in the recovery of community, and this was deeply felt and at times all consuming. And because they committed their time and energies to a particular cause, they were able to accomplish what Louisiana politicians alone could not. This group sounded a constant drumbeat reminding national lawmakers of the disaster. Participants helped shape the political discourse about the disaster and the place of New Orleans in relation to the nation. They sought to draw out connections to place and make them explicit, focusing not only on Louisiana's culture and history but also on issues that resonated with those far removed from New Orleans, such as economics and national security.

I've often been asked if the group accomplished what it set out to achieve. If success is measured by having every member of Congress visit New Orleans, then the group fell short of its original goals. Nonetheless, the group believed it brought about some significant change. When WOS formed, only 23 senators and 36 members of the House had visited Katrina's destruction. After the group's first trip to Washington, dozens of members of Congress, including those on a trip led by Speaker of the House Dennis Hastert and House Minority Leader Nancy Pelosi, visited New Orleans. By September 2006, shortly after the first-year anniversary of Hurricane Katrina, 55 members of the Senate and 107 members of the House had visited New Orleans and coastal Louisiana, according to the group's count.[7] The group kept a detailed record of visits, and members targeted committee chairs in Congress, noting that 10 of 16 committee chairs in the House of Representatives had not visited and that 6 of 10 Senate committee chairs had not made the trip. Years later, in 2012, and in the wake of the BP oil spill, the group claimed that 57 senators (28 Democrats, 28 Republicans, and 1 Independent) and 142 representatives (84 Democrats and 58 Republicans) had visited.[8] Clearly, they believed that they were at least partly responsible for making these visits happen. Perhaps more importantly, they were involved in a kind of post-Katrina record keeping that attempted to quantify broader sentiments in Washington, based on the assumption that a visit to the scene of destruction expressed a willingness to consider the requests and perspectives of those affected by the storms.

Legislation is another way of measuring WOS's influence on U.S. history and politics. For example, not long after the group's first trip to Washington, Congress approved full federal funding for the Road Home housing recovery program.[9] Shortly after the group's second trip, Congress approved measures that provided federal revenue sharing from oil and gas drilling along the Gulf Coast's Outer Continental Shelf, a portion of which would be directed toward coastal restoration projects. In addition to playing a key role in the passage of the Gulf of Mexico Energy Security Act, signed into law by President Bush in December 2006, the group is credited by some observers as helping pass the RESTORE Act, signed by President Obama on July 6, 2012. Under the RESTORE Act, 80 percent of the civil penalties collected from those responsible for the oil spill would be directed to a newly created trust fund for "ecological and economic restoration." A press release from the U.S. Department of Treasury estimated that by 2014 more than $653 million in civil penalties and interest had already been deposited into the fund.[10] It would be impossible to measure the precise influence of WOS on particular policy decisions, but that has not been my goal. Ascertaining exactly how much credit could be given to this group rather than others that similarly pressed Congress in the wake of these disasters would require different methods from those employed here. But the fact that so many lawmakers accepted the group's invitations and that the group was repeatedly mentioned in media accounts and congressional records suggests that WOS has played a significant role in the Gulf Coast recovery.

Scholars of social movement groups often focus on tangible and material outcomes, overlooking more subtle and everyday group accomplishments. That WOS members secured meetings in the masculine spaces of Washington at all is another accomplishment. As Mary Landrieu noted, "Washington, D.C., is a very difficult place to navigate, but the Women of the Storm found a way to steer their ship over very choppy waters and helped to pass the RESTORE Act."[11] As Landrieu suggests, not all civil society groups are granted lawmakers' time or attention, so even gaining access to these powerful figures to start the conversation tells us a great deal about the women's success at political maneuvering. Media sources documented numerous lawmakers shifting their positions on recovery funding as a result of WOS's work, and congressional records show senior politicians such as Nancy Pelosi and Hillary Clinton praising the group's efforts, aligning themselves with a women's group they deemed worthy of endorsing.

An analysis that maps networks of power is only one part of the picture that I've shown here. There is also the issue of understanding the processes by which subjects make their lives meaningful, interpret actions, and produce narratives about themselves and their relations with others. This study has focused not only on what women did but also on who they are and how they see their lives. Given the structural location of those in this study, how can we understand their actions and identities? An ethnographic and microhistorical study like this can help fill in the gaps.

What motivated these women to come together? It seems easy to argue, as the group's post-BP critics did, that these women were simply guided by economic self-interest, and that in doing so they advanced what Naomi Klein has called "disaster capitalism," in which elites use free-market economic policies to "impose unwanted economic shock therapy" in the wake of disaster as part of the "perpetual quest for clean sheets and blank slates on which to build model states."[12] And there is no doubt that WOS was situated within a broader context that anthropologist Vincanne Adams calls the "affect economy," in which there is a "coalescing of interests and institutional arrangements in which charity, faith, patronage, and for-profit capitalism are knitted together."[13] According to Adams, philanthrocapitalism, venture philanthropy, and charity "appear as new mechanisms of redistribution for taking care of those in need." Adams writes, "We are all asked to participate in this affect economy in new ways, with new demands on our time—both paid and unpaid—in the effort to take care of those in need."[14] WOS's unpaid work and time commitments reinforced this affect economy.

The stories in this book both add to and complicate narratives about philanthropy and disaster capitalism. While it remains true that many participants had direct and indirect economic interests in the rebuilding of the Gulf Coast, their voices can't be reduced to expressions of false consciousness speaking in the interest of market forces, class hegemony, or the men in their lives. The women were much more than puppets for neoliberal economic policies. Their reasons for coming together were not determined solely by macro-level processes in the "quest for unfettered capitalism," although market relations clearly both enabled and constrained their civic activism. The narratives in this book show that there are no simple or blanket explanations that can fully account for WOS's individual and collective actions, which were shaped by complex life experiences, social forces, and moral commitments. The women were engaged in collective activities and in self-reflexive processes that took place over many months and years.

As I investigated WOS's activities, I found that their political efforts to aid the rebuilding of the Gulf Coast were only one part of the women's stories. They were simultaneously rebuilding their identities and moral selves. They wanted to do community work that allowed them to see themselves as good people committed to worthy causes. They wanted to fill their lives with meaning and direction, and they sought to contribute to public life in positive ways. It would be easy to dismiss this identity work as inconsequential given the enormity of the Gulf Coast recovery efforts after multiple extreme events over the years. But I view these moral identities as central not only to the reproduction of self but also to the reproduction of a host of other group and institutional arrangements. Recovery work—on the self and for the community—becomes an important analytic concept for discussing how individual and societal concerns overlap and how participants see themselves, their activities, and their relations to others. In the context of small group participation in recovery efforts, the individuals in WOS were involved in the meaning-making processes of reconstructing selfhood and community through the negotiation of social relations and moral bonds. This, in turn, reproduced group and institutional arrangements.

Social scientists who draw on the symbolic interactionist tradition have described the self as arising out of group life and micro-level social interaction. Such an ongoing process was clearly articulated in how participants spoke about their experiences, revealing that many aspects of the self, rather than being static, were being repaired through carefully managed conduct and interaction. Despite the fact that women from diverse backgrounds were recruited based on seemingly fixed racial and ethnic identities, narratives reveal that these differences were in a constant state of being produced and reproduced, problematized and reinscribed, through social interactions and the formation of new structural and organizational arrangements. Group emergence provided an arena for a reconstruction of a moral self, a process guided by a commitment to a greater social good. At stake was what Rebecca Anne Allahyari has referred to as "moral selving," which she understands as "the creation of oneself as a more virtuous, and often more spiritual, person" or what Sherryl Kleinman has called a "moral identity," an "identity that people invest with moral significance"; for Kleinman, "our belief in ourselves as good people depends on whether we think our actions and reactions are consistent with that identity."[15] Participation in WOS became, for many members, a sign of good character. The emergent group provided individuals space to engage in moral identity work in a period of "identity discontinuity that has resulted from *displacement*, or the involuntary disruption of place attachment."[16] Participation thus also reflected a wider investment in a moral community. Because these interactions occurred in an emerging small group context, the women more explicitly examined their place in the world and their relations to one another. While some individuals in the group certainly experienced enhanced social status, many members crafted moral selves by seeking to establish "new forms of moral responsibility."[17] Although this book has focused on the public aspects of the group's civic actions after disaster, it also has aimed to trace out this process of moral self-reconstruction.

In constructing new forms of moral responsibility in the context of catastrophe, WOS participants grappled with representing themselves and others through their words and actions, especially as they tried to build alliances to counter the racism and classism that are particularly strong in New Orleans. There were some great risks involved in these bridge-making efforts. In the conclusion to a study of how religious civic organizations seek to cross social divides, sociologist Paul Lichterman argues, "Failures to bridge do more than weaken alliances, lose campaigns, or hurt feelings; they may squander the good reputation that groups and their leaders spent years accumulating and make the next alliance project more difficult."[18] For WOS, the moral foundations of these disaster-related issues informed the group's internal diversification and their efforts to partner with external groups and organizations. These practices, in turn, created a sense of group solidarity whereby differences were addressed (though by no means eliminated) through their women-centered alliances and concerted efforts toward inclusion.

It is important to note that the women's moral selving took place in a group context. In this sense, the emergent group is one location where identity, culture, and social movements coincide. Participation in WOS allowed members to see themselves as part of a broader community, united by their shared commitment to place. Many felt their lives were interconnected by virtue of the unprecedented devastation of the place they called home. One black woman I interviewed, a middle-class rather than elite participant, described the women's mutually dependent and interrelated lives: "My [WOS partner's] house may not have been destroyed by the storm, but her destiny is still tied up with my destiny. No matter which perspective we came from, all of us needed the same thing. One of us—we can't do it without the other at this point." For her, as with others I interviewed, the struggle for collective survival was played out in a group context rather than individually. She discussed strength in numbers and the need for collective rather than individual action: "So the powerless became powerful because we were united. We were powerless if we would have gone individually, but we became powerful. And I think the proof is in the pudding, because since the trip, the visits that we have received from senators who were conscious, who were awakened because of our visit."

Anne Milling, like many WOS participants, expressed similar sentiments about the power of working together as women. This collective work even allowed some of them to align themselves with a feminist politics, albeit cautiously. In an oral history interview from 2012, Newcomb College undergraduate Kaitlin Splett asked Milling whether or not she considered herself a feminist. Seemingly caught off guard by the directness of Splett's question, Milling let out a brief laugh and then said, "I don't know. That's tricky." She continued by saying that she enjoyed working side by side with women and men in numerous organizations over the course of her career and that she had never lingered over the question "Am I a feminist?" But since Katrina and her participation with those in WOS, Milling reflected, she has grown in appreciation and affection for these women and what women can do. "Is that being a feminist? Well, if you want to say so, then maybe I am." Speaking about what women could accomplish collectively, she said, "I am just in awe. I feel so fortunate to have this experience, of being with them, of being in a leadership role with Women of the Storm. All of us working in concert for the good of the community. It's just blown my mind to see what women can do. And so if that's being a feminist, then I am."[19]

This link between the individual and the collective was also evident in the words of another WOS interviewee, a woman of color whose focus wavered between self-transformation and collective efforts to rebuild New Orleans:

> If I could think of something to do to help with the disaster, this would be the best. This is absolutely—this is my finest hour. Because as one person, there is not anything major you can do on your own that I know. I mean, you can't—there's no way for a person to ride in on a white charger in this situation. But as a group, this was really a significant thing that we can be proud of and we can feel like—I feel like I did the very best that I could do in the situation, and I'm very thankful for the opportunity to do the very best that we could do. We are the kind of women who want to do something significant, and this gave us that opportunity. That is what warms my heart, that at the end of the day, that's what makes me feel good, that I was a part of something that was significant and positive. I'm not out to make history. I'm out to feel good at the end of the day about my contribution to the rebuilding of New Orleans.

In many ways this response exemplifies how the group's civic actions were inextricable from repair of the self. At the same time that the participant remarked on the limits of individual approaches to rebuilding New Orleans, highlighting the importance of collective action, the outcome was also personal. Like many other women who experienced a great sense of personal efficacy, she described her group involvement as her "finest hour." Her individual transformation was shaped by the women's community work and organizing across race, class, and gender.[20]

When WOS first traveled to Washington in January 2006, coming together as women and attempting to bridge social difference in the wake of disaster, they did not set out to remake themselves. But many did. And while they did not set out to make history, the women also left a lasting mark on the historical record. Ultimately, the catastrophe wrought by hurricanes Katrina and Rita was the occasion for them to engage in new forms of civic activism and to rebuild their individual and collective lives.

Acknowledgments

This book has been a decade in the making. I began data collection while a PhD student in sociology at the University of Colorado Boulder (CU). Over ten years later, I've come full circle, with a difference, completing the final manuscript as a faculty member in the Department of Women and Gender Studies at the same institution. In that time my personal and intellectual journey has been meandering and full of disruptions and delight. Throughout the process, I found myself building incredible relationships with those who supported, in various ways, my efforts to write about the Hurricane Katrina recovery. Ultimately, this project was a collective endeavor and would not have been completed without the steadfast support provided by so many people. I am thus grateful to everyone who offered encouragement along the way.

First, I would like to extend my most sincere appreciation to all the women who agreed to be interviewed for this book. They welcomed me into their lives and allowed me to witness their collective efforts to help rebuild New Orleans and the Gulf Coast after Katrina. Without their trust, confidence, and generosity, this book would not have been possible.

I am thankful to several funders of my research. The initial fieldwork was funded by the Natural Hazards Center at CU under the center's Quick Response grant program supported by the National Science Foundation. I'm grateful for this valuable program, which allowed me to document some of the early moments of the recovery in New Orleans beginning in October 2005. Without the center's support, this book would not exist. Once in New Orleans, I benefited from advice and encouragement from the faculty and staff at the Newcomb College Center for Research on Women at Tulane University as well as support from Newcomb's Emily Schoenbaum Research and Community Development Grant. Generous awards from CU's Department of Sociology and the Arts and Sciences Dean's Fund for Excellence helped with travel and the transcriptions of my interviews. Sandy Grabowski deserves special thanks for transcribing more than one thousand single-spaced pages of interviews; she did so with wonderful skill and precision, and it was a pleasure to work with her. In the 2007–2008 academic year, I received support as a graduate student fellow at CU's Center for Humanities and the Arts, where I participated in a yearlong seminar with several other fellows from whom I received valuable suggestions and feedback. The Eugene M. Kayden Award at CU provided funds to help offset the costs for images and permissions. Portions of this book also appeared in *NWSA Journal* and *International Journal of Mass Emergencies and Disasters*.

Several people wholeheartedly welcomed me into their homes during the course of my fieldwork: John Clark, Lisa Di Stefano, Julie Schumacher Grubbs, Ellen Selvidge, and Brien Watson. I am grateful for their invitations and for their hospitality. I am also grateful to Harriet Swift, who, in addition to housing me for several months in early 2006, generously read through the entire manuscript many years later with an eye for the details and peculiarities of New Orleans.

Numerous friends, colleagues, and interlocutors have offered feedback, suggestions, and words of encouragement at various phases of the project, including Jake Amoroso, Scarlet Bowen, Matt Brown, Marcio Correia Campos, Juliann Couture, Jaclyn Darrouzet-Nardi, Jeffrey DeShell, Kristine De Welde, Susanne B. Dietzle, Kelly Elliot, Cynthia Enloe, Michaele Ferguson, Florence Fetterer, Alice Fothergill, Alison Hatch, Allison Hicks, Leslie Irvine, Carla Jones, Jessica Kahle, Marcus Kondkar, Anthony Ladd, Christopher Laferl, Jeanne Liotta, Leith Lombas, Katherine Martinez, Courtney McDonald, Carole McGranahan, Daniel McKernan, Bryce Merrill, Sanyu Mojola, Bruce Montgomery, Keri Oldham, Tara Opsal, Lori Peek, Hillary Potter, Mary Robertson, AnnJanette Rosga, Mario Rugerio, Kelly Sears, Elisabeth Sheffield, Gillian Silverman, Rebecca Snedeker, Rebecca Solnit, Teresa Toulouse, Beth Willinger, Sue Zemka, Michael Zimmerman, and Naida Zukic. I am grateful to them all and to the many others whose names I may have forgotten to include here.

Elissa Auther not only provided incisive feedback on earlier chapters but also offered encouraging words when I needed them most. Keri Brandt helped me find my voice in the text and read multiple drafts with a red pen in hand. Jade Aguilar was an excellent writing partner and helped push my ideas in new directions. Edward Dimendberg helped me refashion the book's narrative structure. Elaine Enarson, a pioneer in the sociological study of gender and disaster, offered valuable advice and support over the years. Allaina Wallace kept my inbox full with updates on recovery efforts in New Orleans, and her love for the city reminds me why New Orleans still matters.

In fall 2005, when I started my fieldwork in New Orleans, I was enrolled in a feminist methods seminar with Joanne Belknap and a feminist geography seminar with Lynn Staeheli. I'm thankful to them both for the incredible support they offered during that challenging semester. Sara Steen and Isaac Reed each contributed to this project in invaluable ways. I'd like to extend a special thanks to my faculty advisors, who not only shaped my intellectual development but also offered encouragement at critical turning points. Edward J. McCaughan molded my thinking at Loyola and first inspired me to pursue graduate studies. Somehow he knew that I would flourish. Kathleen Tierney opened my eyes to the field of disaster sociology and encouraged me to get into the ethnographic field as soon as possible. One afternoon, as we went over my fieldwork plan in her living room, she and her husband, Peter Park, announced that I was ready, giving me the confidence to enter the field and explore many possibilities. Janet Jacobs has been an unwavering source of inspiration and stability. Without a doubt, her compassion and friendship made this book possible. I benefited from her advice to remain focused on how participants made sense of their lives; the end result, I hope, reflects a deep capacity for sociology to humanize the ethnographic subject.

Many thanks are due to Jill McCorkle and my former colleagues in the Department of Sociology and Criminology at Villanova University. Colleagues in the Department of Women and Gender Studies at CU were especially supportive in the final stretch: Lorraine Bayard de Volo, Robert Buffington, Sam Bullington, Alison Jaggar, Deepti Misri, Celeste Montoya, and Robert Wyrod. I am also very grateful to Alicia Turchette and Valerie Bhat for all of their assistance.

Numerous librarians assisted me during my research. In October 2005, when huge swaths of New Orleans were still without electricity, let alone internet access or reliable cell phone service, I rode my bicycle to the Monroe Library at Loyola University, where librarians and staff set me up with computer access so that I could stay connected. I have since lost the piece of paper with the names of those who helped me, but I have not forgotten their kind gestures. Librarians at CU, Regis University, Auraria Library, and the University of Denver have all helped me track down hard-to-find materials. Toward the end of my research, Chloe Raub, head of Archives and Special Collections at the Newcomb College Institute of Tulane University, was particularly generous, and I am grateful to her and the staff at Newcomb for their archival research assistance. Karen T. Leathem and Wayne Phillips, both at the Louisiana State Museum, helped me clarify some points about Carnival history and culture.

It has been a pleasure to work with the current and former staff of the University of Illinois Press. I am particularly indebted to Dawn Durante, whose editorial expertise and keen eye for the readerly experience helped me sharpen the argument and narrative. She shepherded the project through peer review, and it emerged transformed for the better. I also want to extend my appreciation to Brigette Brown and Angela Burton, who assisted with permissions; to Jennifer Comeau, who guided design and production; to Kevin Cunningham in marketing; to Jill Hughes, a wonderful copyeditor; and to Larin McLaughlin, who initially accepted this project. Two external reviewers provided warm words of encouragement, some helpful criticisms, and on-point suggestions for revision, all of which have made this a stronger book.

For all of their support, I would like to thank my family, especially my brother, Eric David; my grandmother, Mae Danzl; my aunts in Colorado, Julie Stoupa and JoAnn Thomas; my uncle in Los Angeles, Erwin David; and my loved ones in Manila—my aunt, Marilyn Ruaro, and the entire Ruaro family, and my uncle, Eric David. Thanks, too, to my late grandparents, Purita David, Honorio David, and Jim Danzl. My mother, Janet Lee, always taught me important life lessons, and her commitment to education, libraries, and social justice has transformed my life as well as those of many people around the world; she even flew to New Orleans in 2006 to volunteer at the Algiers Regional Branch of the New Orleans Public Library. My father, Enrico David, reminded me not to work too hard and to save time for a meal together on weekends; he, too, visited me in post-Katrina New Orleans, as did my brother, Eric, and I'm grateful that they did. Both of my parents provided unconditional love and support, and they encouraged me to see the world, even though these adventures took me far away from home. It is serendipitous, then, that I managed to make my way back to Colorado. Finally, to Patrick Greaney, thanks for everything.

Notes on Method

When I began this project, there was very little information available on WOS other than a single newspaper article that listed the names of a few key members. After all, the group had just formed, and it would be several months before its members launched a website. Plus, with New Orleans in shambles in the wake of disaster, the internet rarely worked, and when it did, it was unreliable and frustrating. Rather than searching for information on the internet, I looked up names the old-fashioned way—using a telephone book—but most phone numbers were unlisted. It became clear that personal contact was necessary. But how would I get in touch?

Two days after WOS's first trip to Washington, I went to a community center in search of an African American woman whose name was printed in the newspaper article. Her name was listed in association with an established cultural institution, so I had a place to start. I went there and introduced myself, and we spoke for about an hour. She said she had gone on the trip, but emphasized that she was not one of the core organizers, just a rank-and-file member. The dynamics were instructive, illustrating a common pattern in field research on elites, in which initial contact is often with a person at the margins of the group.[1]

As I left this first interview, the woman gave me a contact list that had been distributed to WOS participants on the trip. I started calling participants from the list and leaving messages about my interest in speaking with them about their experiences. One of the first people I reached was a core member, who informed me that I had called at the start of their first meeting after their return from Washington. I told her that I was interested in learning more about the group as part of my research. She said if I was interested in studying the group, I would probably want to start attending their meetings. Initially surprised by the open invitation, I said I would love to interview as many of the women as possible. She said she would "bring this to the table." Almost immediately she called back to say that she had discussed my project with the group and emphasized that it would be good to "strike while the iron was hot." I agreed.

Days later I began observing the group's steering committee meetings, which I sat in on for several months. In addition, I attended the group's press conferences when congressional leaders visited New Orleans; I accompanied group members on drives through the city as they planned routes for the land tours of the affected areas; and on a couple of occasions I was even invited to observe private, closed-door meetings with elected officials, under the agreement that I would use this only as background information. Throughout my fieldwork, I recorded detailed field notes on organizational structures, group interactions, and the group's goals, strategies, and tactics.

As mentioned in the Introduction, this book is also based on forty-one open-ended interviews with WOS participants. I also interviewed nine women who were part of the same loose social network of civic activists and philanthropists and who participated in women-led emergence groups, like Citizens for One Greater New Orleans and Katrina Krewe, among others. Three of these nine women would go on to join WOS after my interviews with them. However, because they talked about the activities of these other groups and did not consider themselves WOS members at the time of our interviews, I have refrained from including them in calculating the total number of WOS members who participated in this study. I consider the remaining six interviewees to be indirectly associated with WOS because of their participation in groups that had significant overlapping membership and cross-pollination with WOS and/or because they belonged to the same social circles and philanthropic networks. I suspect but cannot verify that they also, at some point or in some capacity, participated in WOS events, even if only as nominal supporters. In this sense, all the women interviewed for this study were chosen because they were part of this larger context of post-Katrina emergence and incipient social movement activity, demonstrating that WOS's emergence did not occur in a vacuum.

To determine WOS membership and participation, I used numerous sources, including public and internal lists. Several lists of members were published in newspapers, magazines, and on the organization's website. The group also maintained an internal spreadsheet with names and contact information of members and supporters. Several typed and handwritten lists were included in the Women of the Storm records donated by Anne Milling to Newcomb in 2015. Depending on the source, the group size increased from the 130 who originally traveled to Washington in 2006 to anywhere between 300 and 600 members several years later.[2] Other people I observed were nominal supporters who attended local actions but whose names never made it onto one of these lists. In these ways, my discussion rests, in part, on notions of membership and participation (used somewhat interchangeably throughout the book) as fluid and situational. All of the interviews were conducted face-to-face; with two exceptions, the interviews were all one-on-one.[3] They were digitally recorded, transcribed, and then coded.

Interview participants were recruited through snowball sampling. When providing additional contacts, usually at the end of the interview, most white women were interested in introducing me to women who, for them, represented racial, ethnic, or economic difference. Some were particularly interested in putting me in contact with members who had lost their homes or those who had an extraordinary story of the storm. I pursued such leads with great interest. Some even tried to put me in touch with residents outside the group who had dramatic experiences of the disaster. For example, one woman wanted me to interview the maintenance worker who, during our interview, was cleaning her backyard pool. When I politely declined to interview him, she told me the story about his extraordinary escape from the rising floodwaters. I decided against pursuing such interviews, because they did not fall within the parameters of my project, which was beginning to coalesce around the experiences of WOS. But this moment revealed that the lives of the privileged were sometimes directly connected (often through employee-employer relations) to many others who suffered loss.

Snowball sampling revealed important findings related to my questions about group relations. Many interviewees used the method as an opportunity for engaging in organizational impression management, in which interviewees highlighted the racial diversity of the group. Disaster sociologist Kathleen Tierney has written about the importance of controlling an organization's image in times of disaster: "Virtually all organizations, both public and private, seek a favorable public image, and one means to accomplish this aim is to exercise control over information, including the kinds of information researchers seek. The need for organizational impression management is probably even more marked in disaster situations than during normal times."[4] This was the case for WOS. Rarely did I encounter backstage behavior, through a few unguarded moments made their way into my interviews and field notes.

In addition to snowball sampling, I used theoretical sampling to maximize variation within the data and define gaps in categories.[5] Many interviewees provided me with contact information that helped me craft a more diverse sample. It is worth noting that on several occasions, participants commented on how my sampling technique resembled the WOS's recruitment process, by which the core group branched out from existing friendship networks and associations to diversify.

In my in-depth interviews, I asked about how they became involved, their reasons for participating, and their reflections on group participation. I sought to understand how WOS members made sense of their collective participation and how they constructed a sense of self and belonging after disaster. Interviews revealed the complex (and often contradictory) meanings the women attributed to their work and to their relations with one another. I have tried to represent what the interviewees told me as accurately as possible. I have tried to remain as critical as possible by pointing out tensions in relation to race, class, and gender while also adhering to the principles of interactionist sociology that aim to view events through the eyes of participants.

In line with my goals to account for the diverse experiences of participants, demographic information (such as age, race, sex, political party affiliation, marital status, personal and household income, level of education, and occupation) was collected during the interviews. I have used this information at times to contextualize the narratives and to provide more aggregate-level description of the group composition.

Determining socioeconomic status was particularly difficult. Interviewees were asked to report individual and household income levels; however, most of them chose not to share this information. Thus, I used several factors to try to ascertain class status, including professional careers, lifestyle, education, sociopolitical connections, residence in areas with high land and property values (most of which did not flood), and membership in exclusive clubs tied to the Carnival tradition in New Orleans.

I collected information on the interviewees' neighborhoods and zip codes. This, too, revealed complexities of researching in a disaster setting. Women whose homes fared well during the storm provided answers without hesitation. Women who had lost their homes, or who were temporarily or permanently displaced, asked me to clarify what information I was interested in obtaining. Some would say, "Do you mean before or after the storm?" In all, I interviewed at least eight women whose homes flooded during Katrina. I learned that there were many more WOS members whose homes flooded, based on accounts in the public record. Over the course of the study, I found that this experience often correlated with the raced geography of New Orleans. For example, two of the three Vietnamese women interviewed reported that their residences had been flooded. Half of the black women in my interview sample (three of six) reported that their homes had been flooded, compared with only three of the thirty white women I interviewed.

The issue of dislocation came up again when I asked about household size. For example, one interviewee clarified by saying that both of her adult children lost their homes in the flood and that they were currently living with her while their homes were being gutted. Another responded to the number-in-household question by making a before-and-after comparison, saying that before the storm there were four in the household, but at the time of the interview several months after the storm, one of her high-school-age children was finishing school in another state.

The interviews took place in a variety of locations, ranging from coffee shops and restaurants to private settings, including respondents' un-flooded residences, gutted homes, or FEMA trailers. In public settings, interviews were situated in a social context where post-disaster reunions were common or where friends and acquaintances unexpectedly saw one another for the first time after the storm. In these settings, interviews were often interrupted when friends and acquaintances would stop by to ask the interviewee about her evacuation and her return to the city. Interruptions took other forms. During one interview that took place outside, we were forced to stop several times by the deafening sound of military helicopters hovering overhead, an occurrence that had been common in the months after the storm. During an interview in a restaurant with a woman who lost her home, our conversation was interrupted several times by phone calls from contractors. Later, in the same interview, one neighbor saw the interviewee for the first time and asked how her displaced mother was doing.

When interviews were conducted in more personal settings, such as flooded homes, interviewees often provided me with extended tours and explained the extent of damage, the height of the floodwater, as well as the progress made in rebuilding. Several respondents also interrupted interviews to retrieve photos of their homes prior to the storm or to gather documents relevant to my interview questions. They often offered copies of these documents, which enabled me to refer to them as I read through the final interview transcripts. Thus, the exact length of interviews often extended well beyond the average two hours to include these pre- and post-interview rituals.

Access to homes during interviews also allowed me see things that remained invisible or difficult to ascertain during interviews conducted in public settings. As discussed throughout the book, socioeconomic class was one issue that was often carefully managed. For example, when asked about income level, one white woman responded in an eloquent Southern accent, "You know, I'm not going to get into the income part. I'd rather believe that y'all don't care about that."

Some white women had paid house help, mostly women and men of color who during our interviews engaged in chores such as washing dishes, preparing food in the kitchen, doing yard work, or cleaning swimming pools. Other white women commented on the displaced domestic labor force and on being required to prepare their own meals, iron clothing, or pick up dry cleaning themselves. For some, this was a matter of inconvenience; for others, it offered a newfound feeling of independence and autonomy. While I did not request information on paid house help, many respondents mentioned the loss of household help as an important dimension of post-Katrina everyday life. Several women shared the storm stories of employees who worked in their homes and who appeared to be close to their families.[6]

There are some limitations to the interviews. First, my research makes no claims to be a random or representative sample of a general population or even of all WOS members. It should be noted that significant proportions of the population were displaced at the time of my fieldwork, and most WOS participants were among the privileged who were able to return to New Orleans within a relatively short period, four to five months, after the storm.[7] While some women from other parts of Louisiana went on the trip, most of my interviewees were drawn from the New Orleans area, and thus my sample is skewed toward those from the city. Second, I did not interview the women who were not invited to participate in the group nor those in the general population, so I cannot make broad claims about how the women were received by members of the community, other than what has been reported in the public record. Third, I don't have data on those who may have declined to participate (though I'm not aware of anyone who did so). In these ways, my interviewees are, to some degree, self-selected.

To provide additional context, I also use documentary and archival sources. The collection of natural documents provides data that fix current events and actions for future inspection.[8] Many disaster researchers have systematically collected and analyzed formal documents such as official reports and memos, as well as mass media content and articles. Other documentary data, though often overlooked in disaster research, constitute an important source of information for yielding sociological insights. I used what E. L. Quarantelli calls "nonreactive items," which include material not frequently obtained by disaster researchers, such as "organizational minutes of meetings, informal group logs, business transaction data, . . . letters, diaries, graffiti and informal signs, bulletin board items, family albums, religious sermons."[9] I tried to collect as much documentary evidence as possible to help enrich the level of detail included in this study. My systematic collection of natural documents and "nonreactive items" yielded an archive of hundreds of items, each of which I stamped with the date and location of my acquisition. Examples of natural documents include informational packets used during the women's Capitol Hill visits, faxes, memos, invitations extended to members of Congress, meeting agendas, and minutes used during weekly gatherings. Other items include tickets to the film screenings handed out to lawmakers, handouts distributed at events, and a gold-foil-embossed fleur-de-lis table napkin that an interviewee placed under my water glass to protect the furniture at her home. I also drew upon online resources, such as blogs and news sites. As I completed the book in 2016, I was able to consult the WOS records donated to Newcomb College by Anne Milling in 2015.[10]

In addition to in-depth interviews, documentary, and archival sources, I engaged in participant observation and field research. This is a widely recognized method, so much so that sociologist Robert Stallings says, "The prototypical method of disaster research has been the field study."[11] After my initial contacts, I was invited to attend various private planning meetings, strategy sessions, and public events. However, unlike active or complete membership, my role could be characterized as shifting between participant-as-observer, observer-as-participant, and peripheral-member researcher.[12] Patricia Adler and Peter Adler define observer-as-participant as "a rather detached, overt role, typically involving brief and highly formalized interactions between researchers and members, with no attempts to establish enduring relationships by either side."[13] I took on the observer-as-participant role in several field settings, especially when group members engaged in collective actions and my participation was relegated to observing or playing minor roles, such as carrying supplies or distributing water. In the context of smaller group interactions, usually with the core group, or during informal interactions before or after organized collective actions, I often took on the role of participant-as-observer, which "is also an overt role, but involves greater contact and intimacy between the researchers and subjects."[14]

There are several reasons why I used participant observation as a method. It yielded important descriptive data that situates interviews within a specific historical and cultural context.[15] Moreover, participant observation provided access to many implicit group meanings and values that characterize social movement groups.[16] During my fieldwork, I attended numerous public demonstrations, including rallies, marches, and educational events, which provided important qualitative data to contextualize WOS's work in a disaster setting. Participant observation yielded over three hundred single-spaced typed pages of field notes on social and political context, group and individual interaction, and the research process.

Interpersonal relations were also a consideration. I found that I needed to establish and maintain rapport with the women with whom I had episodic or regular contact. The conditions for this rapport were related to socioeconomic class. I was aware of the awkward gap between my middle-class background and the class of many of the women I interviewed. Without a car, I arrived at most interviews by bicycle, rain or shine. And even when I dressed up for special occasions, it was clear that we didn't shop at the same kind of stores (not to mention that I was still episodically following radical volunteer groups and found myself tweaking my style for each audience, sometimes changing from dark hoodies to collared shirts, or sometimes trying to figure out a nondescript outfit suitable for both research sites). In addition to dressing for occasions, I tried to maintain rapport by minding my manners. After in-depth interviews, for example, I was sure to send thank-you cards. This correspondence was particularly important because it helped show respect and gratitude and complemented my efforts to "polish" my manners during my face-to-face interactions. For example, I learned to regularly use the formal address "yes, ma'am" when interacting with many of the older women, which showed them that I understood social conventions of deference. In reviewing my field notes several years later, I saw an entry that remarked upon my transition from studying the radical volunteer group to studying elite women. In that note, I observed that I had begun to shower more often and give extra consideration to hygiene. Taken together, this demonstrates how all sorts of "relearning and resocialization" occur in the fieldwork process.[17]

My research activities and relationships with participants were not flawless. I was not only resocialized but also, in some cases, actively disciplined by participants. Despite efforts to mind my manners, group members also exerted powerfully felt mechanisms of social control, both formally and informally, on several occasions. In other words, I was not a neutral, fly-on-the-wall ethnographer, but often an active participant in the coproduction of these ethnographic moments. When my efforts fell short, or if members were concerned about my words or actions, I definitely heard about it. There were times I overdressed, but more often than not I underdressed for the occasions, showing that I clearly did not understand the unspoken expectations for a given situation. Some quietly eyed the hole in my jeans or the dirt on my shoes, while one woman discreetly recommended that I wear a suit jacket to a specific event, an item of clothing I did not have in New Orleans at the time.

There were embarrassing encounters and mishaps. On the plane returning from one of the trips in Washington, I clumsily bumped a participant, sending an entire glass of red wine all over her crisp white blouse. Mortified, I sheepishly returned to my seat. In this case, no discipline was needed. My only saving grace was that this blunder occurred on the plane ride home rather than before their meetings with lawmakers. Years later I made visits to New Orleans for the book launch of my edited volume on women and Katrina and, to my regret, didn't invite group members, thinking that the anthology didn't directly relate to them (it only reprinted a previously released essay about the group). When participants found out and showed up at the book release, I was told that I should have let them known in advance. "Not to act like your mother," one woman said to me moments before I was to speak before the audience, "but you should have called." Through these disciplinary practices and acts of self-cultivation, I found that I had entered a world not of my own making, a world in which existing cultures, practices, and codes of conduct carried great meaning in the making of the ethnographic scene. Ethnographers often tend to write up glowing accounts of their activities, writing out the messiness, the mistakes, the embarrassments. But there is much to learn about the everyday connections we make (and sometimes break) with participants.

Similarly, there were also age and gender dynamics to be negotiated. After spending time with the group, I began to be introduced by the women, sometimes with great enthusiasm, as their "own graduate student," or as an honorary "Man of the Storm." They also gave me items to show support for the group. On one occasion I decided not to wear their button in public and was met with the question "Where is your button?" Although the women aligned me with the group through a slight modification of the group's name, however playful or affectionate this title may have been, there was little chance of anyone actually mistaking me as a complete group member. Despite my outsider status, which was commented on during several interviews, my pre-storm ties to New Orleans, as a graduate of Loyola University, carried great weight and bestowed a sort of insider status on me. Many women hoped that I would stay in the city as a young working professional. They'd say things like "we need you here," or "we need every young person we can get."

Social location and "positionality" mattered in my fieldwork.[18] I believe my age, gender, and status as a doctoral student worked to my advantage. I benefited from male privilege, experiencing a sort of "glass escalator" effect as a young man in the fields of sociology and gender studies.[19] Numerous women were intrigued that I would make a women's group the focus of my research. Another researcher, a white woman about the same age as many WOS participants, attempted to gain access to the group and to some degree was successful. But she was met with some suspicion by several group members who were concerned that she was trying to "dig up dirt" or find an embarrassing "angle" to report. Some participants made observing the group more difficult for her than for me. It is quite possible that they saw me as less threatening because of my student status.

Race and ethnicity were also at play in my fieldwork. On several occasions, my background as a Filipino American figured prominently in my fieldwork. Light skin color gave me some added social capital in the field, allowing me to move through the research setting relatively unhindered.[20] For some participants, I appeared racially ambiguous, and this became a topic of conversation. For example, one woman asked if I was Cajun, another if I was from South America. Yet another commented, "I mean I can't tell what you are. I'm looking at you going, 'what are you?'"[21] Race and ethnicity was also a liability for me as an ethnographic field-worker. On one occasion during my research, I was stopped by law enforcement as I was cycling through a Katrina-devastated neighborhood. After hearing sirens, then the voice on the patrol vehicle's loudspeaker commanding me to dismount and get on the ground, I was required to sit on the curb while the officers checked my identification. I was finally let go after showing papers with my institutional affiliation that explained that I was in New Orleans conducting research. Perhaps I was in the wrong place at the wrong time, and on a bicycle at that, but I can't help but think that ideas of race and ethnicity (and age and gender) were all part of the reasons I was stopped. After reading accounts of interactions with law enforcement in Katrina's wake, such as those chronicled by writers like Dave Eggers in his book *Zeitoun*, I feel I was quite lucky in my encounter.[22]

The particulars of fieldwork matter because the processes by which it unfolds tells us something about the topic at hand. As Robert Emerson explains, "The very processes of getting on in the field, of dealing with recurrent problems such as entrée, access, and rapport, reveal critical substantive and theoretically relevant features of the setting under study."[23] This point holds for my study, because every twist and turn in my fieldwork was shaped by the uncertainty of the disaster context and the dynamic social interactions with this emerging group. Had I not been both an outsider and a quasi-insider with a very different background from most participants, I might not have gained access to this group in the first place. Perhaps most importantly, my entrée was situated within a narrow window of opportunity. Had I not been in New Orleans at the time, I would never have had the chance to follow these rapidly changing developments or this group of women.

Notes

Prologue

1. Laura Nader, "Up the Anthropologist: Perspectives Gained from Studying Up," in *Reinventing Anthropology*, ed. Dell Hymes, 284–311 (New York: Pantheon Books, 1972).

2. Manav Tanneeru, "Baton Rouge Swells with Evacuees," CNN.com, September 9, 2005.

Introduction

1. Editorial, "Death of an American City," *New York Times*, December 11, 2005, C11. With its focus on recovery and rebuilding efforts, this book does not offer an in-depth account of Katrina at the height of the crisis. For that overview, see Douglas Brinkley, *The Great Deluge: Hurricane Katrina, New Orleans, and the Mississippi Gulf Coast* (New York: Harper Collins, 2006).

2. Elisabeth Bumiller, "Bush Pledges Federal Role in Rebuilding Gulf Coast," *New York Times*, September 16, 2005, A1. On Katrina's militarized response, see Ann Scott Tyson, "Troops Back from Iraq Find Another War Zone; In New Orleans, 'It's Like Baghdad on a Bad Day,'" *Washington Post*, September 6, 2005, A10.

3. "Death of an American City."

4. Richard Campanella, "An Ethnic Geography of New Orleans," *Journal of American History* 93, no. 3 (2007): 704–715.

5. See Lynn Weber and Lori Peek, eds., *Displaced: Life in the Katrina Diaspora* (Austin: University of Texas Press, 2012).

6. "Death of an American City."

7. Tom Wooten, *We Shall Not Be Moved: Rebuilding Home in the Wake of Katrina* (Boston: Beacon Press, 2012), xv.

8. Associated Press, "Many in Louisiana, Texas Lament 'Amnesia,'" *USA Today*, January 25, 2006, http://usatoday30.usatoday.com/news/nation/2006-01-25-rita_x.htm; Doug Simpson, "Rita Plays Second Fiddle to Katrina," *Times-Picayune*, January 29, 2006, A8.

9. "Many in Louisiana."

10. Kathleen Blanco, "Gov. Blanco's Speech to the Louisiana Legislature," special session of the Legislature, February 6, 2006.

11. Following social science conventions, I protect the identities of interviewees. However, I use real names when presenting historical information that is a matter of public record, or when those named, following Eric Klinenberg's approach, "were impossible to disguise, either because the significance of their accounts is related to the roles they played . . . or because they are already on record for their involvement in the event." See Klinenberg, *Heatwave: A Social Autopsy of Disaster in Chicago* (Chicago: University of Chicago Press, 2002), xvii. On the politics of naming names and places, see Alexandra Murphy and Colin Jerolmack, "Ethnographic Masking in an Era of Data Transparency," *Contexts* 15, no. 2 (2016): 14–17.

12. Bruce Alpert, "Louisiana Women Storm Washington," *Times-Picayune*, January 31, 2006, 4.

13. Two days after Katrina's landfall, Hastert received criticism for saying, "It looks like a lot of that place could be bulldozed." Charles Babington, "Hastert Tries Damage Control after Remarks Hit a Nerve," *Washington Post*, September 3, 2005, A17.

14. Adam Nossiter, "A Big Government Fix-It Plan for New Orleans," *New York Times*, January 5, 2006, A1.

15. Jonathan Tilove, "Women of the Storm Urge Congress to Devote BP Penalties to Coastal Restoration," *Times-Picayune*, March 29, 2011, http://www.nola.com/politics/index.ssf/2011/03/women_of_the_storm_urge_congre.html.

16. To the extent that it has become institutionalized over time, the group has increasingly become a social movement organization. For a discussion of emergent groups as social movement organizations, see David Neal and Brenda Phillips, "Female-Dominated Local Social Movement Organizations in Disaster-Threat Situations," in *Women and Social Protest*, ed. Guida West and Rhoda Lois Blumberg, 243–55 (New York: Oxford University Press, 1990).

17. I use the phrase "emergent groups" in place of "emergent citizen groups" to demonstrate that legal status is not a prerequisite for participation in disaster response and recovery efforts. On emergent groups, see Russell R. Dynes, *Organized Behavior in Disasters* (Lexington, MA: Lexington Books, 1970); Robert A. Stallings, "The Structural Patterns of Four Types of Organizations in Disaster," in *Disasters: Theory and Research*, ed. E. L. Quarantelli, 87–103 (London: Sage Publications, 1978); Kathleen Tierney, Michael Lindell, and Ronald Perry, *Facing the Unexpected: Disaster Preparedness and Response in the United States* (Washington, DC: Joseph Henry Press, 2001).

18. Kathleen Tierney, "Research Overview: Emergency Response," *Proceedings of the NEHRP Conference and Workshop on the Northridge, California, Earthquake of January 17, 1994* (Richmond: California Universities for Research in Earthquake Engineering, 1998), 9–15.

19. Joan Alway, Linda Liska Belgrave, and Kenneth J. Smith, "Back to Normal: Gender and Disaster," *Symbolic Interaction* 21, no. 2 (1998): 175–95.

20. Arlie Russell Hochschild, *The Commercialization of Intimate Life: Notes from Home and Work* (Berkeley: University of California Press, 2003), 16.

21. Thomas E. Drabek and David A. McEntire, "Emergent Phenomena and the Sociology of Disaster: Lessons, Trends and Opportunities from the Recent Literature," *Disaster Prevention and Management* 12, no. 2 (2003): 97–112.

22. Vered Vinitzky-Seroussi, *After Pomp and Circumstance: High School Reunion as an Autobiographical Occasion* (Chicago: University of Chicago Press, 1998), 3.

23. Sherryl Kleinman, *Opposing Ambitions: Gender and Identity in an Alternative Organization* (Chicago: University of Chicago Press, 1996); Rebecca Anne Allahyari, *Visions of Charity: Volunteer Workers and Moral Community* (Berkeley: University of California Press, 2000).

24. Kathleen M. Blee, *Democracy in the Making: How Activist Groups Form* (New York: Oxford University Press, 2012), 8.

25. Ibid.

26. Ibid.

27. Ibid., 35, 92.

28. Ibid., 35.

29. Kathleen M. Blee, "The Hidden Weight of the Past: A Microhistory of a Failed Social Movement Group," in *Small Worlds: Method, Meaning, and Narrative in Microhistory*, ed. James F. Brooks, Christopher R. N. DeCorse, and John Walton, 37–52 (Santa Fe, NM: School for Advanced Research Press, 2008). See also *What Is Microhistory? Theory and Practice*, ed. Sigurður Gylfi Magnússon and István M. Szijártó (New York: Routledge, 2013).

30. Loretta Pyles and Judith Lewis, "Women of the Storm: Advocacy and Organizing in Post-Katrina New Orleans," *Affilia* 22, no. 4 (2007): 385–89; Pamela Tyler, "The Post-Katrina, Semiseparate World of Gender Politics," *Journal of American History* 94, no. 3 (2007): 780–88; Roberta Brandes Gratz, *We're Still Here Ya Bastards: How the People of New Orleans Rebuilt Their City* (New York: Nation Books, 2015), 299–317; Melinda Henneberger, *If They Only Listened to Us: What Women Voters Want Politicians to Hear* (New York: Simon and Schuster, 2007), 67–80.

31. James Perry, "Work of New Orleans Advocates Honors Martin Luther King's Legacy," *Facing South: A New Voice for a Changing South*, Institute for Southern Studies, April 5, 2008, https://www.facingsouth.org/2008/04/work-of-new-orleans-advocates-honors-martin-luther-kings-legacy.html.

32. For an exception, see Edward J. Blakely, *My Storm: Managing the Recovery of New Orleans in the Wake of Katrina* (Philadelphia: University of Pennsylvania Press, 2012), 104.

33. A writer for the *New Orleans Tribune* described WOS as an "overwhelmingly white group of Uptown women who formed immediately after Hurricane Katrina and took the early lead with local media help in establishing what they thought the city's agenda would be going forward. That is until realizing their membership looked nothing like the major portion of the city that had just been devastated." See Lovell Beaulieu, "Dillard Mayoral Debate Defines the Campaign," *New Orleans Tribune* 26, no. 2 (2010): 7, 14.

34. Greg Palast, *Vultures' Picnic Deluxe: In Pursuit of Petroleum Pigs, Power Pirates, and High Finance Carnivores* (New York: Penguin, 2011), 156.

35. Blee, *Democracy in the Making*, 12.

36. Ibid., 13.

37. Ibid.

38. Blee, "Hidden Weight," 42; emphasis in original.

39. Blee, *Democracy in the Making*, 53.

40. Sara Ahmed, *On Being Included: Racism and Diversity in Institutional Life* (Durham, NC: Duke University Press, 2012), 1.

41. Ibid., 53.

42. Ibid., 137–38.

43. Those familiar with discourses of intersectionality will notice the omission of sexuality, among other categories. This is not because it is absent from my thinking, but because,

empirically, sexuality was not part of the discussion. Race, class, and gender, on the other hand, were categories that were regularly taken up.

44. On intersectional theory, see bell hooks, *Feminist Theory: From Margin to Center* (Boston: South End Press, 1984); Patricia Hill Collins, *Black Feminist Thought: Knowledge, Consciousness, and the Politics of Empowerment* (New York: Routledge, 2000); Hae Yeon Choo and Myra Marx Ferree, "Practicing Intersectionality in Sociological Research: A Critical Analysis of Inclusions, Interactions, and Institutions in the Study of Inequalities," *Sociological Theory* 22, no. 2 (2010): 129–49.

45. On the depoliticizing of intersectionality, see Sirma Bilge, "Intersectionality Undone," *Du Bois Review: Social Science Research on Race* 10, no. 2 (2013): 405–424.

46. Gerda Lerner, *The Majority Finds Its Past: Placing Women in History* (Chapel Hill: University of North Carolina Press, 2005).

47. Chester Hartman and Gregory Squires, *There Is No Such Thing as a Natural Disaster: Race, Class, and Hurricane Katrina* (New York: Routledge, 2006).

48. For an exception in the context of Hurricane Katrina in which a journalist focuses on the power elite of New Orleans, see Christopher Cooper, "Old-Line Families Escape Worst of Flood and Plot the Future; Mr. O'Dwyer, at His Mansion, Enjoys Highball with Ice; Meeting with the Mayor," *Wall Street Journal*, September 8, 2005, A1.

49. Shamus Rahman Khan, *Privilege: The Making of an Adolescent Elite at St. Paul's School* (Princeton, NJ: Princeton University Press, 2011), 4, 39. See also Richard L. Zweigenhaft and G. William Domhoff, *Diversity in the Power Elite: How It Happened, Why It Matters* (Lanham, MD: Rowman and Littlefield, 2006).

50. Khan, *Privilege*, 4–5.

51. Shamus Rahman Khan, "The Sociology of Elites," *Annual Review of Sociology* 38, no. 1 (2012): 362.

52. Diana Kendall, *Members Only: Elite Clubs and the Process of Exclusion* (Lanham, MD: Rowman and Littlefield, 2008); George Marcus, ed., *Elites: Ethnographic Issues* (Albuquerque: University of New Mexico Press, 1983); Laura Nader, "Up the Anthropologist: Perspectives Gained from Studying Up," in *Reinventing Anthropology*, ed. Dell Hymes, 284–311 (New York: Pantheon Books, 1972); Mike Savage and Karel Williams, eds., *Remembering Elites* (Malden, MA: Blackwell, 2008); Kahn, *Privilege*; Paul Sullivan, "Wealth Matters: Scrutinizing the Elite, Whether They Like It or Not," *New York Times*, October 16, 2010, B6.

53. Colin Jerolmack and Shamus Khan, "Toward an Understanding of the Relationship between Accounts and Action," *Sociological Methods and Research* 43, no. 2 (2014): 236–47; Colin Jerolmack and Shamus Khan, "Talk Is Cheap: Ethnography and Attitudinal Fallacy," *Sociological Methods and Research* 42, issue 2 (2014): 178–209.

54. Cynthia Enloe, *Bananas, Beaches, and Bases: Making Feminist Sense of International Politics*, 2nd ed. (Berkeley: University of California Press, 2014), 5–6.

55. Diana Kendall, *The Power of Good Deeds: Privileged Women and the Social Reproduction of the Upper Class* (Lanham, MD: Rowman and Littlefield, 2002); Kathleen D. McCarthy, ed., *Women, Philanthropy, and Civil Society* (Bloomington: Indiana University Press, 2001); Susan Ostrander, *Women of the Upper Class* (Philadelphia: Temple University Press, 1984); Lois Benjamin, "Black Women Achievers: An Isolated Elite," *Sociological Inquiry* 52, no. 2 (1982): 141–51.

56. For an exception, see Elizabeth Hayes Turner, *Women, Culture, and Community: Religion and Reform in Galveston, 1880–1920* (New York: Oxford University Press, 1997).

57. Elaine Enarson, Alice Fothergill, and Lori Peek, "Gender and Disaster: Foundations and Directions," in *Handbook of Disaster Research*, ed. Havidán Rodríguez, Enrico L. Quarantelli, Russell R. Dynes, 130–46 (New York: Springer, 2007), 132.

58. Elaine Enarson and Maureen Fordham, "Lines that Divide, Ties that Bind: Race, Class and Gender in Women's Flood Recovery in the U.S. and U.K.," *Australian Journal of Emergency Management* 15, no. 4 (2004): 43–52; Alice Fothergill, *Heads above Water: Gender, Class, and Family in the Grand Forks Flood* (Albany: State University of New York Press, 2004); Maureen Fordham, "The Intersection of Gender and Social Class in Disaster: Balancing Resilience and Vulnerability," *International Journal of Mass Emergencies and Disasters* 17, no. 1 (1999): 15–36.

59. Khan, "Sociology of Elites," 362.

60. Ibid.

61. Ibid.

62. Max Weber, *Economy and Society*, ed. Guenther Roth and Clause Wittich (Berkeley: University of California Press, 2013), 302–307; Cecilia L. Ridgeway, "Why Status Matters for Inequality," *American Sociological Review* 79, no. 1 (2014): 1–16.

63. Felice Batlan, "Weathering the Storm Together (Torn Apart by Race, Gender, and Class)," *NWSA Journal* 20, no. 3 (2008): 163–84; Andrea Wilbon Hartman, Erica Dudas, and Jennifer Day-Suly, "It's Raining Men: Gender and Street Harassment in Post-Katrina New Orleans," in *Rethinking Disaster Recovery: A Hurricane Katrina Retrospective*, ed. Jeannie Haubert, 27–38 (Lanham, MD: Lexington Books, 2015).

64. William F. Falk, Matthew O. Hunt, and Larry L. Hunt, "Hurricane Katrina and New Orleanians' Sense of Place: Return and Reconstitution or 'Gone with the Wind,'" *Du Bois Review* 3, no. 1 (2006): 115–28, 116; White House Report, *The Federal Response to Hurricane Katrina: Lessons Learned* (Washington, DC: U.S. Government Printing Office, 2006).

65. Paul Lichterman and Nina Eliasoph, "Civic Action," *American Journal of Sociology* 123, no. 4 (2014): 798–863, 809.

66. Ibid., 811.

67. Herbert Blumer, *Symbolic Interaction: Perspective and Method* (Berkeley: University of California Press, 1969); Erving Goffman, *The Presentation of Self in Everyday Life* (New York: Doubleday, 1959); George Herbert Mead, *Mind, Self, and Society: From the Standpoint of a Social Behaviorist*, ed. Charles W. Morris (1934; Chicago: University of Chicago Press, 1967).

68. Émile Durkheim, *The Elementary Forms of Religious Life*, trans. Karen E. Fields (1912; New York: Free Press, 1995).

69. Michael Burawoy, "For Public Sociology," *American Sociological Review* 70 (2005): 4–28.

70. Lila Abu-Lughod, *Writing Women's Worlds: Bedouin Stories* (Berkeley: University of California Press, 1993), 25–36.

71. Ibid., 8.

72. Ibid., 9.

73. Ibid., 29–30.

74. Ibid., 31.

75. Jane Addams, *Twenty Years at Hull-House; with Autobiographical Notes* (Champaign: University of Illinois Press, 1990); João Biehl, *Vita: Life in a Zone of Social Abandonment* (Berkeley: University of California Press, 2013); Chad Broughton, *Boom, Bust, Exodus: The Rust Belt, the Maquilas, and a Tale of Two Cities* (New York: Oxford University Press, 2015). See also Jennifer C. Hunt, *Seven Shots: An NYPD Raid on a Terrorist Cell and Its Aftermath* (Chicago: University

of Chicago Press, 2010); Robert Jackall, *Wild Cowboys: Urban Marauders and the Forces of Order* (Cambridge, MA: Harvard University Press, 1997); Kenneth T. MacLeish, *Making War at Fort Hood: Life and Uncertainty in a Military Community* (Princeton, NJ: Princeton University Press, 2013); Kirin Narayan, "Tools to Shape Texts: What Creative Nonfiction Can Offer Ethnography," *Anthropology and Humanism* 32, no. 2 (2007): 130–44; Mary Romero, *The Maid's Daughter: Living Inside and Outside the American Dream* (New York: New York University Press, 2011); Christine Walley, *Exit Zero: Family and Class in Post-Industrial Chicago* (Chicago: University of Chicago Press, 2013). On the use of narrative in a microhistorical study of a single group, see Daniel Burton Rose, *Guerrilla USA: The George Jackson Brigade and the Anticapitalist Underground of the 1970s* (Berkeley: University of California Press, 2010). Like in Michael Schwalbe's work, which combines elements of biography, social history, and narrative nonfiction, much of my analysis is found between the lines. See Michael Schwalbe, *Remembering Reet and Shine: Two Black Men, One Struggle* (Jackson: University Press of Mississippi, 2004).

76. Dan Baum, *Nine Lives: Mystery, Magic, Death, and Life in New Orleans* (New York: Spiegel & Grau, 2009); Tom Wooten, *We Shall Not Be Moved: Rebuilding Home in the Wake of Katrina* (Boston: Beacon Press, 2012); Rebecca Solnit, *A Paradise Built in Hell: The Extraordinary Communities That Arise in Disaster* (New York: Penguin, 2009).

77. For an excellent example of building character profiles with documentary sources, see Cynthia Enloe, *Nimo's War, Emma's War: Making Feminist Sense of the Iraq War* (Berkeley: University of California Press, 2010).

Chapter 1. Emergence

1. On the conceptual differences between disaster and catastrophe, see E. L. Quarantelli, "Catastrophes Are Different from Disasters: Some Implications for Crisis Planning and Managing Drawn from Katrina," *Understanding Katrina: Perspectives from the Social Sciences,* June 11, 2006, http://understandingkatrina.ssrc.org/Quarantelli.

2. Emmet Mayer III, "Ups and Downs; Current Population Estimates of the Seven-Parish New Orleans Area," staff map printed in the *Times-Picayune,* January 1, 2006. Estimates from the Brookings Institution put the January 2006 total at approximately 156,141. See Bruce Katz, Matt Fellowes, and Mia Mabanta, "Katrina Index: Tracking Variables of Post-Katrina Reconstruction," working paper, Brookings Institution, Washington, DC, 2006.

3. Mayer, "Ups and Downs."

4. Institute for Southern Studies, "The Mardi Gras Index: The State of New Orleans by Numbers Six Months after Hurricane Katrina," *Southern Exposure* 34, no. 1 (2006): 7.

5. Brian Thevenot, "Stop and Go," *Times-Picayune,* January 15, 2006, Metro section, 1.

6. Katz, Fellowes, and Mabanta, "Katrina Index."

7. Arlene Kaplan Daniels, *Invisible Careers: Women Civic Leaders from the Volunteer World* (Chicago: University of Chicago Press, 1998).

8. This account of Anne Milling's early years is based on numerous print sources, as well as her oral history on file at the Newcomb College Institute. See Anne Milling, interview by Kaitlin Splett, April 5, 2012, Newcomb Oral History Collection, Newcomb Archives and Vorhoff Library Special Collections, Newcomb College Institute, Tulane University.

9. "The Men behind the Desks," *Monroe Morning World,* August 5, 1951, 2; Student Records of Hilda Marie Wasserman, Manuscript Collection UA.54, Newcomb Archives and Vorhoff Library Special Collections, Newcomb College Institute, Tulane University.

10. This information is drawn from the pages of the 1958 edition of *The Monroyan*, the yearbook for Neville High School in Monroe, Louisiana.

11. Many details from this period of Anne McDonald's life come from the following sources: "Miss McDonald's Betrothal to Mr. Milling Is Announced," *Times-Picayune*, March 15, 1964, section 4, 3; "Mrs. Roswell King Milling," *Times Picayune*, June 23, 1964, section 3, 2.

12. I am indebted to Harriet Swift for drawing my attention to the hierarchies within the New Orleans elite and the social importance of the debutante season in shaping the politics of Carnival, and for sending me a copy of Millie Ball, "The Carnival Stratum: Not All Debutantes Are Created Equal," *Times-Picayune*, February 13, 1983, section 2, 4–5.

13. Margaret Fuller, "'Turn On the Pumps!' S&WB President Pro Tem Accustomed to the Jokes," *Times-Picayune*, August 23, 1983, section 4, 4.

14. Ibid. This description of McGehee comes from "Come on Down to 'Nawlins,'" *W Magazine*, April 2008, 255.

15. G. William Domhoff, "How to Do Power Structure Research," Who Rules America?, http://whorulesamerica.net/methods/how_to_do_power_structure_research.html, first posted May 2009; updated October 2012.

16. Fuller, "'Turn On the Pumps!'"; Susan Feeney, "S&WB Flood-Buster May Turn the Tide," *Times-Picayune*, October 7, 1985, A4.

17. Fuller, "'Turn On the Pumps!'"

18. "Anne McDonald Milling Interview," AJLI Video, May 18, 2012, https://www.youtube .com/watch?v=VxmMB1pGoFc.

19. Ibid.

20. Terry Flettrich, "The Beautiful Activist," *Times-Picayune*, March 11, 1973, section 4, 11. For a brief history of media framing of the upper classes, see "Twenty-Four-Karat Gold Frames: Lifestyles of the Rich and Famous," in Diana Kendall, *Framing Class: Media Representations of Wealth and Poverty in America* (Lanham, MD: Rowman and Littlefield, 2005), 21–58.

21. Flettrich, "Beautiful Activist."

22. Feeney, "S&WB Flood-Buster."

23. Ibid. Marc Chagall appears to have been popular among New Orleans collectors, especially after the New Orleans Museum of Art held an exhibition in 2000 titled "Marc Chagall in New Orleans." See Ian McNulty, "Museum Discovers the Fine Art of Sponsorship Marketing," *New Orleans CityBusiness* 22, no. 10 (2001): 13; Ian McNulty, "Chagall Shows Up," *New Orleans CityBusiness* 21, no. 3 (July 2000): 1.

24. Feeney, "S&WB Flood-Buster."

25. Ibid.

26. Daniels, *Invisible Careers*, 127.

27. Nell Nolan, "Parenting Center Party Gives Grown-Ups a Turn," *Times-Picayune*, November 10, 1980, 2; Fuller, "'Turn On the Pumps!'"

28. Fuller, "'Turn On the Pumps!'"; Betty Guillaud, "Between the Braque and the Bouzouki, a Gala Evening for All," *Times-Picayune*, November 3, 1983, 2.

29. Fuller, "'Turn On the Pumps!'"; Nell Nolan, "LNC Benefit a Soaring Success," *Times-Picayune*, November 13, 1982, section 4, 3.

30. Quoted in AJLI Video, "Anne Milling—Mary Harriman Award Winner," April 25, 2012, https://www.youtube.com/watch?v=Z3lK5Q2CMBc.

31. "History of the Organization," Project Lazarus, http://www.projectlazarus.net/history .htm.

32. John Pope, "Anne Milling Receives 1995 T-P Loving Cup," January 14, 2009; updated April 2, 2010, http://www.nola.com/living/index.ssf/2009/01/anne_milling_receives_1995_t-p.html.

33. Susan Stinson, "Anne Milling," *New Orleans CityBusiness*, November 24, 2008, 55.

34. "Anne McDonald Milling Interview," AJLI Video.

35. "Anne Milling—Mary Harriman Award Winner," AJLI Video.

36. Ibid.

37. Sue Strachan, "Project Lazarus Guardian Angel Award Gala Honors David Cortez and Anne Milling," *Times-Picayune*, June 22, 2016, http://www.nola.com/society/index.ssf/2016/06/project_lazarus_guardian_angel.html.

38. Kathy Hogan Trocheck, "Good Times a Religion in New Orleans," *Atlanta Journal and Constitution*, September 7, 1987, C1.

39. Lily Jackson, "Preparing for the Pope," *Times-Picayune*, August 9, 1987, D3.

40. Bruce Nolan, "New Orleans Archbishop Philip Hannan Was a Vivid, Public Force for His Flock," *Times-Picayune*, September 29, 2011, http://www.nola.com/religion/index.ssf/2011/09/archbishop_philip_hannan_was_a.html.

41. Hugh H. Mulligan, "Pope's Visit to New Orleans Called 'One-Man Mardi Gras,'" *St. Petersburg Times*, September 12, 1987, 4E.

42. Pope, "Anne Milling Receives 1995 T-P Loving Cup."

43. Marjorie Roehl, "Meeting the Pope? Just Act Naturally," *Times-Picayune*, September 8, 1987, A4.

44. Ed Anderson, "Roemer Dinner Scheduled," *Times-Picayune*, December 3, 1987, B11.

45. Sheila Grissett, "Walking among Us; Local Catholics Remember When 'The Holiest Person Walking the Earth' Touched Down at New Orleans' Airport and Spent 36 Hours in Their Midst," *Times-Picayune*, April 3, 2005, 1; Leslie Williams, "Storming D.C.," *Times-Picayune*, January 26, 2006, A1, A8; Sonya Stinson, "Anne Milling," *New Orleans CityBusiness*, November 24, 2008, 55; Fuller, "'Turn On the Pumps!'"

46. No awards were given in 1908 or 1909.

47. Susan Tucker and Beth Willinger, "Part III: Lives," in *Newcomb College, 1886–2006: Higher Education for Women in New Orleans*, ed. Susan Tucker and Beth Willinger (Baton Rouge: Louisiana State University Press), 263–64; James Hodge, "Rosa Keller Given Times-Picayune Cup," *Times-Picayune*, October 7, 1985, A1, A6. For a discussion of Rosa Keller, see Pamela Tyler, *Silk Stockings and Ballot Boxes: Women and Politics in New Orleans, 1920–1963* (Athens: University of Georgia Press, 1996), chap. 6.

48. Melinda Henneberger, *If They Only Listened to Us: What Women Voters Want Politicians to Hear* (New York: Simon and Schuster, 2007), 67–80, 79. On Sheehan, see Richard W. Stevenson, "Of the Many Deaths in Iraq, One Mother's Loss Becomes a Problem for the President," *New York Times*, August 8, 2005, http://www.nytimes.com/2005/08/08/politics/of-the-many-deaths-in-iraq-one-mothers-loss-becomes-a-problem-for.html.

49. The social characteristics of Audubon are quite revealing. According to 2000 census data, the Audubon neighborhood was 86.1 percent white, 5.1 percent black or African American, and 4.4 percent Hispanic (any race). Of the occupied housing units, 54.3 percent were owner occupied, while 45.7 percent were renter occupied. Just over 31 percent of household reported total income of over $100,000, including 15 percent that reported total income of $200,000 or more (compared to 2.2 percent in Orleans Parish and 2.4 percent across the United States). See the Data Center analysis of data from U.S. Census 2000 Summary File 3 (SF3), http://www.datacenterresearch.org/data-resources/neighborhood-data/district-3/Audubon.

50. John R. Logan, "The Impact of Katrina: Race and Class in Storm-Damaged Neighborhoods," January 2006, Providence, Rhode Island, Brown University, https://s4.ad.brown.edu/Projects/Hurricane//report.pdf. While some parts of the Audubon/University neighborhoods did flood, the concentration of wealth and resources helped ensure that the recovery would take place relatively quickly.

51. Diana Kendall, *Members Only: Elite Clubs and the Process of Exclusion* (Lanham, MD: Rowman and Littlefield, 2008), 45. See also Diana Kendall, *The Power of Good Deeds: Privileged Women and the Social Reproduction of the Upper Class* (Lanham, MD: Rowman and Littlefield, 2002), 152–53.

52. Core member Peggy Laborde is not to be confused with Peggy Scott Laborde, another prominent New Orleans personality, who hosts a weekly television program. To my knowledge Peggy Scott Laborde was not part of WOS. WOS member Peggy Laborde, mentioned in the text, was married to Jack Laborde, an oil and gas industry executive, whose father was Alden "Doc" Laborde, the co-founder of ODECO (Ocean Drilling and Exploration Company) and also Tidewater Inc., a company best known for revolutionizing the offshore oil and gas industry when it developed a moveable offshore drilling rig. See "Alden 'Doc' Laborde Interview— Co-founder of ODECO," *Offshore Magazine*, video interview, presented by the George Bush Presidential Library and Museum, http://www.offshore-mag.com/topics/m/video/92828421/alden-doc-laborde-interview-co-founder-of-odeco.htm. In 2014 Jack Laborde was named Rex, King of Carnival. See also Dominic Massa, "Rex Royalty Revealed: Jack Laborde and Carroll Gelderman Are King and Queen of Carnival," WWL-TV.com, March 2, 2014.

53. Joe M. Richardson, "Edgar B. Stern: A White New Orleans Philanthropist Helps Build a Black University," *Journal of Negro History* 82, no. 3 (1997): 328–42, 339. See also Stephanie Deutsch, *You Need a Schoolhouse: Booker T. Washington, Julius Rosenwald, and the Building of Schools for the Segregated South* (Evanston, IL: Northwestern University Press, 2011). Edith Rosenwald Stern (1895–1980), daughter of Sears Roebuck founder Julius Rosenwald, is described as a "philanthropist, community leader, and civil rights activist," whose activities in New Orleans included voter education and registration efforts as well as working with African American communities to help build Dillard University. See Marion Shulevitz, "Edith Rosenwald Stern," *Jewish Women: A Comprehensive Historical Encyclopedia*, Jewish Women's Archive, March 20, 2009, http://jwa.org/encyclopedia/article/stern-edith-rosenwald; Gerda Weissmann Klein, *A Passion for Sharing: The Life of Edith Rosenwald Stern* (Chappaqua, NY: Rossel Books, 1984); John Pope, "Edith Rosenwald Stern," in *Getting Off at Elysian Fields: Obituaries from the New Orleans* Times-Picayune (Jackson: University Press of Mississippi, 2015), 9–13.

54. Kimberley Singletary, "Beverly Church, 2015 New Orleans Top Female Achiever," *New Orleans Magazine*, July 2015, http://www.myneworleans.com/New-Orleans-Magazine/July-2015/Beverly-Church-2015-New-Orleans-Top-Female-Achiever.

55. Williams, "Storming D.C." On the Longue Vue House and Gardens, see its website, http://www.longuevue.com/index.php/about-longue-vue/longue-vue-history.

56. On the reconstruction of everyday life, see Joan Alway, Linda Liska Belgrave, and Kenneth J. Smith, "Back to Normal: Gender and Disaster," *Symbolic Interaction* 21, no. 2 (1998): 175–95.

57. Jeffrey Alexander, "Toward a Theory of Cultural Trauma," in *Cultural Trauma and Collective Identity*, ed. Jeffrey C. Alexander, Ron Eyerman, Bernhard Giesen, Neil J. Smelser, and Piotr Sztompka, 1–30 (Berkeley: University of California Press, 2004).

58. James Kendra and Tricia Wachtendorf, "Elements of Resilience after the World Trade Center Disaster: Reconstituting New York City's Emergency Operations Center," *Disasters*

27, no. 1 (2003): 37–53; Tricia Wachtendorf and James Kendra, "Improvising Disaster in the City of Jazz: Organizational Response to Hurricane Katrina," *Understanding Katrina: Perspectives from the Social Sciences*, June 11, 2006, http://understandingkatrina.ssrc.org/Wachtendorf_Kendra.

59. Kendall, *Power of Good Deeds*, 31–42.

60. Phil Magers, "Analysis: Blanco Wants Cut of Oil Revenue," http://www.upi.com/Analysis-Blanco-wants-cut-of-oil-revenue/84571101773720, November 29, 2004.

61. Jason P. Theriot, *American Energy, Imperiled Coast: Oil and Gas Development in Louisiana's Wetlands* (Baton Rouge: Louisiana State University Press, 2014), 190–96.

62. Ibid.

63. Henneberger, *If They Only Listened to Us*, 78. Connections like these led some to consider AWF's deeply embedded ties to the oil and gas industry. Shell Oil, for example, is a "World Sponsor" of the America's WETLAND. See hppt://www.shell.us/home/content/usa/environment_society/respecting_the_environment/americas_wetland.

64. Naming is an important turning point in the trajectory of emergent activist groups; it is one moment where a field of open possibilities begins to narrow over time. Blee writes, "However names are chosen, they freeze the group in time. Names imply stasis, even when a group is in flux." See Kathleen M. Blee, *Democracy in the Making: How Activist Groups Form* (New York: Oxford University Press, 2012), 13.

65. Bruce Alpert, "In Congress, Vast Majority Yet to See Ruins," *Times-Picayune*, January 11, 2006, A1, A9.

66. Ibid.

67. Kendall, *Framing Class*, 35.

Chapter 2. Bridgework

1. Kathleen M. Blee, *Democracy in the Making: How Activist Groups Form* (New York: Oxford University Press, 2012), 69–70.

2. There are varying accounts in the media and my interviews with respect to the exact number of women who flew to Washington, ranging from as low as 80 to as many as 140. Some interviewees reported that there were about a dozen members of the press and 140 available seats. Moreover, even though there was a final list of participants distributed to the women, a few dropped out at the last minute and a few were added in their place. This shows the degree to which the group continued to take shape, even up until the day of the Washington trip.

3. On membership caps and identifying specific categories of membership, see Diana Kendall, *Members Only: Elite Clubs and the Process of Exclusion* (Lanham, MD: Rowman and Littlefield, 2008), 45.

4. Ibid.

5. Blee, *Democracy*, 55.

6. On diversity as a form of public relations, see Sara Ahmed, *On Being Included: Racism and Diversity in Institutional Life* (Durham, NC: Duke University Press, 2012), 143.

7. Blee, *Democracy*, 55–56.

8. Janita Poe, "Jack and Jill Fights Label of 'Black Elite," *Chicago Tribune*, November 27, 1992, http://articles.chicagotribune.com/1992-11-27/news/9204180518_1_jack-and-jill-black

-children-chapters. See also Monte Williams, "Is There a Black Upper Class?" *New York Times*, March 7, 1999, section 9, 1.

9. There were racial asymmetries in pivotal figures who did "bridgework," to borrow a phrase from cultural sociologist Paul Lichterman. This burden seems to have fallen upon elite women of color who participated in elite white women's activities and organizations more often than the other way around. On "bridgework," see Paul Lichterman, *Elusive Togetherness: Church Groups Trying to Bridge America's Divisions* (Princeton, NJ: Princeton University Press, 2005).

10. "About Us," The Links, Incorporated, http://www.linksinc.org/about.shtml. See also Kijua Sanders-McMurtry and Nia Woods Haydel, "The Links, Incorporated; Advocacy, Education, and Service in the African American Community," in *Uplifting a People: African American Philanthropy and Education*, ed. Marybeth Gasman and Katherine V. Sedgwick, 101–118 (New York: Peter Lang, 2005).

11. "The History of The Links, Incorporated," *Linked Magazine* 2, no. 1 (2012): 8–11.

12. "About Us," The Links, Incorporated. See also Gasman and Sedgwick, *Uplifting a People*.

13. Lawrence Otis Graham, *Our Kind of People: Inside America's Black Upper Class* (New York: HarperCollins, 1999), 102.

14. Ibid.

15. Ibid., 109.

16. Ibid., 111.

17. Ibid., 103.

18. Ibid., 105–106.

19. On August 30, 2005, the day after Katrina's landfall, Margaret Thompson Johnson, the southern area director of The Links, initiated a nationwide search to account for displaced Links members. Soon after, Dr. Gladys Gary Vaughan, national president of The Links, encouraged chapters across the country to "open their homes and their hearts to provide resources to our Sister Links as well as other persons who are in need." See "LINKS, Inc. Take Action—Offer Disaster Assistance; Nation Wide Search for Members of Links Affected by Katrina," West Palm Beach Chapter of The Links, Incorporated, http://www.wpblinks.org/linkstakeaction.htm; "Link Lines Hurricane Relief Letter," West Palm Beach Chapter of The Links, Incorporated, August 30, 2005, http://www.wpblinks.org/hurkatrina.htm.

20. See Edward Bonilla-Silva, *Racism without Racists: Color-Blind Racism and the Persistence of Racial Inequality in the United States* (Lanham, MD: Rowman and Littlefield, 2006), 75. Many commentators have suggested that the word "articulate" is rarely used to discuss white people; instead it is often seen as a descriptor or a "compliment" for someone who isn't expected to be "well-spoken." See Richard Delgado and Jean Stefancic, "Images of the Outsider in American Law and Culture: Can Free Expression Remedy Systemic Social Ills," *Cornell Law Review* 77, no. 6 (1992): 1258–97, 1283.

21. See Lichterman, *Elusive Togetherness*.

22. On the moral obligations of protecting the "secrets of the team" see Erving Goffman, *The Presentation of Self in Everyday Life* (Garden City, NY: Doubleday, 1959), 212.

23. Janelle L. White, "New Orleans and Women of Color: Connecting the Personal and Political," *Satya*, November 2005, http://www.satyamag.com/nov05/white.html.

24. Testimony of Tanya Harris, Association of Community Organizations for Reform Now, before the Committee on Health, Education, Labor, and Pensions of the United States Senate, March 7, 2006, http://www.help.senate.gov/imo/media/doc/harris2.pdf. For more on

Harris's experiences of Katrina, see John Atlas, *Seeds of Change: The Story of ACORN, America's Most Controversial Antipoverty Community Organizing Group* (Nashville: Vanderbilt University Press, 2010), 165.

25. "Hurricane Katrina: Voices from Inside the Storm," Select Bipartisan Committee to Investigate the Preparation for and Response to Hurricane Katrina, December 6, 2005, https://www.c-span.org/video/?190199-1/gulf-coast-evacuees-hurricane-katrina.

26. On the post-Katrina public housing movement, see John Arena, *Driven from New Orleans: How Nonprofits Betray Public Housing and Promote Privatization* (Minneapolis: University of Minnesota Press, 2012). For an analysis of how women struggled with post-Katrina public housing changes, see Jane M. Henrici, Allison Suppan Helmuth, and Angela Carlberg, "Doubly Displaced: Women, Public Housing, and Spatial Access after Katrina," in *The Women of Katrina: How Gender, Race, and Class Matter in an American Disaster*, ed. Emmanuel David and Elaine Pitt Enarson, 142–54 (Nashville: Vanderbilt University Press, 2012).

27. "Hurricane Katrina: Voices from Inside the Storm."

28. Jed Horne, *Breach of Faith: Hurricane Katrina and the Near Death of a Great American City* (New York: Random House, 2006), 109.

29. Rod West would become president and chief executive of Entergy. See Eric Hansen, "Rebuilding Big Easy West Sat Tight through Katrina, Looking Ahead," *SouthBend Tribune*, December 24, 2006; Pete LaFleur, "Champions in Life," University of Notre Dame Athletics, http://www.und.com/ot/60bca-champions-life.html.

30. Kathleen D. McCarthy, *Noblesse Oblige: Charity and Philanthropy in Chicago, 1849–1929* (Chicago: University of Chicago Press, 1982); Kendall, *Framing Class*, 50. For a historical account of how women's clubs figured into the progressive era and post-disaster reforms, see Elizabeth Hayes Turner, *Women, Culture, and Community: Religion and Reform in Galveston, 1880–1920* (New York: Oxford University Press, 1997).

31. Quoted in *Women of the Storm*, a film directed, edited, and produced by Wesley Shrum (Liars and Madmen Productions, 2015).

32. Robin Shannon, "Women of the Year: Dolly Simpson," *New Orleans CityBusiness*, November 19, 2007, 54. See also "Links, Inc. National Assembly, The Links, Incorporated, 30th National Assembly, July 1996: Celebrating 50 Years, 1946–1996," book 1996, The Portal to Texas History, University of North Texas Libraries, http://texashistory.unt.edu/ark:/67531/metapth305912, crediting University of Texas at San Antonio.

33. I arrived at this number through interviews and by comparing the list of WOS participants with membership rosters posted on The Links websites.

34. This figure is based on 2000 census data. Nihal Shrinath, Vicki Mack, and Allison Plyer, "Who Lives in New Orleans and Metro Parishes Now?" The Data Center, October 16, 2014, http://www.datacenterresearch.org/data-resources/who-lives-in-new-orleans-now.

35. "Anne McDonald Milling Interview," AJLI Video, YouTube.

36. Florence L. Herman, "Women of the Storm Storm D.C.," *Clarion Herald: Official Newspaper of the Archdiocese of New Orleans* 45, no. 5 (2006): 1; "Women of the Storm Team Captains," January 30, 2006, Women of the Storm Records, Manuscript Collection NA.020, Newcomb Archives and Vorhoff Library Special Collections, Newcomb College Institute, Tulane University (hereafter cited as "WOS Records"). On the post-Katrina environmental activism of the Vietnamese community, see Charles H. Rowell and Kim Dung Nguyen, "Kim Dung Nguyen," *Callaloo* 29, no. 4 (2006): 1082–87.

37. "Anna Gershanik," Puentes New Orleans, http://puentesno.org/puentes/staff-board -of-directors.

38. I'm not aware of anyone declining the invitation, though it is quite possible that this occurred.

39. For a cross-group comparison, see Pamela Tyler, "The Post-Katrina, Semiseparate World of Gender Politics," *Journal of American History* 94, no. 3 (2007): 780–88; Pamela Tyler, "Louisiana Women and Hurricane Katrina: Some Reflections on Women's Responses to the Catastrophe," in *Louisiana Women: Their Lives and Times*, ed. Janet Allured and Judith F. Gentry, 324–42 (Athens: University of Georgia Press, 2009).

40. On the 9/11 widows, see Dan Barry, "As Sept. 11 Widows Unite, Grief Finds Political Voice," *New York Times*, November 25, 2001, A1; Kristen Breitweiser, *Wake-Up Call: The Political Education of a 9/11 Widow* (New York: Warner Books, 2006).

41. A correspondence shared with me reveals that the initial idea for a post-Katrina women's group was "instigated by a male friend" who drew inspiration from the women who mobilized after 9/11. However, the person responsible for organizing this effort was a woman, as were most of those invited to meetings before the group dissolved.

42. On crowded social movements sectors, see Benita Roth, *Separate Roads to Feminism: Black, Chicana, and White Feminist Movements in America's Second Wave* (New York: Cambridge University Press, 2004).

43. I'm grateful to Harriet Swift for pointing out that the women's use of the word "captains" replicated the organizational structure of Carnival krewes, another example of the group's use of Southern culture.

44. E. L. Quarantelli et al., *Emergent Citizen Groups in Disaster Preparedness and Recovery Activities: An Interim Report* (Newark: University of Delaware, Disaster Research Center, 1983); R. A. Stallings, E. L. Quarantelli, "Emergent Citizen Groups and Emergency Management," *Public Administration Review* 45 (1985): 93–100.

45. Beverley Reese Church, "A Note from Bev," *St. Charles Avenue*, March 2006, 7. In 2015 Christian T. Brown reigned as Rex, King of Carnival. When the Rex organization announced the 2015 Carnival royalty, he listed among his credentials being an "original member of the steering committee of Women of the Storm." See "Rex Announces 2015 Carnival Royalty," Rex, February 14, 2015, http://www.rexorganization.com/News/index.php?id=U49BE1.

46. Core members often called me "a man of the storm," which clearly marked me as not part of the group but aligned me with it through the speech of naming. As I met additional women at various WOS events, several of the core membership introduced me as "an honorary Man of the Storm," which elicited smiles and laughter.

47. I made requests to interview both men but was unsuccessful in my attempts. One man agreed to my interview, but our meeting never materialized. The other request went unanswered. Thus, I have little data on the men's participation.

48. Beth Willinger, "The Effects of Katrina on the Employment and Earnings of New Orleans Women," in *Katrina and the Women of New Orleans*, ed. Beth Willinger (New Orleans: Tulane University, 2008), 32–49.

49. On anonymity of donors, see Kendall, *Framing Class*, 34, 37–38.

50. "Women of the Storm General Ledger," July 18, 2008, WOS Records.

51. Gregory Ben Johnson to Janet Brown, March 19, 2007, WOS Records.

52. Leslie Williams, "Storming D.C.," *Times-Picayune*, January 26, 2006, A1, A8.

Chapter 3. Making Plans, Going Public

1. As with many emergent activist groups, WOS participants needed to define problems and propose solutions. On defining problems, see Kathleen M. Blee, *Democracy in the Making: How Activist Groups Form* (New York: Oxford University Press, 2012), 93–94. Women of the Storm oscillated between defining the problem as "unique" and as "representative."

2. "Women of the Storm Talking Points," n.d., in author's collection. A copy of the entire packet used on the trip to Washington was given to me on March 20, 2006.

3. Ibid.

4. Tyler Priest, "Extraction Not Creation: The History of Offshore Petroleum in the Gulf of Mexico," *Enterprise and Society* 8, no. 2 (2007): 236; Tyler Priest, *The Offshore Imperative: Shell Oil's Search for Petroleum in Postwar America* (College Station: Texas A&M Press, 2007).

5. Priest, "Extraction Not Creation," 36.

6. Ibid., 37. On the life of Leander Perez, see Glenn Jeansonne, *Leander Perez: Boss of the Delta* (Baton Rouge: Louisiana State University Press, 1977).

7. Editorial, "A Share for Us," *Times-Picayune*, December 9, 2006, Metro section, 6. See also Bill Walsh, "States Take Long Road to Share in Oil Revenue; Louisiana Rejected Truman's 1949 Offer," *Times-Picayune*, December 10, 2006, National section, 1.

8. Bill Walsh, "Congress Approves Offshore Revenue Sharing; It Will Provide Money for Coastal Restoration," *Times-Picayune*, December 9, 2006, National section, 1; Walsh, "States Take Long Road." In the 1980s the parish government sued the Perez family on charges that the Delta Development Corporation, owned by the Perezes, had stolen millions in mineral royalties from oil-rich Plaquemines Parish. The case went to the Louisiana Supreme Court, where it was overruled. This decision resulted in the parish dropping the $80 million in claims against the family, who nevertheless had to pay $12 million and give up control of the parish lands. See "Leander Perez Jr. Is Dead at 68," *New York Times*, October 6, 1988, http://www.nytimes.com/1988/10/06/obituaries/leander-perez-jr-is-dead-at-68.html.

9. Priest, "History of U.S. Oil and Gas Leasing," 29.

10. Theriot, *American Energy, Imperiled Coast*, 82–84.

11. Ibid., 190.

12. "Women of the Storm Talking Points."

13. Adam Nossiter, "Rejection of Building Plan Causes Dismay in Louisiana," *New York Times*, January 26, 2006, http://www.nytimes.com/2006/01/26/us/nationalspecial/rejection-of-building-plan-causes-dismay-in-louisiana.html.

14. Adam Nossiter, "A Big Government Fix-It Plan for New Orleans," *New York Times*, January 5, 2006, A1.

15. Oren Dorell, "White House Rejects La. Buyout Proposal," *USA Today*, January 25, 2006, A3.

16. Nossiter, "Big Government Fix-It Plan."

17. Robert D. Bullard and Beverly Wright, *The Wrong Complexion for Protection: How the Government Response to Disaster Endangers African American Communities* (New York: New York University Press, 2012). See also Dorell, "White House Rejects La. Buyout Proposal."

18. Nossiter, "Big Government Fix-It Plan."

19. Unpublished Women of the Storm document, in author's collection.

20. Scott Cowen, *The Inevitable City: The Resurgence of New Orleans and the Future of Urban America* (New York: Palgrave Macmillan, 2014), 133.

21. "To" and "From" form letter distributed to WOS members to request congressional appointments. Distributed by e-mail on January 24, 2006, by Anne Milling; used with permission.

22. Leslie Williams, "Storming D.C.," *Times-Picayune*, January 26, 2006, A1, A8.

23. Jacki Schneider, "Local Woman Brings Storm Stories to D.C.," *Times-Picayune*, April 2, 2006, 21. Arceneaux died in a tragic automobile accident on July 25, 2006. See "Tammany activist dies in wreck—She may have had heart attack," *Times-Picayune*, July 26, 2006, National section, 1.

24. Jed Horne, *Breach of Faith: Hurricane Katrina and the Near Death of a Great American City* (New York: Random House, 2006), 342.

25. David Skinner, "Walter Isaacson Biography," Awards and Honors: 2014 Jefferson Lecturer, National Endowment for the Humanities, http://www.neh.gov/about/awards/jefferson -lecture/walter-isaacson-biography. See also "Isaacson to Leave CNN, Join Aspen Institute," CNN, January 13, 2003, http://www.cnn.com/2003/US/01/13/isaacson.cnn.

26. Walter Isaacson, foreword to Tom Wooten, *We Shall Not Be Moved* (Boston: Beacon, 2012), ix–xiii. Outside New Orleans, Isaacson is perhaps best known for his 2011 biography of Steve Jobs, the co-founder of Apple.

27. Horne, *Breach of Faith*, 342–43.

28. Donald E. Powell, "Rebuilding Wisely," *Washington Post*, February 2, 2006, http://www .washingtonpost.com/wp-dyn/content/article/2006/02/01/AR2006020101834.html.

29. Ibid.

30. The Baker Bill also had critics. In contrast to WOS, the group Color of Change saw the Baker Bill as an effort to purge poor and black residents from their homes. In an online petition that circulated in early 2006, Color of Change sought to stop the passage of the Baker Bill, calling on supporters to "oppose federally-funded gentrification." For an in-depth discussion of privatization and market-driven governance after Katrina, see Vincanne Adams, *Markets of Sorrow, Labors of Faith: New Orleans in the Wake of Katrina* (Durham, NC: Duke University Press, 2013).

31. Nossiter, "Big Government Fix-It Plan."

32. Quoted in Bruce Alpert, "Hastert, Pelosi Urged to Visit," *Times-Picayune*, January 28, 2006, 13.

33. On gender, appearance, and beauty ideology, see Diane Barthel, *Putting on Appearance* (Philadelphia: Temple University Press, 1988); Debra Gimlin, *Bodywork: Beauty and Self-Image in American Culture* (Berkeley: University of California Press, 2002); Blain Roberts, *Pageants, Parlors, and Pretty Women: Race and Beauty in the Twentieth-Century South* (Chapel Hill: University of North Carolina Press, 2014).

34. See Diana Kendall, *The Power of Good Deeds: Privileged Women and the Social Reproduction of the Upper Class* (Lanham, MD: Rowman and Littlefield, 2002), 62.

35. Evelyn Brooks Higginbotham, *Righteous Discontent: The Women's Movement in the Black Baptist Church, 1880–1920* (Cambridge, MA: Harvard University Press, 1994), 187. On the geographies of niceness and respectability in New Orleans, see LaKisha Michelle Simmons, *Crescent City Girls: The Lives of Young Black Women in Segregated New Orleans* (Chapel Hill, NC: University of North Carolina Press, 2015).

36. It is important to note that these were not just constructions of white femininities. Among The Links, there are very specific protocols that govern attire during ceremonies. For example,

during induction, chartering, and memorial services, Links members are often required to wear "uninterrupted white." Juanda Maxwell, chair of rituals, writes, "Uninterrupted white is all white attire from your head to the toe. Flesh and white colored hosiery may be worn." See Juanda Maxwell, "Proper Protocol Is the Heart of Successful Rituals," *Southern Area Advantage* 2, no. 1 (n.d.), 7.

37. Higginbotham, *Righteous Discontent*, 187.

38. On the social functions of jewelry, see Georg Simmel, *The Sociology of Georg Simmel*, trans. Kurt H. Wolff (New York: Free Press, 1950), 339, 342.

39. For a historical overview of the role of the *Times-Picayune* in New Orleans, see S. L. Alexander, Frank D. Durham, Alfred Lawrence Lorenz, and Vicki Mayer, *The* Times-Picayune *in a Changing Media World: The Transformation of an American Newspaper* (Lanham, MD: Lexington Books, 2014).

40. Williams, "Storming D.C." The same article appeared online ahead of print the previous day under a different title; see Leslie Williams, "'Women' to Personally Invite Congressmen to Tour City," *Times-Picayune*, January 25, 2006.

41. Brian Denzer, "Conversation with Lauren Anderson," Community Gumbo, WTUL–New Orleans, February 11, 2006, http://communitygumbo.blogspot.com/2006/02/21106-community-gumbo.html.

42. Richard Campanella, *Bourbon Street: A History* (Baton Rouge: Louisiana State University Press, 2014), 124–25.

43. Mimi Hall, "'Women of the Storm' Push for More Katrina Funding," *USA Today*, January 31, 2006, A2.

44. Priscilla Greear, "'Women of the Storm' to Blitz Washington Again," *Georgia Bulletin: The Newspaper of the Catholic Archdiocese of Atlanta*, September 14, 2006, http://www.georgiabulletin.org/local/2006/09/14/storm.

45. Williams, "Storming D.C."

46. "Women of the Storm Participants," n.d., WOS Records, Tulane University.

47. Mandy Chocheles, letter to the editor, *Times-Picayune*, January 29, 2006, 6.

48. Evelyn Bryan, letter to the editor, *Times-Picayune*, January 29, 2006, 6.

Chapter 4. The Flight

1. Felicity Barringer and Donald G McNeil Jr., "Grim Triage for Ailing and Dying at a Makeshift Airport Hospital," *New York Times*, September 3, 2005. For a firsthand account by a doctor who stayed at Charity Hospital for six days and nights after Katrina, see Ruth Berggren, "Unexpected Necessities, Inside Charity Hospital," in *The Women of Katrina: How Gender, Race, and Class Matter in an American Disaster*, ed. Emmanuel David and Elaine Enarson, 39–42 (Nashville: Vanderbilt University Press, 2012). See also Sheri Fink, *Five Days at Memorial: Life and Death in a Storm-Ravaged Hospital* (New York: Crown Publishers, 2013).

2. Sean Payton and Ellis Henican, *Home Team: Coaching the Saints and New Orleans Back to Life* (New York: New American Library, 2010), 47.

3. An e-mail from one of the core members to the participants advised that the name tags were to be worn only in the morning and on the plane, not during the press conference or during the Hill visits.

4. Pam Bryan, "Women of the Storm Panel Discussion," podcast audio, March 7, 2006, Newcomb Archives and Vorhoff Library Special Collections, Newcomb College Institute,

Tulane University; Erin Healan, "Local Women Bring Leaders to New Orleans," *Tulane Hullabaloo*, March 10, 2006, 7.

5. A few weeks earlier, on January 6, also known as Twelfth Night, New Orleans entered the first Carnival season after the storm, and still had a month before Mardi Gras day, or Fat Tuesday, the last day of Carnival, which in 2006 was in late February.

6. Unpublished Women of the Storm supporting materials, in author's collection.

7. Jarvis DeBerry, "The Pride of New Orleans," *Boston Globe*, August 28, 2008, A11.

8. Alina Cho, "Women of the Storm," *American Morning*, CNN, January 30, 2006.

9. Ruth Mahony, "After the Storm: Barbara Blackwell's Odyssey," *De Novo: The Newsletter of the Law Library of Louisiana* 4, no. 1 (2006): 7.

10. "Dillard Neighborhood Snapshot," Greater New Orleans Community Data Center, http://www.datacenterresearch.org/pre-katrina/orleans/6/27/snapshot.html.

11. Mahony, "After the Storm." See also Laura Hertzfeld, "Katrina Home: An 'Unwavering, Persistent Angel,'" posted on Stay Human Message Board, September 16, 2005, http://www.spearhead-home.com/phpBB2_StayHuman/viewtopic.php?t=2938.

12. Mahony, "After the Storm."

13. United States, *Hurricane Katrina: A Nation Still Unprepared*, Special Report of the Committee on Homeland Security and Governmental Affairs, United States Senate, Together with Additional Views (Washington, DC: U.S. Government Printing Office, 2006), 154, 364.

14. Ibid., 364.

15. Ibid.

16. Ibid., 9.

17. Ibid., 70–71.

18. Mahony, "After the Storm."

19. Ibid.

20. Spencer S. Hsu, "Post-Katrina Promises Unfulfilled," *Washington Post*, January 28, 2006.

21. Information about Cecile Tebo is drawn from numerous published sources, including Fritz Esker, "Cecile Tebo," *New Orleans CityBusiness*, November 19, 2007, 59; Maryn McKenna, "After the Deluge," *More Magazine*, April 2008, 74; and several interviews on broadcast television stations such as CNN. Tebo left the NOPD in 2011 and rejoined after three years of retirement to become the director of the Officer Assistance Program as well as the community coordinator of the Crisis Intervention Team, which trains officers to deal with people with mental illness.

22. Quoted in McKenna, "After the Deluge."

23. The flood also destroyed all of her adoption case records, which she had planned to use as source materials for a book she dreamed of writing. See McKenna, "After the Deluge."

24. Leslie Irvine, *Filling the Ark: Animal Welfare in Disasters* (Philadelphia: Temple University Press), 34.

25. McKenna, "After the Deluge." See also Paula A. Madrid and Stephanie J. Schacher, "A Critical Concern: Pediatrician Self-Care after Disasters," *Pediatrics* 117, no. 5 (2006): S454–S457.

26. McKenna, "After the Deluge."

27. "Katrina: We Are Not OK," transcript, *CNN: American Morning*, December 2, 2005, http://www.cnn.com/TRANSCRIPTS/0512/02/ltm.07.html. Used with Cecile Tebo's permission.

28. Quoted on WWL-TV Eyewitness News with Jonathan Betz, January 14, 2006.

29. Leslie Eaton, "Rooted in New Orleans, and Riding Out the Storm," *Wall Street Journal* Blogs, September 1, 2008, http://blogs.wsj.com/stormtracker/2008/09/01/rooted-in-new-orleans-and-riding-out-the-storm.

30. Michelle Goldberg, "Saving the Neighborhood," Salon.com, February 24, 2006, http://www.salon.com/2006/02/24/broadmoor; Tom Wooten, *We Shall Not Be Moved: Rebuilding Home in the Wake of Katrina* (Boston: Beacon Press, 2012), 216.

31. Karl F. Seidman, *Coming Home to New Orleans: Neighborhood Rebuilding after Katrina* (New York: Oxford University Press, 2013).

32. David Winkler-Schmit, "Call to Action," *Gambit Weekly*, March 14, 2006. See also Ian McNulty, "Gambit's 40 under 40," *Gambit Weekly*, November 7, 2006.

33. Goldberg, "Saving the Neighborhood."

34. Seidman, *Coming Home*, 66.

35. Ibid., 75.

36. Traci Farrell, "New Orleans' Broadmoor Is Model for Disaster Recovery," *Belfer Center Newsletter*, Harvard University, Summer 2008.

37. Goldberg, "Saving the Neighborhood."

38. Ibid.; Mahony, "After the Storm."

39. Cho, "Women of the Storm."

Chapter 5. The Press Conference

1. Pam Bryan, "Women of the Storm Panel Discussion," podcast audio, March 7, 2006, Newcomb Archives and Vorhoff Library Special Collections, Newcomb College Institute, Tulane University.

2. Alina Cho, "Women of the Storm," *American Morning*, CNN, January 30, 2006.

3. One interviewee told me the first order of umbrellas was botched. The group's logo appeared in red, which could hardly be seen against the blue fabric. Someone quietly placed another order, this time with a white logo, and absorbed the cost of the rushed custom order.

4. Quoted in "'Women of the Storm' Documentary Makes Debut," WWL-TV Channel 4, February 28, 2015.

5. See Beverly Reese Church, *Seasonal Celebrations* (New Orleans: Entertaining Celebrations, 2005); Beverly Reese Church and Bethany Ewald Bultman, *The Joys of Entertaining* (New York: Abbeville Press, 1998); Beverly Reese Church and Kristina Petersen, *Entertaining Celebrations: Celebrate Each Month with Pizzazz!* (New Orleans: Entertaining Celebrations, 1999).

6. On the strategic use of space and place in women's activism, see Ruth Fincher and Ruth Panelli, "Making Space: Women's Urban and Rural Activism and the Australian State," *Gender, Place, and Culture: A Journal of Feminist Geography* 8, no. 2 (2001): 129–48.

7. Liz Reyes, ABC-WGNO 26 News, January 30, 2006.

8. On the links between performance, social movements, and political protest, see Ron Eyerman, "Performing Opposition or How Social Movements Move," in *Social Performance: Symbolic Action, Cultural Pragmatics, and Ritual*, ed. Jeffrey C. Alexander, Bernhard Giesen, and Jason L. Mast, 193–217 (New York: Cambridge University Press, 2006); Deborah B. Gould, *Moving Politics: Emotion and ACT UP's Fight against AIDS* (Chicago: University of Chicago Press, 2009); Harry J. Elam Jr., *Taking It to the Streets: The Social Protest Theater of Luis Valdez and Amiri Baraka* (Ann Arbor: University of Michigan Press, 2001); Diana Taylor, *The Archive and the Repertoire: Performing Cultural Memory in the Americas* (Durham, NC: Duke University Press, 2003).

9. These elements include systems of collective representation, actors, observers/audience, means of symbolic production, mise-en-scène, and social power. Jeffrey C. Alexander,

"Cultural Pragmatics: Social Performance between Ritual and Strategy," in Alexander et al., *Social Performance*, 29–90.

10. Ibid., 35.

11. One woman I spoke with later said she wished the umbrellas had been "flat" to represent the roofs of homes.

12. Joseph Roach observes that the "umbrella seems to represent an icon in the atlas of cultural difference" and that it is "evocative of prestige, luxury, and pampered excess," especially when held overhead by others. See Joseph Roach, "The Global Parasol: Accessorizing the Four Corners of the World," in *The Global Eighteenth Century*, ed. Felicity A. Nussbaum (Baltimore: Johns Hopkins University Press, 2003), 95, 105.

13. On performative success and failure, see Jeffrey C. Alexander, "From the Depths of Despair: Performance, Counterperformance, and September 11," in Alexander et al., *Social Performance*, 91–114.

14. Joseph Roach, *Cities of the Dead: Circum-Atlantic Performance* (New York: Columbia University Press, 1996), 278.

15. Angelo Coclanis and Peter Coclanis, "Jazz Funeral: A Living Tradition," *Southern Cultures* 11, no. 2 (2005): 86–92; Roach, *Cities of the Dead*; Joseph Roach, "Cutting Loose: Burying the 'First Man of Jazz,'" in *Joyous Wakes, Dignified Deaths: Issues in Death and Dying*, ed. Robert Harvey (Stony Brook, NY: Humanities Institute, 2001), 3–14; "Jazz Origins in New Orleans," National Park Service, https://www.nps.gov/jazz/learn/historyculture/history_early.htm.

16. Helen Regis, "Second Lines, Minstrelsy, and the Contested Landscapes of New Orleans Afro-Creole Festivals," *Cultural Anthropology* 14, no. 4 (1999): 472–504; Helen Regis, "Blackness and the Politics of Memory in the New Orleans Second Line," *American Ethnologist* 28, no. 4 (2001): 752–77.

17. On defining the scope of a problem, see Kathleen M. Blee, *Democracy in the Making: How Activist Groups Form* (New York: Oxford University Press, 2012), 84.

18. On diversity discourses as public relations, see Sara Ahmed, *On Being Included: Racism and Diversity in Institutional Life* (Durham, NC: Duke University Press, 2012).

19. Mary Rickard, "A New Orleans Dollhouse Gets a Makeover in Miniature," Nola.com, January 24, 2013, http://www.nola.com/homegarden/index.ssf/2013/01/a_new_orleans_dollhouse_gets_a.html.

20. Her father, Charles C. Teamer, cofounded Dryades Savings Bank in the early 1990s and became president of the World Trade Center of New Orleans in the early 2000s. In addition to serving as vice president of fiscal affairs at Dillard University and Clark Atlanta University, he is director of Entergy New Orleans. See "Charles Teamer," The History Makers: The National Largest African American Video Oral History Collection, interview date, March 28, 2008, http://www.thehistorymakers.com/biography/charles-teamer-41.

21. See Alpha Phi Alpha, "A Statement of Public Policy," *The Sphynx* (Fall 1985): 39–44.

22. "Landrieu Announces National Advisory Board for Cultural Economy, Tourism, and Hospitality in Louisiana," press release, State of Louisiana Office of the Lieutenant Governor, September 20, 2005.

23. Whitney Pierce Santora, "2005 Women of the Year: Cheryl Teamer," *New Orleans City-Business*, January 23, 2006, 57. In 2012 Teamer would become the first female chairperson of the New Orleans Aviation Board. See Richard Rainey, "New Orleans Aviation Board Chooses Its First Female Chair," *Times-Picayune*, May 17, 2013.

24. Blee, *Democracy in the Making*, 120.

25. Ibid.

26. Ibid.

27. Wolf Blitzer, "The Situation Room," January 30, 2006, http://www.cnn.com/TRAN-SCRIPTS/0601/30/sitroom.01.html.

28. Clancy Dubos, "Undaunted by the Odds," *Gambit Weekly*, January 31, 2006, 15.

29. Ibid.

30. Bruce Alpert, "Louisiana Women Storm Washington," *Times-Picayune*, January 31, 2006, 4.

31. "Women of the Storm Push for Hurricane Relief," *CNN Live Today*, January 30, 2006.

32. "Speaking with One Voice," *Nightwatch*, WWL4 Eyewitness News with Shauna Sanford, January 30, 2006.

33. WGNO-ABC26 News with Liz Reyes, January 30, 2006.

34. Gloria C. Love, "A Katrina Recovery Initiative: Dillard University Student Projects, January-July 2006," *Journal of African American History* 93, no. 3 (2008): 402–409.

35. Information about Marvalene Hughes was compiled from the following sources: Scott Dyer, "New Orleans' Black College Prepare to Reopen in January," *Black Issues in Higher Education* 9, no. 2 (2005): 9; Marvalene Hughes, "Dillard Renews Promise, Rebuilding after Storm: A Guest Column by Dr. Marvalene Hughes," *Times-Picayune*, August 28, 2010; Sam Dillon, "Educators Offer Classrooms to Many Displaced Students," *New York Times*, September 1, 2005; "Hurricane Katrina's Devastating Effect on African-American Higher Education," *Journal of Blacks in Higher Education* (2005), http://www.jbhe.com/features/49_hurrican_katrina.html.

36. Duane A. Gill, Anthony E. Ladd, and John Marszalek, "College Students' Experiences with Hurricane Katrina: A Comparison between Students from Mississippi State University and Three New Orleans Universities," *Journal of the Mississippi Academy of Sciences* 52, no. 4 (2007): 262–80.

37. Interview with Marvalene Hughes, "Katrina Update," *Black Collegian* 36, no. 2 (2006): 10–12.

38. "Women of the Storm Push for Hurricane Relief," transcript, *CNN: Live Today*, January 30, 2006, http://transcripts.cnn.com/TRANSCRIPTS/0601/30/lt.02.html.

39. Ahmed, *On Being Included*, 143.

40. "Women of the Storm Invitation," n.d., in author's collection. Used with permission.

41. On the cultural politics of the invitation, see Rebecca Snedeker's film *By Invitation Only* (New Day Movies, 2006). Focusing on the old-line Carnival krewes, the film is centered on Snedeker's struggle to understand the krewes' exclusive practices. During my fieldwork, one WOS interviewee mentioned Snedeker's name to me, indicating that she and presumably those in her social circle were well aware of the film, which at the time was still in production. For an analysis of the film, see Catherine Clinton, "Scepter and Masque: Debutante Rituals in Mardi Gras New Orleans," in *Manners and Southern History*, ed. Ted Ownby (Jackson: University Press of Mississippi, 2007), 92; Billy Sothern, *Down in New Orleans: Reflections from a Drowned City* (Berkeley: University of California Press, 2007), 250–51. Jane Dailey, "Remarks," in *Manners and Southern History*, 141. On the racial desegregation of Carnival krewes, see Barbara Vennman, "Boundary Face-Off: New Orleans Civil Rights Law and Carnival Tradition," *Drama Review* 37, no. 3 (1993): 76–109.

42. J. L. Austin, *Philosophical Papers* (New York: Oxford University Press, 1961); J. L. Austin, *How to Do Things with Words* (Cambridge, MA: Harvard University Press, 1962); John Searle, *Speech Acts* (Cambridge, UK: Cambridge University Press, 1969).

43. Austin, *Philosophical Papers*, 231.

44. Ibid., 224–25.

Chapter 6. Hill Visits

1. Leslie Williams, "Storming D.C.," *Times-Picayune*, January 26, 2006, A1, A8.

2. Bevil Knapp and Mike Dunne, *America's Wetland: Louisiana's Vanishing Coast* (Baton Rouge: Louisiana State University Press, 2005).

3. Alina Cho, "Women of the Storm," *American Morning*, CNN, January 30, 2006.

4. Cecile Tebo, "Women Take the Word to D.C.," *Times-Picayune*, February 2, 2006, B7.

5. Cho, "Women of the Storm."

6. Tebo, "Women Take the Word to D.C."

7. Pam Bryan, "Women of the Storm Panel Discussion," podcast audio, March 7, 2006, Newcomb Archives and Vorhoff Library Special Collections, Newcomb College Institute, Tulane University.

8. Rukmini Callimachi, "'Women of the Storm' Lobby Washington for More Help," *St. Louis Post-Dispatch*, January 31, 2006, A2.

9. Bryan, "Women of the Storm Panel Discussion."

10. Rukmini Callimachi, "New Orleans Women Travel to D.C.," *Houston Chronicle*, January 31, 2006, 9.

11. Callimachi, "'Women of the Storm' Lobby Washington."

12. Callimachi, "New Orleans Women Travel to D.C."

13. Bruce Alpert, "Louisiana Women Storm Washington," *Times-Picayune*, January 31, 2006, 4.

14. Ibid.

15. Bryan, "Women of the Storm Panel Discussion."

16. Callimachi, "'Women of the Storm' Lobby Washington."

17. Ibid.

18. Callimachi, "New Orleans Women Lobby Congress for Aid"; Priscilla Greear, "'Women of the Storm' to Blitz Washington Again," *Georgia Bulletin: The Newspaper of the Catholic Archdiocese of Atlanta*, September 14, 2006, http://www.georgiabulletin.org/local/2006/09/14/storm.

19. Laura McKnight, "Four Locals Join Women's Group's Visit to D.C.," *Courier*, January 29, 2006; Laura McKnight, "Local Women Score Mixed Results on Capitol Hill," *Courier*, February 1, 2006.

20. Ibid.

21. McKnight, "Four Locals Join Women's Group Visit"; Restore or Retreat, http://www.restoreorretreat.org/about-us.

22. Ibid.

23. Lili LeGardeur, "The East: Concerns about the Future," *Gambit Weekly*, November 8, 2005.

24. Ibid.

25. "Read Blvd East Neighborhood: People and Household Characteristics," Greater New Orleans Community Data Center, July 25, 2006, http://www.datacenterresearch.org/pre-katrina/orleans/9/52/people.html.

26. LeGardeur, "The East." See also "Dooky Chase '67 Honored as 2012 Alumnus of the Year," Jesuit High School of New Orleans, October 12, 2012, http://www.jesuitnola.org/2012/10/12/dooky-chase-of-the-class-of-67-honored-as-2012-alumnus-of-the-year.

27. "Speaking with One Voice," *Nightwatch*, WWL4 Eyewitness News with Shauna Sanford, January 30, 2006.

28. Ibid.

29. Jeanette Bell, "Women of the Storm Panel Discussion," podcast audio, March 7, 2006, Newcomb Archives and Vorhoff Library Special Collections, Newcomb College Institute, Tulane University; Patti Lapeyre, "Contact Form," n.d., WOS Records.

30. bell hooks, "A Place Where the Soul Can Rest," in *Etiquette: Reflections on Contemporary Comportment*, ed. Ron Scapp and Brian Seitz, 174–75 (New York: State University of New York Press, 2007).

31. Sara Mills, "Gender and Impoliteness," *Journal of Politeness Research* 1, no. 2 (2005): 274.

32. bell hooks writes, "The etiquette of civility then is far more than the performance of manners: it includes an understanding of the deeper psychoanalytic relationship to recognition as that which makes us subjects to one another rather than objects." See hooks, "Place Where the Soul Can Rest," 175.

33. John F. Kasson, "Taking Manners Seriously," in *Manners and Southern History*, ed. Ted Ownby (Jackson: University Press of Mississippi, 2007), 153.

34. Ibid.

35. Pierre Bourdieu, *Outline of a Theory of Practice*, trans. Richard Nice (New York: Cambridge University Press, 1977), 95; emphasis in original.

36. Hazel Barnes, "Take Clothes, for Example," in Scapp and Seitz, *Etiquette*, 240.

37. Jeffrey C. Alexander, "Toward a Theory of Cultural Trauma," in *Cultural Trauma and Collective Identity*, ed. Jeffrey C. Alexander, Ron Eyerman, Bernhard Giesen, Neil J. Smelser, and Piotr Sztompka, 1–30 (Berkeley: University of California Press, 2004), 1.

38. Editorial, "Louisiana in Limbo," *New York Times*, January 30, 2006.

39. "Speaking with One Voice," *Nightwatch*, WWL4 Eyewitness News with Shauna Sanford, January 30, 2006.

40. "Contact Form," n.d., WOS Records.

41. WOS's plane ride itself was important, reflecting what Larry Isaac describes as the social movement phenomena of the "migration of people as carriers of movement 'mail.'" See Larry Isaac, "Movement of Movements: Culture Moves in the Long Civil Rights Struggle," *Social Forces* 87, no. 1 (2008): 37.

Chapter 7. Noblesse Oblige

1. Women of the Storm, "Reps Not Being Met," n.d., WOS Records, Tulane University.

2. On the politics of the RSVP, see Peggy Post, *Emily Post's Etiquette* (New York: Harper-Collins, 1997), 356.

3. Anne Milling, e-mail message to Women of the Storm participants, February 1, 2006; used with permission.

4. Ibid.

5. Micaela di Leonardo, "The Female World of Cards and Holidays: Women, Families, and the Work of Kinship," *Signs* 12, no. 3 (1987): 440–53.

6. U.S. Congress, *Tax Relief Extension Reconciliation Act of 2005*, pp. S413–14 (Senate, February 1, 2006). For a sociological critique of the "9/11 Commission Report," see Kathleen Tierney, "The 9/11 Commission and Disaster Management: Little Depth, Less Context, Not Much Guidance," *Contemporary Sociology* 34, no. 2 (2005): 115–20.

7. Members from Citizens for One Greater New Orleans attributed Blanco's move to New Orleans as a result of its levee reform movement, in which the "Ladies in Red" pressured the state government to consolidate the multiple levee boards.

8. Associated Press, "Governor Proposes Relief Measures for New Orleans," *New York Times*, February 7, 2006.

9. "Gov. Blanco's Speech to the Louisiana Legislature," Office of the Governor, Kathleen Babineaux Blanco, State of Louisiana, February 6, 2006. See also Associated Press, "Governor Proposes Relief Measures."

10. Anne Milling, e-mail message to Women of the Storm participants, February 6, 2006; used with permission.

11. Petula Dvorak, "Hurricane Victims Demand More Help," *Washington Post*, February 9, 2006. See also Bill Walsh, "Capitol Offensive: Hurricane Katrina Victims Rally in Washington to Urge Bush, Congress to Step Up Recovery," *Times-Picayune*, February 10, 2006, B1.

12. "ACORN Builds for the Future of New Orleans," The Katrina Reader, http://katrina reader.org/sites/katrinareader.org/files/Katrina-II-C-Housing-FEMA-10.pdf.

13. Leslie Williams, "Women of the Storm Await 1st Guests; Georgia, New Jersey Lawmakers to Visit," *Times-Picayune*, February 10, 2006, 10; Walsh, "Capitol Offensive."

14. Kathleen M. Blee, *Democracy in the Making: How Activist Groups Form* (New York: Oxford University Press, 2012), 69.

15. Anne Milling, e-mail message to Women of the Storm participants, February 12, 2006; used with permission.

16. On women's disaster activism, see David Neal and Brenda Phillips, "Female-Dominated Local Social Movement Organizations in Disaster-Threat Situations," in *Women and Social Protest*, ed. Guida West and Rhoda Lois Blumberg, 243–55 (New York: Oxford University Press, 1990). See also Elaine Enarson and Betty Hearn Morrow, "Women Will Rebuild Miami: A Case Study of Feminist Response to Disaster," in *The Gendered Terrain of Disaster: Through Women's Eyes*, ed. Elaine Enarson and Betty Hearn Morrow (Westport, CT: Greenwood, 1998), 192, 198.

17. Ruth Mahony, "After the Storm: Barbara Blackwell's Odyssey," *De Novo: The Newsletter of the Law Library of Louisiana* 4, no. 1 (2006): 7.

18. It was also not long before participation in WOS was added to the credentials of those who would become queens of Carnival social clubs in the years that followed. See "Mystic Goes to Gotham; Ball Re-creates a Party Hosted by New York Society 'Royals' in 1913," *Times-Picayune*, February 2, 2008, 1; "The Reign in Spain; The Mystic Club's Ball Masque Bows to Queen Isabella and King Ferdinand," *Times-Picayune*, February 22, 2009, 1; Nell Nolan, "Isabella Sails Again," *Times-Picayune*, March 2, 2009, 2. "Mystic queens are members' wives, but all are chosen for their roles because of their community works," said John Magill of the Historic New Orleans Collection, who in 1997 curated a display titled "Mystical Bal Masque: 75 Years of the Mystic Club." Quoted in Mary Lou Atkinson, "Unmasking Mystic's Mystiques Exhibit Celebrates Mystic Club's 75th Anniversary and Salutes Carnival's Behind-the-Scenes Players," *Times-Picayune*, January 12, 1997, E1.

19. Diana Kendall, *The Power of Good Deeds: Privileged Women and the Social Reproduction of the Upper Class* (Lanham, MD: Rowman and Littlefield, 2002), 30. Another reporter described the women as "dressed for political combat in pastel power suits, smart skirt outfits and discreet jewelry." See Ann M. Simmons, "Storming Capitol Hill to Help Louisiana," *Los Angeles Times*, October 21, 2006, A12.

20. Kendall, *Power of Good Deeds*, 30.

21. Shulamit Reinharz, "Women as Competent Community Builders: The Other Side of the Coin," in *Social and Psychological Problems of Women: Prevention and Crisis Intervention*, ed. Annette U. Rickel, Meg Gerrard, and Ira Iscoe (Harper & Row: New York, 1984), 20.

22. Kathleen D. McCarthy, *Noblesse Oblige: Charity and Philanthropy in Chicago, 1849–1929* (Chicago: University of Chicago Press, 1982), ix.

Chapter 8. Divergent Paths

1. Rosary O'Neill, *New Orleans Carnival Krewes: The History, Spirit and Secrets of Mardi Gras* (Charleston, SC: History Press, 2014).

2. Mary LaCoste, "Fashions Made from Blue Tarps a Big Hit at Show to Help Wetlands Recover," *Louisiana Weekly*, February 27, 2006.

3. "Brief History of Krewe du Vieux," http://www.kreweduvieux.org/History.html.

4. Ibid.

5. Krewe du Vieux, "Krewe du Vieux says 'C'est Levee,'" *Le Monde de Merde* 15, no. 1, February 11, 2006. "Le Monde de Merde" is French for "The World of Shit."

6. Karen Sommer Shalett, "Tangled Up in Blue; Tongue Firmly Planted in Cheek, Some of the City's Best Designers Made Very Serious Clothing Out of Very Unserious Blue Tarp, All Part of an Effort to Raise Money for Tourism Promotion and Wetlands Restoration," *Times-Picayune*, February 22, 2006, 1.

7. Ibid.

8. Ibid; Jeff Duncan, "Musicians, Revelers Jam the Quarter, Riverfront," *Times-Picayune*, February 28, 2006, 1.

9. Shalett, "Tangled Up in Blue."

10. LaCoste, "Fashions Made from Blue Tarps a Big Hit."

11. "Blue Tarp Fashion All the Rage in La," *Advocate*, February 15, 2006, 8.

12. Diana Kendall, *The Power of Good Deeds: Privileged Women and the Social Reproduction of the Upper Class* (Lanham, MD: Rowman and Littlefield, 2002), 65.

13. Evelyn Poitevent, "Here Comes the Rain Again," *Times-Picayune*, April 7, 2006, 5.

14. Kendall, *Power of Good Deeds*, 64–65.

15. Ibid., 77.

16. Kathleen M. Blee, *Democracy in the Making: How Activist Groups Form* (New York: Oxford University Press, 2012), 73.

17. Data from the 2000 census reveal numerous pre-Katrina social vulnerabilities for Gert Town residents. Like many New Orleans neighborhoods, Gert Town was highly segregated by race, with blacks or African Americans making up 94.5 percent of residents, the majority of whom, 60.7 percent, were women. Of the 1,541 occupied housing units in the neighborhood, 75.8 percent were renter occupied. The average household income was about $23,000 ($31,224 in 2015 dollars), or about half of the average reported for Orleans Parish, and 40.2 percent of households reported total income of less than $10,000. See the Data Center analysis of data from U.S. Census 2000 Summary File 3 (SF3), http://www.datacenterresearch.org/data-resources/neighborhood-data/district-4/Gert-Town.

18. Antoinette D. Handy, *Jazz Man's Journey: A Biography of Ellis Louis Marsalis, Jr.* (Lanham, MD: Scarecrow Press, 1999).

19. Allen Toussaint, "The House with 88 Keys," *Wall Street Journal*, September 26, 2013.

20. Country Club of Louisiana Property Owners Association, http://www.cclapoa.com/outside_home.asp.

21. April Capochino, "New Orleans Nonprofit Director Gains New Family," *New Orleans CityBusiness*, October 10, 2005.

22. April Capochino, "Gert Town Turns into a Ghost Town," *New Orleans CityBusiness*, January 9, 2006, 1.

23. Louisiana Department of Environmental Quality—Remediation Services Division, "Basis for Decision for No Further Action." June 5, 2008, http://www.deq.louisiana.gov/portal/Portals/0/RemediationServices/NFA%20documents%20for%20Thompson%20Hayward%20with%20pictures.pdf.

24. Capochino, "Gert Town Turns into a Ghost Town."

25. Phil Brown and Faith Ferguson, "'Making a Big Stink': Women's Work, Women's Relationships, and Toxic Waste Activism," *Gender and Society* 9 (1995): 145–72; Celine Krauss, "Women of Color on the Front Line," in *Unequal Protection: Environmental Justice and Communities of Color*, ed. Robert D. Bullard, 256–71 (San Francisco: Sierra Club Books, 1997). On environmental racism and Katrina, see Robert D. Bullard and Beverly Wright, *The Wrong Complexion for Protection: How the Government Response to Disaster Endangers African American Communities* (New York: New York University Press, 2012).

26. Capochino, "Gert Town Turns into a Ghost Town."

27. Louisiana Department of Environmental Quality, "Basis for Decision for No Further Action."

28. Ian Wilhelm, "When the Helpers Need Help," *Chronicle of Philanthropy*, February 23, 2006, 48–51.

29. Ibid.

30. Ibid.

31. For documentation of solidarity between Vietnamese Americans and black residents after Katrina, see Eric Tang, "A Gulf Unites Us: The Vietnamese Americans of Black New Orleans East," *American Quarterly* 63, no. 1 (2011): 117–49; Karen J. Leong, Christopher A. Airriess, Wei Li, Angela Chia-Chen Chen, and Verna M. Keith, "Resilient History and the Rebuilding of Community: The Vietnamese American Community in New Orleans East," *Journal of American History* 94 (December 2007): 770–79.

32. Charles H. Rowell and Vien Nguyen, "Father Vien Nguyen," *Callaloo* 29, no. 4 (2006): 1071–81.

33. Ibid.

34. Florence L. Herman, "Women of the Storm Storm D.C.," *Clarion Herald: Official Newspaper of the Archdiocese of New Orleans* 45, no. 5 (2006): 1.

35. "Women and Business Presents the Women of the Year: Tina Owen," *New Orleans CityBusiness* 22, no. 24 (2001): 19A.

36. Rowell and Nguyen, "Father Vien Nguyen," 1078.

37. Leslie Eaton, "A New Landfill in New Orleans Sets Off a Battle," *New York Times*, May 6, 2006.

38. Richard A. Webster, "Desire Community Built on Toxic Dumpsite Demands Answers, Relief," *Times-Picayune*, September 26, 2014.

39. Testimony of Beverly Wright, Director, Deep South Center for Environmental Justice and Co-Chair, National Black Environmental Justice Network, before the Subcommittee on

Environment and Hazardous Materials Committee on Energy and Commerce, United States House of Representatives, September 29, 2005, https://www.gpo.gov/fdsys/pkg/CHRG -109hhrg24251/html/CHRG-109hhrg24251.htm.

40. Webster, "Desire Community."

41. Ibid.

42. Wright, testimony.

43. "Three Displaced New Orleans Residents Discuss Race and Hurricane Katrina," *Democracy Now!*, September 7, 2005; "Going Home: The *Satya* Interview with Dr. Beverly Wright," *Satya*, November 5, 2006; Ronald Roach, "Unequal Exposure," *Black Issues in Higher Education* 22, no. 21 (2005); Lottie L. Joiner, "Q&A Beverly Wright," *Crisis* 118, no. 2 (2012): 7.

44. "Going Home: The *Satya* Interview." Wright's experiences were not unlike the subjects in Alice Fothergill's study of middle-class women who experienced downward economic mobility after the 1997 Red River flood in Grand Forks, North Dakota, and negotiated the stigma of charity after receiving government aid. See Alice Fothergill, *Heads above Water: Gender, Class, and Family in the Grand Forks Flood* (Albany: State University of New York Press, 2004).

45. "Crescent City's Beverly Wright Releases New Book," *Advantage* 3, no. 1 (n.d.): 41.

46. Browen Wyatt, "Sheila Webb," *New Orleans Magazine* 40, no. 9 (2006): 50–51.

47. National Association of Community Health Centers, "Legacy of Disaster: Health Centers and Hurricane Katrina; One Year Later" (Washington, DC: National Association of Community Health Centers, 2006), 13, http://www.smrrc.org/PDF%20files/katrinareport.pdf.

48. Wyatt, "Sheila Webb."

Chapter 9. Invitations Accepted

1. This non-response was seen as a violation of a moral expectation. In other words, "shame" really meant "He *should* be ashamed of himself." For a microsociological account of shame, see Thomas J. Scheff, "Shame and Conformity: The Deference-Emotion System," *American Sociological Review* 53, no. 3 (1988): 395–406; Thomas J. Scheff, "Shame and Related Emotions: An Overview," *American Behavior Scientist* 38 (1995): 1053–59.

2. Jeff Duncan, "House Visitors Tour Katrina Ruins," *Times-Picayune*, February 20, 2006.

3. Becky Zaheri, WOS participant and founder of Katrina Krewe, remembered meeting with Garrett's staff in Washington: "When we first went into Garrett's office, the first person who came out looked like a twelve-year-old," who was "very nice and listened to what we had to say." See Leslie Williams, "Women of the Storm Await 1st Guests; Georgia, New Jersey Lawmakers to Visit," *Times-Picayune*, February 10, 2006, 10.

4. Jeff Duncan, "'Women of the Storm' Show the Face of Recovery," *Times-Picayune*, February 19, 2006, 1.

5. Ivor van Heerden, "The Failure of the New Orleans Levee System Following Hurricane Katrina and the Pathway Forward," *Public Administration Review* 67, no. 1 (2007): 24–35. See also Committee on the Future of Coastal Louisiana, *Saving Coastal Louisiana: Recommendations for Implementing an Expanded Coastal Restoration Program* (Baton Rouge: Governor's Office of Coastal Activities, 2002).

6. Van Heerden, "Failure of the New Orleans Levee System."

7. Duncan, "'Women of the Storm' Show the Face of Recovery."

8. As described in one woman's voicemail left for me on the morning of the lawmakers' trip.

9. Duncan, "'Women of the Storm' Show the Face of Recovery."

10. Ibid.

11. For a discussion of how racial familiarity can encourage empathy, see Michael Eric Dyson, *Come Hell or High Water: Hurricane Katrina and the Color of Disaster* (New York: Basic Civitas Books, 2006).

12. Duncan, "'Women of the Storm' Show the Face of Recovery."

13. Ibid.

14. "Editorial: Seeing Is Believing," *Times-Picayune*, February 21, 2006, 4.

15. Ibid.

16. Ibid.

17. Ibid.

18. Jeffrey C. Alexander. "Toward a Theory of Cultural Trauma," in *Cultural Trauma and Collective Identity*, ed. Jeffrey C. Alexander, Ron Eyerman, Bernhard Giesen, Neil J. Smelser, and Piotr Sztompka, 1–30 (Berkeley: University of California Press, 2004), 1.

19. Ibid., 11–12.

20. Ibid., 13–14

21. Rukmini Callimachi, "New Orleans Women Seek Congress' Support," *Washington Post*, January 31, 2006; Thayer Evans, "Football's First Family," *New York Times*, February 1, 2010.

22. John Lynkwiler and Michele Wilson, "The Code of the New Southern Belle: Generating Typifications to Structure Social Interaction," in *Southern Women*, ed. Caroline Matheny Dillman (New York: Taylor and Francis, 1988), 113–25. On studies of deference, see Erving Goffman, "The Nature of Deference and Demeanor," *American Anthropologist* 58, no. 3 (1956): 473–502; Janet M. Wedel, "Ladies, We've Been Framed! Observations on Erving Goffman's 'The Arrangements between the Sexes," *Theory and Society* 5, no. 1 (1978): 113–25.

23. Benita Roth, *Separate Roads to Feminism: Black, Chicana, and White Feminist Movements in America's Second Wave* (New York: Cambridge University Press, 2004), 53–54.

24. Nancy Naples, *Grassroots Warriors: Activist Mothering, Community Work, and the War on Poverty* (New York: Routledge, 1998); Lynn Staeheli and Meghan Cope, "Empowering Women's Citizenship," *Political Geography* 13 (1994): 443–60.

25. "Women of the Storm Working to Rebuild New Orleans," CNN, February 21, 2006.

26. Ibid.

27. Ibid.; see also Donna Soper, "Q&A / Rep. Lynn Westmoreland: Seeing Hurricane Devastation an Eye-opener," *Atlanta Journal-Constitution*, March 9, 2006, JI1.

Chapter 10. New Orleans at Six Months

1. Institute for Southern Studies, "The Mardi Gras Index: The State of New Orleans by Numbers Six Months after Hurricane Katrina," *Southern Exposure* 34, no. 1 (2006): 3.

2. Ibid., 9.

3. Ibid., 3.

4. Ibid., 25.

5. Thom Patterson, "Let the Good Times Roll (but Not Too Much): Big Easy Struggles with Post-Katrina Mardi Gras," CNN, February 27, 2006.

6. The Krewe of Muses usually parades on the Wednesday night preceding Mardi Gras. On Muses, see Ian McNulty, "New Krewe Follows Muses," *New Orleans CityBusiness*, February

19, 2001, 1, 56; R. Stephanie Bruno, "Carnival Enthusiast Virginia Saussy Relishes Her New Home—Where Else?—On the Uptown Parade Route," *Times-Picayune*, February 11, 2012; Robin Roberts, "New Orleans Mardi Gras and Gender in Three Krewes: Rex, the Truck Parades, and Muses," *Western Folklore* 65, no. 3 (2006): 303–328.

7. Morgan Packard, "The Spirit of New Orleans," *New Orleans Living Magazine*, May 1, 2006, http://www.livingneworleans.com/?p=62. In 2007, Rita Benson LeBlanc would be honored as an Honorary Muse. And in 2010 Mary Matalin, a regular CNN contributor and WOS member, was given the honor.

8. Dave Walker, "Muses Explained: The Colorful Krewe Featured in 'Treme's' Season-Two Mardi Gras Episode," *Times-Picayune*, June 5, 2011. See also Packard, " Spirit of New Orleans."

9. "First Mardi Gras Celebration after Hurricane Katrina," CNN *American Morning* with Miles O'Brien, February 28, 2006.

10. Ibid.

11. Ibid.

12. Anne Milling, "Five Steps to Starting a Grassroots Movement," *Vibrant Nation*, June 18, 2008, http://www.vibrantnation.com/live-it-lists/5-steps-to-starting-a-grassroots-movement.

13. Jeff Duncan, "Prayer Kicks off 3-Day Katrina Tour," *Times-Picayune*, March 3, 2006, A6.

14. "Congress Members Greet 9th Ward Activists," *Times-Picayune*, March 3, 2006, nola.com community photo archives, http://photos.nola.com/8001200/gallery/congress_members_greet_9th_ward_activists/index.html#/0.

15. Duncan, "Prayer Kicks off 3-Day Katrina Tour."

16. Michelle Krupa, "Lawmakers Wrap up Storm Tour," *Times-Picayune*, March 5, 2006, 1.

17. "Do Your Homework," *Times-Picayune*, editorial, March 22, 2006, 6; "Clueless on the Hill," *Times-Picayune*, editorial, March 15, 2006, 6.

18. Rukmini Callimachi, "Women's Mission Accomplished as Congressional Leaders Tour City," Associated Press, March 4, 2006.

19. Ibid.

20. Ibid.

21. Krupa, "Lawmakers Wrap up Storm Tour."

22. Pam Bryan, "Women of the Storm Panel Discussion," podcast audio, March 7, 2006, Newcomb Archives and Vorhoff Library Special Collections, Newcomb College Institute, Tulane University.

23. Newt Gingrich and John M. Barry, "Why New Orleans Needs Saving," *Time* 167, no. 10 (2006): 41.

24. Ibid.

25. Gwen Filosa, "One Last Look for Bodies Planned," *Times-Picayune*, March 5, 2006, B1.

26. Shaila Dewan, "In Attics and Rubble, More Bodies and Questions," *New York Times*, April 11, 2006.

27. Sean Callebs, "Katrina Victim's Body Found in Attic," CNN, March 6, 2006.

28. Dewan, "In Attics and Rubble."

29. Ibid.

30. Jeanette Bell, "Women of the Storm Panel Discussion," podcast audio, March 7, 2006, Newcomb Archives and Vorhoff Library Special Collections, Newcomb College Institute, Tulane University.

31. Data Center analysis of data from U.S. Census 2000 Summary File 1 (SF1), http://www.datacenterresearch.org/data-resources/neighborhood-data/district-2/central-city.

32. Data Center analysis of data from U.S. Census 2000 Summary File 3 (SF3), http://www.datacenterresearch.org/data-resources/neighborhood-data/district-2/central-city.

33. Faith Dawson, Christina Masciera, and Margaret O'Connor, "The Ibbys," *New Orleans Magazine* 31, no. 9 (1997).

34. Ibid.

35. Anne Raver, "From the Scars of Katrina, Green Shoots and Blossoms," *New York Times,* February 16, 2006.

36. "Hurricane Katrina's Impact on the Historic Gardens of New Orleans," *Magnolia* 77, no. 2 (2005).

37. Kristin Kelly and Joan Weinstein, "Rethinking Crescent City Culture: New Orleans Two and a Half Years Later," *Conservations: The Getty Conservation Newsletter* 23, no. 1 (2008): 16–19.

Chapter 11. The Breach

1. April Capochino, "Stormers Not Ready to Stop Congress Push," *New Orleans CityBusiness,* June 12, 2006.

2. Gwen Filosa, "Students Rally for Category 5 Levee Protection," *Times-Picayune,* January 13, 2006.

3. Joe Gyan Jr., "McCain, Graham Visit N.O. Disaster Areas," *Advocate,* March 11, 2006, 1.

4. Kathleen Blee addresses how newcomers are typically regarded by emergent activist groups: "Their appearance is usually regarded by current members as more disruptive than welcome." In my observation, the newcomers were welcomed at this press event to the extent that they helped give the appearance of a large crowd, but very little effort was made to draw these women, some of whom used their lunch break to attend the press conference, into everyday group operations. This resonates with Blee's conclusions very well: "They did not fit the group's sense of what members should be like." See Kathleen M. Blee, *Democracy in the Making: How Activist Groups Form* (New York: Oxford University Press, 2012), 73–75.

5. Bruce Alpert, "3 More Senators Coming to See Destruction," *Times-Picayune,* March 9, 2006, 8.

6. The April 2006 edition of *Heartline On-Line: The E-mail Newsletter of the Academy of the Sacred Heart,* featured color photographs of Sacred Heart students with McCain. Coverage of the event in the *Times-Picayune,* however, differed; the photographs of the event were carefully cropped so as not to include the girls.

7. Author's transcription of digital audio recorded at press conference.

8. Ibid.

9. Jeff Duncan, "Two Key Senators Go to Bat for N.O.," *Times-Picayune,* March 11, 2006, A1, A13.

10. Quoted in Bruce Alpert and Bill Walsh, "On the Hill; News from the Louisiana Delegation in the Nation's Capital," *Times-Picayune,* March 12, 2006, 7.

11. Ibid.

12. Ibid.

13. Anne Milling, e-mail message to Women of the Storm participants, March 23, 2006; used with permission.

14. "Pair of Bodies Found in Yard," *Times-Picayune,* March 25, 2006, B1.

15. "Mission and History," McGehee School, http://mcgeheeschool.com/discover-mcgehee/mission-history; obituary of Bradish Johnson, *New York Times,* November 5, 1892;

Bette Roth Young, *Emma Lazarus in Her World: Life and Letters* (Philadelphia: Jewish Publication Society, 1995), 48–49.

16. Eileen F. Powers, "Letter from Eileen #17," *McGehee News*, March 16, 2006.

17. G. William Domhoff, "The Women's Page as a Window on the Ruling Class," in *Hearth and Home: Image of Women in the Mass Media*, ed. Gaye Tuchman, Arlene Kaplan Daniels, and James Benét (New York: Oxford University Press, 1978), 169.

Chapter 12. Going National

1. Anne Milling, e-mail message to Women of the Storm participants, March 26, 2006; used with permission.

2. Robert A. Stallings, "The Structural Patterns of Four Types of Organizations in Disaster," in *Disasters: Theory and Research*, ed. E. L. Quarantelli, 87–103 (London: Sage Publications, 1978).

3. "Women of the Storm Gains Big Support," *Times-Picayune*, March 29, 2006, 1.

4. "Editorial: After the Storm," *Times-Picayune*, March 30, 2006, 6.

5. "NCJW Joins with Women of the Storm to Urge Congress to Witness New Orleans," National Council of Jewish Women press release, March 29, 2006, http://www.ncjw.org/html/News/PressReleases/060329.

6. Women of the Storm, "National Women's Groups Join Women of the Storm, Urge Congress to Visit New Orleans and South Louisiana," press release, March 29, 2006.

7. Ibid. This appears to be the number of lawmakers who actually accepted WOS's inviation rather than the total number of congressional visits after the storm.

8. Nathan Jones, "Women Storm the Nation," *Times-Picayune*, letter to the editor, March 31, 2006, 6.

9. Whitney Pierce Santora, "Women of the Year: Diana Pinckley," *New Orleans CityBusiness*, November 13, 2006, 55.

10. "Allen to Reschedule Trip to New Orleans," press release, April 7, 2006, http://allen.senate.gov/public/index.cfm.

11. "Arkansas Senator to View Devastation Caused by Hurricane Katrina," *New Orleans CityBusiness*, April 19, 2006, 1; Bruce Alpert and Bill Walsh, "On the Hill; News from the Louisiana Delegation in the Nation's Capital," *Times-Picayune*, April 23, 2006, 7.

12. Associated Press, "Voting Rights for the Displaced Is the Rally Cry in New Orleans," *New York Times*, April 2, 2006, A18.

13. Quoted in Michelle Krupa, Gordon Russell, and Frank Donze, "Women Voters Remain Major Force," *Times-Picayune*, April 22, 2006, 1.

14. Anne Milling, e-mail message to Women of the Storm participants, April 21, 2006; used with permission.

15. See Congressional Distinguished Service Award, May 10, 2006, C-Span Archives, http://www.c-spanarchives.org/program/192450-1&start=2973.

Chapter 13. Storm Warnings

1. During the first Storm Warning event, on June 1, 2005, America's WETLAND dramatized a flooding in the French Quarter to warn of vulnerability to flooding caused by hurricanes; according to Women of the Storm, this "proved eerily prophetic three months later when

Hurricane Katrina struck, inundating many other parts of the city with water." See "Women of the Storm Raise Hurricane Storm Warnings: First Day of Hurricane Season Used to Illustrate Lack of Congressional Interest in Post-Katrina New Orleans and Increased Threat Caused by Loss of America's WETLAND," press release, June 1, 2006, http://americaswetland.com/article.cfm?id=382. See also Shirley Laska, "What If Hurricane Ivan Had Not Missed New Orleans?" *Natural Hazards Observer* 29, no. 2 (2005): 5–6.

2. Carolyn Kousky and Richard Zeckhauser, "JARing Actions that Fuel the Floods," in *On Risk and Disaster: Lessons from Hurricane Katrina*, ed. Ronald J. Daniels, Donald F. Kettl, and Howard Kunreuther, 59–73 (Philadelphia: University of Pennsylvania Press, 2006); Ivor van Heerden, "The Failure of the New Orleans Levee System Following Hurricane Katrina and the Pathway Forward," *Public Administration Review* 67, no. 1 (2007): 24–35.

3. Author's transcription of digital audio recorded at press event.

4. Women of the Storm, "Women of the Storm Raise Hurricane Storm Warnings."

5. Emile Durkheim, *The Elementary Forms of Religious Life*, trans Karen E. Fields (1912; New York: Free Press, 1995), 393.

6. "Workers Find Body in Flooded Home," *Times-Picayune*, June 18, 2006, 1; "Another Katrina Victim Found," *Times-Picayune*, August 1, 2006, 3.

7. Quoted in "Women Say 6 States Have Yet to Visit New Orleans," *Beaumont Enterprise*, June 2, 2006, A13. See also Rukmini Callimachi, "Utah Delegation Still Hasn't Visited Orleans," *Deseret News*, June 2, 2006, A2; "Editorial: A Sight to See," *Times-Picayune*, June 2, 2006, 6. See also FOX 8 News, June 1, 2006. Others interviewed include Jane Arnette, Alexis Duvall, and Becky Currence.

8. Leslie Williams, "Blanco Firm on Threat to Block Gulf Lease Sale," *Times-Picayune*, June 2, 2006, 1.

9. Joe Gyan Jr., "Experts: Redirect River," *Advocate*, June 2, 2006, 1. For an in-depth discussion of Blanco's efforts to force legal action against federal agencies, see Jason P. Theriot, *American Energy, Imperiled Coast: Oil and Gas Development in Louisiana's Wetlands* (Baton Rouge: Louisiana State University Press, 2014), 202–209.

10. Bruce Alpert, "Billions of Relief Dollars Secured for State," *Times-Picayune*, June 9, 2006, 1.

11. Quoted in Christina Bellantoni, "White House Suitors Deluge New Orleans," *Washington Times*, July 2, 2006, http://www.washingtontimes.com/news/2006/jul/2/20060702-121944-6600r.

12. Ibid.

13. Christina Bellantoni, "Senators Back Big Easy Rebuilding," *Washington Times*, June 24, 2006, A2. See also Bellantoni, "White House Suitors Deluge New Orleans."

14. "Women's Leadership Initiative—United Way for the Greater New Orleans Areas," July/August 2006, Brown Digital Repository, Katrina Collection, https://repository.library.brown.edu/studio/item/bdr%3A67777.

15. Lee Davidson, "Bennett Finally Sees Devastation," *Deseret News*, July 18, 2006, B2.

16. Gwen Filosa, "2 More Senators Get Look at Storm Damage," *Times-Picayune*, July 15, 2006, 1.

17. Davidson, "Bennett Finally Sees Devastation."

18. Robert Gehrke, "1st New Orleans Visit," *Salt Lake Tribune*, July 15, 2006.

19. Ibid.

20. Davidson, "Bennett Finally Sees Devastation."

21. Gehrke, "1st New Orleans Visit."

22. Davidson, "Bennett Finally Sees Devastation."

23. Filosa, "2 More Senators Get Look at Storm Damage."

24. Jeff Zeleny, "Obama Joins Parade to See New Orleans," *Chicago Tribune*, July 22, 2006, 1.

Chapter 14. Women of the Storm Return

1. William H. Fray, Audrey Singer, and David Park, "Resettling New Orleans: The First Full Picture from the Census," report from the Brookings Institution, Special Analysis in Metropolitan Policy, Washington, D.C., September 12, 2007.

2. Ibid. See also Elizabeth Fussell, "Construction New Orleans, Constructing Race: A Population History of New Orleans," *Journal of American History* 94 (2007): 846–55.

3. Fray, Singer, and Park, "Resettling New Orleans," 11.

4. Beth Willinger and Janna Knight, "Setting the Stage for Disaster: Women in New Orleans Before and After Katrina," in *The Women of Katrina: How Gender, Race, and Class Matter in an American Disaster*, ed. Emmanuel David and Elaine Pitt Enarson, 64 (Nashville: Vanderbilt University Press, 2012).

5. John Pope, "Leaders Hopeful about Recovery," *Times-Picayune*, August 29, 2006, 1; Gerard Shields, "Katrina Art on Display in D.C.," *Advocate*, August 28, 2006, 7.

6. Priscilla Greear, "'Women of the Storm' to Blitz Washington Again," *Georgia Bulletin*, September 14, 2006.

7. Ibid.

8. "Editorial: Come on Down," *Times-Picayune*, September 9, 2006, 6.

9. "Messages and Supporting Material: Women of the Storm D.C. Trip—Sept. 20, 2006," n.d., WOS Records.

10. Greear, "'Women of the Storm' to Blitz Washington Again."

11. "Women of the Storm General Ledger," July 18, 2008, WOS Records.

12. Greear, "'Women of the Storm' to Blitz Washington Again."

13. Diana Pinckley, "WOS Master List," October 10, 2010, WOS Records.

14. "Sign-In Sheet," September 20, 2006, WOS Records.

15. Ann M. Simmons, "Storming Capitol Hill to Help Louisiana," *Los Angeles Times*, October 21, 2006, A12.

16. "Washing Away" admittance ticket, September 20, 2006, WOS Records.

17. Quoted in Ana Radelat, "A Year after Hurricane Rita, Victims Lobby for Coastal Restoration Money," *Gannett News Service*, September 21, 2006, 1.

18. Sue Strachan, "Persona: Rita Benson LeBlanc," *New Orleans Magazine*, 41, no. 12 (2007): 22–25. For more on LeBlanc, see Jill Gottesman, "Top Female Achievers: Rita LeBlanc," *New Orleans Magazine* (June 2004): 51–52; Greg LaRose, "Women of the Year: Rita Benson LeBlanc," *New Orleans CityBusiness*, November 8, 2004, 9A. Years later, in 2014, Rita Benson LeBlanc was fired by her grandfather. She and mother and brother were engaged in a much talked about legal battle with Tom Benson over the inheritance of the Saints and Pelicans franchises, which he announced that he would leave to his wife, Gayle Benson. See Ken Belson, "Saints' Owner Marches out of Step with His Heirs' Expectations," *New York Times*, March 6, 2015.

19. Brian Solomon, "Billionaire Tom Benson Benches Granddaughter, Presumed Heir, for Her 'Sense of Entitlement,'" *Forbes*, April 23, 2012, 4.

20. Mark Schleifstein, "Rita Benson LeBlanc," *Times-Picayune*, March 20, 2014.

21. Ibid.

22. Author's documentation of the speeches at the public reception.

23. Ibid. On John Breaux's efforts in the 1990s to establish a cost-sharing program for coastal restoration, which culminated in the passage of the Coastal Wetlands Planning, Protection, and Restoration Act, also known as the "Breaux Act," see Jason P. Theriot, *American Energy, Imperiled Coast: Oil and Gas Development in Louisiana's Wetlands* (Baton Rouge: Louisiana State University Press, 2014), 165–71.

24. Author's documentation of the speech at the public reception.

25. For an in-depth biography of Leah Chase, see Carol Allen, *Leah Chase: Listen, I Say Like This* (Gretna, LA: Pelican Publishing, 2002).

26. PBS, "New Orleans," *American Experience* (2007), http://www.pbs.org/wgbh/amex/neworleans/filmmore/pt.html.

27. "Safe Haven at Dooky Chase," *New Orleans Magazine* 45, no. 5 (2011): 39.

28. PBS, "New Orleans."

29. Allen, *Leah Chase: Listen, I Say Like This*, 70.

30. Kim Severson, "In New Orleans, Knives, Forks, and Hammers," *New York Times*, August 23, 2006.

31. In 2007 the city of New Orleans and the Housing Authority of New Orleans won a lawsuit allowing the demolition of Lafitte and three other public housing developments, which resulted in a loss of more than three thousand pre-Katrina apartment units for low-income residents. According to researchers at the Institute for Women's Policy Research, who analyzed data from the U.S. Department of Housing and Urban Development, the vast majority—77 percent—of household residents in the area's public housing are women. See Jane Henrici, Allison Suppan Helmuth, and Rhea Fernandes, "Mounting Losses: Women and Public Housing after Hurricane Katrina," Institute for Women's Policy Research (August 2010), IWPR #D491.

32. Quoted in Associated Press, "Reflecting on Lessons Storm Taught about Race and Poverty," Associated Press Newswires, August 16, 2006.

33. Frank Bruni, "Obama's Red Scare," *New York Times*, November 17, 2008, dinersjournal.blogs.nytimes.com/2008/11/17/obamas-red-scare; Donna Battle Pierce, "Hungry for History: Leah Chase of Dooky Chase Restaurant," *Ebony*, May 6, 2016, http://www.ebony.com/life/soul-food-leah-chase.

34. Chelsea Brasted, "In 'Lemonade,' Beyonce Returns to New Orleans for Visual Album," Nola.com, April 23, 2016, www.nola.com/music/index.ssf/2016/04/beyonce_lemonade_hbo_new_orlea.html.

35. *Washing Away: Losing Louisiana*, directed by Christina Hendrick Melton, narrated by Susan Sarandon (Baton Rouge: Louisiana Public Broadcasting, 2006), DVD.

36. Quoted in Joe Gyan Jr., "Blanco, Activists Rally for Amendments 1–4,"*Advocate*, September 27, 2006, 4.

37. Quoted in John Pope, "Levee, Wetlands Initiatives Win Big," *Times-Picayune*, October 2, 2006, 1.

38. Lolis Eric Elie, "More Loss Comes from a Break," *Times-Picayune*, October 2, 2006, 1.

39. "Jazz and Razz," *Times-Picayune*, November 12, 2006, 6.

40. "Women of the Storm in Final Push for Royalty Deal," *New Orleans CityBusiness*, November 16, 2006, 1.

41. Melinda Deslatte, "Offshore Drilling Royalties Law will Bring Billions to La," Associated Press, December 20, 2006. See Bruce Alpert and Bill Walsh, "On the Hill: News from the Louisiana Delegation in the Nation's Capital," *Times-Picayune*, December 17, 2006, 18.

42. Deslatte, "Offshore Royalties Bill."

43. Bill Walsh, "Congress Approves Offshore Revenue Sharing," *Times-Picayune*, December 9, 2006; Bill Walsh, "State Takes Long Road to Share in Oil Revenue," *Times-Picayune*, December 10, 2006.

Chapter 15. The Presidential Debate

1. Robert A. Stallings, "The Structural Patterns of Four Types of Organizations in Disaster," in *Disasters: Theory and Research*, ed. E. L. Quarantelli, 87–103 (London: Sage Publications, 1978).

2. "Women of the Storm: Executive Committee Bios," March 17, 2007, WOS Records.

3. Ibid.

4. Anne Milling, letter to Ms. Janet Brown, March 19, 2007; available on Women of the Storm's website, accessed September 24, 2007.

5. Mary Landrieu, letter to Chairmen Fahrenkopf and Kirk, March 22, 2007.

6. "Editorial: A Fitting Debate Site," *Times-Picayune*, March 23, 2007, 6; "New Orleans as Debate Site," *Advocate*, April 2, 2007, 6.

7. "Louisiana Recovery Authority Lobbies for Presidential Debate in New Orleans," *New Orleans CityBusiness*, October 2, 2007.

8. Bruce Alpert, "Letter Touts N.O. as Site for Debate," *Times-Picayune*, March 23, 2007, 19; "Editorial: A Fitting Debate Site"; "Where to Discuss the Nation's Ills," editorial, *New York Times*, July 18, 2007, 18.

9. "Debating in New Orleans," *Washington Post*, August 29, 2007, A16.

10. "A Non-Debatable Choice," *USA Today*, September 5, 2007, 12A.

11. "The Long Slog after Katrina," *Boston Globe*, August 29, 2007, A16.

12. Richard Stengel, "Why We Returned to New Orleans," *Time* 170, issue 7 (2007): 6.

13. John Pope, "Recovery Groups' Organizers Are Newcomb's Top Alumnae," *Times-Picayune*, April 21, 2007, 1.

14. John Pope, "Bond, Thornburgh Will Speak to Loyola Grads," *Times-Picayune*, April 27, 2007, 2. In 2010 R. King Milling also received an honorary doctorate from Loyola University.

15. John Pope, "Triumph of Spirit," *Times-Picayune*, May 20, 2007, 1.

16. Hillary Clinton to Anne Milling, June 8, 2007, WOS Records.

17. Doreen Massey, *Space, Place, and Gender* (Minneapolis: University of Minnesota Press, 1994), 156.

18. America's WETLAND Foundation, "Leaders Land in Dubuque to Dramatize Links between America's Wetland and America's River," *U.S. Newswire*, September 7, 2007; Lynne Jensen, "Group Will Carry Hurricane Alarm to Upriver States," *Times-Picayune*, May 31, 2007, 1; Leslie Williams, "Women of the Storm on the Road Again," *Times-Picayune*, June 1, 2007, 1; Melinda Morris, "Salvaging Wetlands Carries Big Price Tag, Speaker Says," *Times-Picayune*, July 19, 2007, 14.

19. Bruce Alpert, "New Orleans Offers Unique Platform for Political Debate," *Newhouse News Service*, June 18, 2007, 1; "Editorial: The Perfect Site," *Times-Picayune*, August 27, 2007, 4.

20. Walter Isaacson, "Boosters Take Our Story to Aspen," *Times-Picayune*, August 20, 2007, B6.

21. Bill Walsh, "Pelosi to Lead Visit to N.O.," *Times-Picayune*, August 8, 2007, 2.

22. Ibid.

23. Michelle Singer, "Rebuilding in New Orleans Is Slow Going," *CBS Evening News*, August 28, 2007, http://www.cbsnews.com/news/rebuilding-new-orleans-is-slow-going; see also "Katrina's Cruisading Women," *CBS Evening News*, September 21, 2007, http://www.cbsnews.com/videos/katrinas-crusading-women.

24. Singer, "Rebuilding in New Orleans."

25. "Katrina's Cruisading Women."

26. Ibid.

27. Katharine Q. Seelye, "Left Off Debate List, New Orleans Sees Politics at Play," *New York Times*, November 24, 2007, A11.

28. Ibid.

29. Seelye, "Panel Picks 4 Debate Sites," A20; see also "Across the Southeast," *Augusta Chronicle*, November 20, 2007, B3.

30. Bruce Alpert, "Well, Why Can't We?," *Times-Picayune*, November 20, 2007, 1.

31. "Editorial: A Shameful Rebuff," *Times-Picayune*, November 20, 2007, 6; Jarvis DeBerry, "A Poor Backdrop for GOP? No Debate," editorial, *Times-Picayune*, November 20, 2007, 7.

32. Ibid.

33. Lolis Eric Elie, "Empty Talk Can't Justify Debate Snub," *Times-Picayune*, November 21, 2007, 1.

34. "Editorial: A Shameful Rebuff."

35. Quoted in Bruce Alpert and Bill Walsh, "On the Hill; News from the Louisiana Delegation in the Nation's Capital," *Times-Picayune*, November 25, 2007, 8.

36. Bill Walsh, "Panel's Decision to Snub N.O. Assailed," *Times-Picayune*, November 21, 2007, 1.

37. Jarvis DeBerry, "Editorial: New Orleans Is in No Mood to Be Dissed," *Times-Picayune*, November 27, 2007, 7.

38. Anne Milling, "Founding Member of New Orleans–Based Women of the Storm Rebuts Presidential Debate Allegations," *New Orleans CityBusiness*, November 27, 2007.

39. Ibid.

40. "Women of the Storm General Ledger," July 18, 2008, WOS Records.

41. Bruce Alpert, "Race for President May Run into N.O.," *Times-Picayune*, April 30, 2008, 1; Stephanie Grace, "We're Fed Up, and We've Got YouTube," *Times-Picayune*, May 1, 2008, 7.

42. "Editorial: The Great Debate," *Times-Picayune*, April 30, 2008, 6.

43. Bruce Alpert, "2nd Chance for Debate in N.O. Fizzles," *Times-Picayune*, August 4, 2008, 1.

44. Anne Milling, "Community United in Presidential Debate Bid," editorial, *Times-Picayune*, August 10, 2008, 6.

45. Anne Milling, "Campaign Season a Chance to Spotlight Recovery," *Times-Picayune*, August 4, 2006. See also Anne Milling, "Testimony to the DNC National Platform Hearing, "April 1, 2008, WOS Records.

46. "Editorial: Make Time for Forum," *Times-Picayune*, August 5, 2008, 6. See also "Editorial: Making Our Case," *Times-Picayune*, August 4, 2008, 3.

47. "Itinerary," August 24–25, 2008, WOS Records; e-mail from Ford Church to Anne Milling, August 18, 2008, WOS Records.

48. Women of the Storm, "Treasurer's Report," October 5, 2008, WOS Records.

49. Friends of New Orleans, "Louisiana Three Years after Katrina," n.d., WOS Records.

50. Stephanie Grace, "Louisiana Takes its Agenda to Denver," *Times-Picayune*, August 26, 2008, 7.

51. Quoted in Bruce Alpert, "Denver Parties with New Orleans Flavor," *Times-Picayune*, August 25, 2008, 1; Keith Spera, "Louisiana Musicians Make Their Point Loud and Clear," *Times-Picayune*, August 25, 2008, 1.

52. Keith Spera, "New Orleans Musicians to Kick Off Democratic Convention," *Times-Picayune*, July 2, 2008, http://blog.nola.com/keithspera/2008/07/new_orleans_musicians_to_kick.html; Marni Kockenberg, "Friends of New Orleans All-Star Jam-Balaya at First Avenue in Minneapolis," *Twin City Blues*, September 1, 2008.

53. Women of the Storm, "Treasurer's Report," October 5, 2008, WOS Records.

54. Quoted in Bruce Alpert, "Debates Almost a Shutout for N.O.," *Times-Picayune*, October 17, 2008, 1.

55. Judy Keen, "Feeling Reach Heightened Pitch in USA," *USA Today*, January 21, 2009, http://usatoday30.usatoday.com/news/nation/2009-01-20-nationwatches_N.htm.

56. "Jazz and Razz," *Times-Picayune*, May 31, 2009, 4.

57. John Pope, "Dr. Martin Luther King Jr. Charter School Prepares for the Ultimate Civics Lesson: President Obama Visits Thursday," *Times-Picayune*, October 13, 2009, 1.

58. Bruce Alpert and Jonathan Tilove, "On the Hill: News from the Louisiana Delegation in the Nation's Capital," *Times-Picayune*, January 31, 2010, A12.

59. Donna Brazile, "Brazile: Enjoying the 'Who Dat Nation,'" *Lowell Sun*, February 20, 2010.

60. Campbell Robertson, "On Anniversary, Signs of Healing," *New York Times*, August 8, 2010; Bruce Nolan, "After Katrina; The Storm of a Lifetime Has Changed Us in Ways We Never Imagined," *Times-Picayune*, August 15, 2010, A1; Gordon Russell, "Superbowl Champion Saints Set New Parade Standard," *Times-Picayune*, February 9, 2010, http://www.nola.com/superbowl/index.ssf/2010/02/super_bowl_champion_saints_set.html. On the New Orleans Saints win, see Brandon D. Haynes, "A Gateway for Everyone to Believe: Identity, Disaster, and Football in New Orleans," PhD diss., University of New Orleans, 2013.

Chapter 16. The BP Oil Spill and Beyond

1. Anne Milling, e-mail message to Women of the Storm participants, June 16, 2010; used with permission.

2. "Editorial: A Personal View of Disaster," *Times-Picayune*, July 12, 2010, B3.

3. Ibid.

4. Cindy Chang, "Message to the World 'Be the One' to Save the Coast," *Times-Picayune*, July 20, 2010, A1.

5. "Women of the Storm Launch 'Be the One' Video," *Gambit Weekly*, http://www.youtube.com/watch?v=qvvfmGziAfM&feature=related, posted July 20, 2010.

6. "Mannings Go about Business amid Saints Mania," Associated Press, July 9, 2010, CNBC, http://www.cnbc.com/id/38175800.

7. Kathleen Parker, "Riders on the Storm," *Washington Post*, July 28, 2010, A15.

8. Bruce Alpert, "Actress Severs Ties with 'Be the One' over Industry Ties," *Times-Picayune*, July 30, 2010, A10.

9. Brendan DeMelle and Jerry Cope, "Wetlands Front Group Funded by Big Oil Wants Taxpayers to Foot the Bill for BP's Gulf Destruction," *Huffington Post*, July 28, 2010, http://www.huffingtonpost.com/brendan-demelle/wetlands-front-group-fund_b_662739 .html.

10. David Itzkoff, "Bullock Wants to Be Removed from Oil-Spill Video," *New York Times*, July 31, 2010, C2.

11. Darwin BondGraham, "Women of the Spill—And the Oil Men Who Love Them," July 30, 2010, http://darwinbondgraham.blogspot.com/2010/07/women-of-spill-and-oil-men -who-love.html.

12. Diana Kendall, *Framing Class: Media Representations of Wealth and Poverty in America* (Lanham, MD: Rowman and Littlefield, 2005), 52–53.

13. Quoted in Bruce Alpert, "Actress Severs Ties."

14. "Editorial: Defenders of the Coast," *Times-Picayune*, July 31, 2010, B4.

15. Ibid.

16. Gary Beauchamp, "Everyone Needs to Be Rational about Oil," *Times-Picayune*, August 1, 2010, B4.

17. Quoted in Diane Loupe, "Year Five: Women of the Storm Re-energized by BP Spill," *Women's E-News*, August 25, 2010, http://womensenews.org/2010/08/year-five-women -storm-re-energized-bp-spill.

18. Bruce Alpert, "Bullock Agrees to Return to Spot in Wetlands Video," *Times-Picayune*, August 11, 2010, A4.

19. Robin Pogrebin, "Bullock to Remain in Oil-Spill Campaign," *New York Times*, August 12, 2010, C3.

20. Alpert, "Bullock Agrees to Return."

21. "Editorial: Our Full Picture," *Times-Picayune*, August 22, 2010, B4.

22. Nancy Marsiglia, "Q&A with Nancy Marsiglia, Women of the Storm," Greater New Orleans Foundation, September 14, 2010, http://www.gnof.org/blog/q-a-with-nancy-marsiglia -women-of-the-storm.

23. The trip was underwritten, in part, by Gloria Kabacoff. See John Pope, "Philanthropist, Civic Activist Gloria Kabacoff Dies at 88," *Times-Picayune*, February 24, 2012, http://www .nola.com/business/index.ssf/2012/02/philanthropist_civic_activist.html.

24. Transcript from audio recorded by the author at Women of the Storm's press conference.

25. "Celebrity Studded Video, E-Petition to Restore Gulf Coast Gain Wide U.S. Support. Sign it! Share it! Be the One!" Women of the Storm handout in author's collection; acquired March 24, 2011, during WOS's third trip to Washington.

26. Ray Mabus, "America's Gulf Coast: A Long Term Recovery Plan for after the Deepwater Horizon Oil Spill," September 2010, 5–6, https://www.restorethegulf.gov/sites/default/files/ documents/pdf/gulf-recovery-sep-2010.pdf.

27. "Deep Water: The Gulf Oil Disaster and the Future of Offshore Drilling." Recommendations, National Commission on the BP Deepwater Horizon Oil Spill and Offshore Drilling, January 2011, 280. https://www.gpo.gov/fdsys/pkg/GPO-OILCOMMISSION/pdf/GPO -OILCOMMISSION.pdf.

28. "Women of the Storm Become Women of the Spill," editorial, *Press Register*, March 29, 2011, http://blog.al.com/press-register-commentary/2011/03/women_of_the_storm_become_wome.html.

29. "Karen Kersting, Owner of Alane Design," http://www.livespergallon.net/Page_17.html.

30. Christina Skagas, "Mayor Moran Travels with Women of the Storm to D.C.," Ocean Springs WLOX, March 31, 2011, http://oceansprings.wlox.com/news/news/mayor-moran-travels-women-storm-dc/46040.

31. Melissa M. Scallan, "Women of the Storm Head for D.C.," Sunherald.com, March 28, 2011, http://www.sunherald.com/2011/03/28/2979858/women-of-the-storm-heads-for-dc.html#disqus_thread.

32. Harlan Kirgan, "Women from the Gulf Coast to Rally in D.C. for BP Fine Money," *Mississippi Press*, March 29, 2011, http://blog.gulflive.com/mississippi-press-news/2011/03/coast_women_to_rally_in_dc_for.html.

33. George Altman, "Infighting Blamed for Inaction on Oil Spill Fines," March 30, 2011, http://blog.al.com/live/2011/03/infighting_blamed_for_inaction.html.

34. "About Mobile Baykeeper," http://www.hotfrog.com/business/mobile-baykeeper_13477111; see also Mobile Baykeeper, http://www.mobilebaykeeper.org.

35. Kirgan, "Women from the Gulf Coast to Rally in D.C."

36. Rose Ann Haven, "Women of the Storm; Lucy Buffett Joins Group of Southern Ladies Fighting to Make Sure the Gulf Coast Receives Fines the Government Collects from BP," March 30, 2011, WKRG-News5, http://www.wkrg.com/gulf_oil_spill/article/women-of-the-storm/1205839/Mar-30-2011_2-49-pm.

37. "Seeking Money for a Good Cause," Houmatoday.com, editorial, March 29, 2011, http://www.houmatoday.com/article/20110329/OPINION/110329447/1030/opinion?p=all&tc=pgall.

38. Nikki Buskey, "Women Will Storm Capital for Restoration," Houmatoday.com, March 28, 2011, http://www.houmatoday.com/article/20110328/ARTICLES/110329490/-1/opinion?p=all&tc=pgall.

39. Ibid.

40. "Women of the Storm Head to D.C. to Lobby for Coastal Restoration Money," WWLTV.com, March 28, 2011, http://www.wwltv.com/eyewitness-morning-news/Women-of-the-Storm-head-to-DC-to-lobby-for-coastal-restoration-money-118764594.html#.

41. Anne Milling, "Women of the Storm Head to D.C. to Urge Gulf Coast Restoration in the Wake of BP Oil Spill," Women of the Storm press release, n.d., in author's collection.

42. Ibid.

43. "Scalise Leads Coalition to Direct 80 Percent of BP Fines to Gulf States for Coast Restoration and Recovery," Press Release, March 29, 2011, in author's collection.

44. Transcript from audio recorded by the author at Women of the Storm's press conference.

45. Ibid.

46. Mark Green, "Both Sides Now w/Huffington and Matalin: The Fog of Wars, Education in America, Palin in Israel," HuffPostRadio, podcast audio, March 27, 2011, http://www.huffingtonpost.com/huff-radio/both-sides-now-w-huffingt_13_b_841204.html.

47. Quoted in "Keep the Gulf RESTORE Act on a Roll in Congress: An Editorial," *Times-Picayune*, March 15, 2012, http://www.nola.com/opinions/index.ssf/2012/03/keep_the_restore_the_gulf_act_1.html.

48. "Gulf Coast Region Can Now Receive RESTORE Act Funding from U.S. Treasury," U.S. Department of the Treasury, October 14, 2014, https://www.treasury.gov/press-center/press-releases/Pages/JL2663.aspx.

Conclusion

1. Nathaniel Rich, "Waterworld: The Most Ambitious Environmental Lawsuit Ever," *New York Times Magazine*, October 5, 2014, http://www.nytimes.com/interactive/2014/10/02/magazine/mag-oil-lawsuit.html.

2. Ibid.

3. Michelle C. Hayes and Madeline E. Heilman, "It Had to Be You (Not Me)! Women's Attributional Rationalization of their Contribution to Successful Joint Work Outcomes," *Personality and Social Psychology Bulletin* 39, no. 7 (2013): 956–69.

4. For more on Lindy Boggs, including her strategic use of gender in politics, see Jill Jordan Sieder, "Women & Co.: Lindy Boggs: A Legacy of Leadership Tough to Beat," *New Orleans CityBusiness* 9, no. 25 (1989): 38; Lindy Boggs, *Washington through a Purple Veil: Memoirs of a Southern Woman* (New York: Harcourt Brace, 1994); Tania Tetlow, "Lindy and Me," in *Newcomb College, 1996–2006: Higher Education for Women in New Orleans*, ed. Susan Tucker and Beth Willinger (Baton Rouge: Louisiana State University Press), 377–83.

5. Randall Collins, "Women and the Production of Status Cultures," in *Cultivating Differences: Symbolic Boundaries and the Making of Inequality*, ed. Michèle Lamont and Marcel Fournier (Chicago: University of Chicago Press, 1992), 226.

6. G. William Domhoff, "The Women's Page as a Window on the Ruling Class," in *Hearth and Home: Image of Women in the Mass Media*, ed. Gaye Tuchman, Arlene Kaplan Daniels, and James Benét (New York: Oxford University Press, 1978), 174.

7. "Women of the Storm Bring Congress to New Orleans," September 10, 2006, unpublished document in author's collection.

8. "Whose [*sic*] Visited," *Women of the Storm: A Gulf Coast Coalition*, http://www.womenofthestorm.com/whose-visited.

9. Diane Loupe, "Year Five: Women of the Storm Re-energized by BP Spill," *Women's E-News*, August 24, 2010, http://womensenews.org/2010/08/year-five-women-storm-re-energized-bp-spill. Historian Pamela Tyler highlighted the class dimensions that enabled the formation of WOS, as well as Katrina Krewe and Citizens for One Greater New Orleans, characterizing members of these emergent groups as "enjoying box seats, not bleachers." She said, "Their lives were such bastions of comfort and security" that they had "the luxury of concentrating first on systematic reform," rather than focusing on other pressing issues such as affordable housing or public education. She also notes that most of this money was directed to homeowners rather than renters. See Pamela Tyler, "The Post-Katrina, Semiseparate World of Gender Politics," *Journal of American History* 94, no. 3 (2007): 788.

10. U.S. Department of the Treasury, "Gulf Coast Region Can Now Receive RESTORE Act Funding from U.S. Treasury," press release, October 14, 2014, http://www.treasury.gov/press-center/press-releases/Pages/JL2663.aspx.

11. Quoted in *Women of the Storm*, a film directed, edited, and produced by Wesley Shrum (Liars and Madmen Productions, 2015).

12. Naomi Klein, *The Shock Doctrine: The Rise of Disaster Capitalism* (New York: Metropolitan Books, 2007), 466.

13. Vincanne Adams, *Markets of Sorrow, Labors of Faith: New Orleans in the Wake of Katrina* (Durham, NC: Duke University Press, 2013), 174.

14. Ibid., 175. On the connections between the state and philanthropy, see Darwin BondGraham, "Building the *New* New Orleans: Foundation and NGO Power," *Review of Black Political Economy* 38, no. 4 (2011): 305–306.

15. Rebecca Anne Allahyari, "The Felt Politics of Charity: Serving 'the Ambassadors of God' and Saving 'the Sinking Classes,'" in *Passionate Politics: Emotions and Social Movements*, eds. Jeff Goodwin, James M. Jasper, and Francesca Polletta (Chicago: University of Chicago Press, 2001), 195; Sherryl Kleinman, *Opposing Ambitions: Gender and Identity in an Alternative Organization* (Chicago: University of Chicago Press, 1996), 5.

16. Melinda J. Milligan, "Displacement and Identity Discontinuity: The Role of Nostalgia in Establishing New Identity Categories," *Symbolic Interaction* 26, no. 3 (2003): 381–403.

17. Jeffrey C. Alexander, "Toward a Theory of Cultural Trauma," in *Cultural Trauma and Collective Identity*, ed. Jeffrey C. Alexander, Ron Eyerman, Bernhard Giesen, Neil J. Smelser, and Piotr Sztompka, 1–30 (Berkeley: University of California Press, 2004), 27.

18. Paul Lichterman, *Elusive Togetherness: Church Groups Trying to Bridge America's Divisions* (Princeton, NJ: Princeton University Press, 2005), 258–59.

19. Anne Milling, interview by Kaitlin Splett, April 5, 2012, Newcomb Oral History Collection, Newcomb Archives and Vorhoff Library Special Collections, Newcomb College Institute, Tulane University.

20. Nancy Naples, *Grassroots Warriors: Activist Mothering, Community Work, and the War on Poverty* (New York: Routledge, 1998); Nancy Naples, ed., *Community Activism and Feminist Politics: Organizing across Race, Class, and Gender* (New York: Routledge, 1998).

Notes on Method

1. Susan Ostrander, *Women of the Upper Class* (Philadelphia: Temple University Press, 1984).

2. Diana Pinckley, "WOS Master List," October 10, 2010, Women of the Storm Records, Manuscript Collection NA.020, Newcomb Archives and Vorhoff Library Special Collections, Newcomb College Institute, Tulane University; Michelle Singer, "Rebuilding is New Orleans is Slow Going," *CBS Evening News*, August 28, 2007, http://www.cbsnews.com/news/rebuilding-new-orleans-is-slow-going/

3. There are two exceptions. In one case I scheduled a meeting and upon my arrival found out that the interviewee had invited a friend who was also a WOS participant. In a second case, the interviewee's husband entered the setting and stayed. In both situations I proceeded with the interviews, with the signed permission of those present, adapting the interview to accommodate their interests.

4. Kathleen Tierney, "The Field Turns Fifty: Social Change and the Practice of Disaster Fieldwork," in *Methods of Disaster Research*, ed. R. A. Stallings (Philadelphia: Xlibris, 2002), 349–74, 359.

5. See Kathy Charmaz, "The Grounded Theory Method: An Explication and Interpretation," in *Contemporary Field Research*, ed. Robert M. Emerson (Prospect Heights, IL: Waveland Press, 1983), 109–126.

6. For a discussion of these dynamics, see Rebecca Sharpless, *Cooking in Other Women's Kitchens: Domestic Workers in the South, 1865–1960* (Chapel Hill: University of North Carolina

Press, 2010). See also Judith Rollins, *Between Women: Domestics and Their Employers* (Philadelphia: Temple University Press, 1985).

7. Among the women I interviewed, all but one had returned to New Orleans, even if they were still living in temporary housing such as a FEMA trailers. One interviewee, displaced to Baton Rouge, scheduled her interview with me on a day trip to New Orleans.

8. See Ian Hodder, "The Interpretation of Documents and Material Culture," in *Handbook of Qualitative Research*, ed. Norman Denzin and Yvonne Lincoln (Thousand Oaks, CA: Sage Publications, 1994), 393–402; Kenneth Plummer, *Documents of Life: An Introduction to the Problems and Literature of a Humanistic Method* (London: Allen and Unwin, 1983); Paul ten Have, "Natural Documents," in *Understanding Qualitative Research and Ethnomethodology* (Thousand Oaks, CA: Sage Publications, 2004), 89–106.

9. E. L. Quarantelli, "A Social Science Research Agenda for the Disasters of the 21st Century: Theoretical, Methodological, and Empirical Issues and Their Professional Implementations," preliminary draft, Disaster Research Center (DRC) preliminary paper, 2003.

10. I found traces of my participation in the WOS records. In one document I was listed as both a WOS "intern" and a member of the "core," and in the master list of participants I saw my name with a note about my thesis. I suspect that it was these documents that resulted in my name (misspelled by one letter) being included in the list of WOS participants in the final credits of Wesley Shrum's 2015 documentary, *Women of the Storm*.

11. Robert Stallings, "Methodological Issues," in *Handbook of Disaster Research*, ed. Havidán Rodríguez, Enrico L. Quarantelli, and Russell R. Dynes (New York: Springer, 2003), 55–82. See also Tierney, "The Field Turns Fifty."

12. Patricia Adler and Peter Adler, *Membership Roles in Field Research* (Newbury Park: Sage Publications, 1987).

13. Ibid., 13.

14. Ibid.

15. Gary Alan Fine, "Field Labor and Ethnographic Reality," *Journal of Contemporary Ethnography* 28, no. 5 (1999): 532–39; John Lofland and Lyn H. Lofland, *Analyzing Social Settings: A Guide to Qualitative Observation and Analysis*, 3rd ed. (New York: Wadsworth Publishing, 1995); Verta Taylor, "Feminist Methodology in Social Movements Research," *Qualitative Sociology* 21, no. 4 (1998): 357–79.

16. Paul Lichterman, "What Do Movements Mean? The Value of Participant Observation," *Qualitative Sociology* 21, no. 4 (1998): 401–418.

17. Rosalie Wax, *Doing Fieldwork: Warnings and Advice* (Chicago: University of Chicago Press, 1971), 20.

18. Jill McCorkel and Kristen Myers, "What Difference Does Difference Make? Position and Privilege in the Field," *Qualitative Sociology* 26, no. 2 (2003): 199–231. For an important discussion of ethnography, disclosure, and the contradictions of feminist standpoint work, see Kimberly Kay Hoang, *Dealing in Desire: Asian Ascendancy, Western Decline, and the Hidden Currencies of Global Sex Work* (Oakland: University of California Press, 2015), 20–24.

19. Christine Williams, "The Glass Escalator: Hidden Advantages for Men in the 'Female' Professions," *Social Problems* 39, no. 3 (1992): 253–67.

20. Margaret L. Hunter, "'If You're Light You're Alright': Light Skin Color as Social Capital for Women of Color," *Gender and Society* 16, no. 2 (2002): 175–93; Evelyn Nakano Glenn,

"Yearning for Lightness: Transnational Circuits in the Marketing and Consumption of Skin Lighteners," *Gender and Society* 22, no. 3 (2008): 281–302.

21. For responses to these types of questions, see Jillian Paragg, "'What Are You?': Mixed Race Responses to the Racial Gaze," *Ethnicities* (December 2015): 1–22.

22. Dave Eggers, *Zeitoun* (San Francisco: McSweeney's Books, 2009).

23. Emerson, *Contemporary Field Research*, 176.

Index

EMMANUEL DAVID is an assistant professor of women and gender studies at University of Colorado Boulder. He is coeditor of *The Women of Katrina: How Gender, Race, and Class Matter in an American Disaster.*

The University of Illinois Press
is a founding member of the
Association of American University Presses.

———————————————————

Composed in 10.75/13 Arno Pro
with Adrianna Extended Pro display
by Kirsten Dennison
at the University of Illinois Press
Cover designed by Dustin J. Hubbart
Cover illustration: A group of women from Louisiana carry
blue-tarp umbrellas as they walk to a news conference on
Capitol Hill, Monday, January 30, 2006, to bring attention to the
lack of funding in the rebuilding effort after Hurricane Katrina.
(AP photo/Susan Walsh)

University of Illinois Press
1325 South Oak Street
Champaign, IL 61820-6903
www.press.uillinois.edu